CLARENDON LAW SERIES

Edited by

PETER BIRKS

CLARENDON LAW SERIES

Introduction to Roman Law
By BARRY NICHOLAS

Legal Reasoning and Legal Theory
By NEIL MCCORMICK

Natural Law and Natural Rights
By JOHN G. FINNIS

The Concept of Law (2nd edition)
By H. L. A. HART

An Introduction to the Law of Contract (5th edition)
By P. S. ATIYAH

Principles of Criminal Law (2nd edition)
By ANDREW ASHWORTH

Playing by the Rules
By FREDERICK SCHAUER

Precedent in English Law (4th edition)
By SIR RUPERT CROSS AND JIM HARRIS

An Introduction to Administrative Law (3rd edition)
By PETER CANE

Policies and Perceptions of Insurance
By MALCOLM CLARKE

An Introduction to Family Law
By GILLIAN DOUGLAS

Discrimination Law
By SANDRA FREDMAN

The Conflict of Laws
By ADRIAN BRIGGS

THE LAW OF PROPERTY

F. H. LAWSON and BERNARD RUDDEN

THIRD REVISED EDITION

by BERNARD RUDDEN

OXFORD
UNIVERSITY PRESS

*This book has been printed digitally and produced in a standard specification
in order to ensure its continuing availability*

OXFORD
UNIVERSITY PRESS

Great Clarendon Street, Oxford OX2 6DP

Oxford University Press is a department of the University of Oxford.
It furthers the University's objective of excellence in research, scholarship,
and education by publishing worldwide in

Oxford New York

Auckland Cape Town Dar es Salaam Hong Kong Karachi
Kuala Lumpur Madrid Melbourne Mexico City Nairobi
New Delhi Shanghai Taipei Toronto

With offices in

Argentina Austria Brazil Chile Czech Republic France Greece
Guatemala Hungary Italy Japan South Korea Poland Portugal
Singapore Switzerland Thailand Turkey Ukraine Vietnam

Oxford is a registered trade mark of Oxford University Press
in the UK and in certain other countries

Published in the United States
by Oxford University Press Inc., New York

ISBN 978-0-19-829993-6

Most of us have heard these principles stated, reasoned upon, enlarged, and explained, till we have been lost in admiration at the strength and stretch of the human understanding.

Buller J, *Lickbarrow* v *Mason* (1787) 2 T.R. 64, 73; 100 E.R. 35, 40.

Preface

The aim of this third edition remains the same as that of its predecessors: to provide a general and explanatory, not a detailed and technical, book on property law. The previous editions were designed for two classes of readers: law students approaching this subject for the first time, and non-lawyers wishing to obtain a rapid and summary view of what is usually regarded as the most obscure part of the common law. This remains the design of the book, but it turns out that lawyers of 'civil-law' jurisdictions, whose whole approach to the subject is traditionally quite different, also found the earlier works helpful.

Although the aim, the themes, and the general approach remain as they were, the text of this third edition has been entirely rewritten. There are two main reasons for this reworking. First of all, the senior author of the previous edition died soon after its publication and so could collaborate in this version only in spirit and by example. Second, the perspective of the law has altered in England and Wales in the last quarter of the twentieth century, thereby to some extent catching up with changes in the distribution and transfer of property and the uses to which it is put. For instance, the machinery for the creation and protection of concurrent and successive interests in land has been much improved by legislation of 1996. These amendments, prompted by the decline of older patterns of endowment and enjoyment, have made it possible to omit much of the elderly learning on settlements, entails, and the like. More recent property statutes continue to streamline other parts of the system.

On the other hand, any simple account has been rendered more elusive by the 'computerization' of interests and transactions in property and by the development of pyramids of custodians and other holders of investment securities. In relation to holdings in the great public companies, and to government bonds and the like, documents have been replaced by data, so that we now speak, not of stocks and shares and bonds, but of 'uncertificated units' in 'financial assets', and of the 'dematerialized instructions' which transfer them. Furthermore, although this is a book about the common law, the world of investment is global and the law applicable is often that of Luxembourg or the USA. Once upon a time there were more markets than countries; now there are more countries than markets.

Within England and Wales this computerization process has reached the machinery for the transfer of interests in land, and the current Land Registration Bill 2001 paves the way for the large-scale, and compulsory, adoption of electronic conveyancing. Under this system transactions will be entered even as they are made and those with access to the network will be empowered directly to effect changes in the Land Register. The counterpart of the electronic transfer of the land is, necessarily, a means of effecting simultaneous electronic payment of the money. Cybercash is here.

The main emphasis of this work remains the general patterns of the subject, and this approach gives rise to certain distinctive features. First of all, the text takes for granted the existence, and legal protection, of private property and does not examine the many philosophical, ethical, and political problems to which this gives rise. Those issues have been debated for thousands of years and have recently formed the subject matter of a number of excellent English-language publications, to which the reader is referred.[1] This book sticks to the humdrum law.

Secondly, in writing such a text, there is an inevitable trade-off between intelligibility and accuracy. By this is meant that most, if not all, of the general propositions explained here are subject to sporadic exceptions, or at least to nuances. If, however, the text were to try to account for them, the important points would swiftly sink in a sea of detail. So in striving to make clear the elements of the subject, the book ignores many exceptions. Furthermore it still refrains from discussing—or even citing—decided cases, a practice which causes uneasiness to some readers, and satisfaction to others.

Thirdly, this is a portrait, or at least a sketch, of the law of property as a whole, eschewing the familiar divisions into land on the one hand and everything else on the other. There are, of course, irreducible differences in the law's treatment of immovable property on the one hand and movable on the other. These differences are noted where they occur, but there is a great deal of doctrine common to both; and the things them-selves are often interchangeable as component parts of the same fund when, for instance, its managers sell the one and invest in the other. It is also argued that, even when land and movables are treated as individual

---

[1] See, for instance, J. W. Harris, *Property and Justice* (OUP 1996); Ugo Mattei, *Basic Principles of Property Law: a comparative legal and economic introduction* (Greenwood Press, Westport, Conn., London, 2000); Stephen R. Munzer, *A Theory of Property* (CUP 1990); James E. Penner, *The Idea of Property in Law* (OUP 1997); Jeremy Waldron, *The Right to Private Property* (OUP 1968).

objects, there is much more in common between them than is usually acknowledged.

Perhaps the greatest difficulty in exposition is caused by the course the common law has taken. In large measure its vocabulary is still that of feudalism, giving the impression that the law of property is mainly concerned with field and farmhouse, crops and cattle. In fact this feudal terminology has long been filled with commercial content and applied to stocks, shares, intellectual property, goodwill, derivatives—in a word to capital which is not merely movable but *mobile*. In an exasperated but illuminating aside, Friedrich Engels once observed that, for our law of property, the relation between the words used and their actual function is as remote as that between the spelling and the pronunciation of the English language. An additional difficulty is that, for much of the twentieth century, the legal machinery applied to the family home was that of commerce and investment rather than of domestic necessity.

Many of the fundamental elements of property law seem to be much alike throughout the developed world. Certainly within the countries of the common-law family there are close similarities in approach, and much of what this book says about basic principle will be true for them; but inevitably parts of the text are concerned with the modern law of England and Wales (Scotland has an entirely different history, vocabulary, and system, and is rarely included in the text which follows). The reader should be aware, however, of the danger of a doggedly insular perspective: namely, that regulatory choices (such as those made by the 1925, 1996, and recent English property legislation) may be taken to be universal axioms, whereas they are actually technical rules which could well be different and which do not apply beyond our shores.

The book was written with the resources, help, and support, of the Librarian and staff at two great law libraries: that of Cornell Law School, and that of the Bodleian at Oxford. Thanks are also due to Arianna Pretto for her help in understanding modern developments in investment securities, and to David Vaver for invaluable assistance with intellectual property. The author is especially grateful to Bill Swadling, who read, commented on, and greatly improved a draft of the entire text. Any remaining mistakes are solely the work of the undersigned.

B. R.

Penzance, 21 August 2001

Contents

PART 1: Introduction

  1. Subject, Setting, and Sources   3

PART 2: Property in General

  2. The Classification of Things   19
  3. The Acquisition of Property Interests   50
  4. Protection of Property Interests   63

PART 3: Common-Law Techniques

  5. Concepts and Categories   77
  6. Ownership and its Fragmentation   90
  7. Land Legislation for England and Wales 1925–2001   101

PART 4: Standard Patterns

  8. Leases and the Like   113
  9. Security   127
10. Real Property: Servitudes   152
11. Succession   159

PART 5: Property as Wealth

12. Wealth   169
13. The Control of Endowment   184
14. Conclusion   192

Index   201

Part 1

Introduction

I

Subject, Setting, and Sources

THE SUBJECT

The subject matter of this book must be seen in the context of other parts of the law, many of which also deal with property. Constitutional law restricts the State's power to take its citizens' property; criminal law seeks to protect our belongings against theft, vandalism, and the like; divorce law gives judges power to reallocate assets by taking property off one spouse and giving it to the other; the law of tort is supposed to ensure compensation for trespass on, or taking of, our land and our goods.

What the above examples have in common is that they are the law's response to something abnormal, something which disturbs the even flow of life in society. In the usual run of events, the government does not take private property, theft and wanton damage are crimes, most marriages last until death, and tort means 'wrong'. But all of us all the time take peacefully for granted the business of getting things and then keeping and utilizing them. A person may acquire something by making it, but is more likely to get it from someone else and to have to pay for it. Buyers want to be sure that they get what they are paying for, but are normally far more concerned with quality and suitability than with worrying whether it was the seller's to sell. They are able to take this for granted in most cases because the law is working, virtually unnoticed, to protect them. The buyer may prefer to pay for the goods or the house by instalments, and in such cases no one would provide credit without security. By means of such devices as mortgage and hire purchase, the law enables the creditor to obtain this security. It thus reduces the risk of giving credit and tends to improve the terms offered, typically by increasing the amount of a loan, by extending the period for which it is made, or by lowering the interest rate. Having got the thing, its owner may keep and use it, or keep and forget about it, or may want to sell it or give it away. The thing may have been acquired for its own sake, like a shirt or a dwelling, or may be merely an investment such as a savings certificate or block of shares. Furthermore—especially if the thing is of a fairly permanent nature like a house or shares—the owner may want to distribute it among others either commercially by charging a rent or by way of gift or bequest to family and friends.

All these, and similar, transactions are entirely normal, peaceful, and useful. The law of property underlies them. Some of its provisions are 'default' rules, which operate unless we expressly design our own scheme, but there are a number of important mandatory rules whose application we cannot avoid—many of them concern the use or transfer of land, especially by way of lease. In general, however, the function of the law relating to private property is to provide us with a bag of tools with which to achieve our wishes.

First of all, it says what counts as property, that is to say what can be the object of its powers and protections. We cannot, for instance, effectively give, sell, lease, or bequeath our reputation, or our surname, or our job: these may be ours, and may be valuable, but they do not count as property so as to form the subject matter of dispositions. The law of property also determines the types of interests which will be treated as proprietary, that is as being more than merely personal, familial, or con-tractual, and it spells out the consequences of a finding that a particular interest is proprietary.[1] It says what we can do with these interests—anything we like, if we like; and it says what others can do with them—nothing, unless we let them. So in conjunction with other branches of law—especially the law of obligations—property law protects the rights of the holders of these interests—owners, co-owners, lessees, charge-holders, trustees, and so on. And, again along with other branches of law, it deals with the transfer of property and the repackaging of proprietary interests whether *inter vivos* or on death. Here we find the formalities needed for certain transactions, and the methods used for altering and amalgamating the various components of, and interests in, property, and for creating complex, if fairly standard, structures of control and enjoyment (leases, co-ownership, security interests, trusts, and so on).

It is these formalities and structures which most concern the law of property. If a field is sold, or leased, or given away, or left by will, the field

---

[1] Perhaps it should be made clear at once that in English law there is no special category of family property. Husband and wife are treated as separate persons each with their own belongings; if they do own anything together it is because they have agreed to do so or because both have contributed to its acquisition or improvement. Children have no auto-matic right to inherit a share of their parents' property. Outside intestacy, the law of property treats family members as strangers, an approach even more true of the households of domestic partners who are not married to each other.

itself does not change at all; looking at it will not tell you whose it is. What changes is the legal relations of persons, changes effected by human decisions expressed in the appropriate formalities. The same is true if the object is a house, a car, a cat, a share in a company, or a government bond. So one of the main difficulties the student of property law encounters at the very threshold is the presence of abstractions rather than physical objects. We are accustomed to this in the law of persons, where companies and other corporate bodies live alongside human beings. Much the same is true of things. Property lawyers take surprisingly little interest in land or ships or machinery or animals as such, but a great deal in abstract notions such as the 'fee simple' in land, trust funds, stocks and shares, security interests, title, and documents of title. These are the instruments which relate the particular object to the rest of the economy. Thanks to them, assets (like the field we mentioned) lead an invisible, parallel life alongside their material existence. A modern economist has recently argued, on the basis of research on the ground, that it is the absence of such instruments, and not the lack of assets or enterprise, that accounts for much of the poverty in the Third World and the former communist nations. 'The inhabitants of these nations do have things, but they lack the process to represent their property and create capital. They have houses but not titles, crops but not deeds, businesses but not statutes of incorporation. It is the unavailability of these essential legal representations that explains why people who have adapted every other Western invention, from the paper clip to the nuclear reactor, have not been able to produce sufficient capital to make their domestic capitalism work.' [2]

SETTING

So far we have been discussing private property, whose law deals with the relations between persons with regard to things. We have not asked why the law permits and protects private property, nor whether it should do so; for that debate, as we have said, the reader is referred to other works.[3] This book will concentrate on the ordinary person's property in both the means of consumption and the means of production, distribution, and exchange. But a few words should be said about the wider setting.

[2] Hernando de Soto, *The Mystery of Capital* (Bantam Press, London, 2000). The quotation above is from his article in *International Herald Tribune*, 5 January 2001.
[3] See the works cited in the Preface footnote.

Public international law

An important and long-standing branch of public international law deals with the relations between sovereign States concerning their lands and their boundaries, their ships, aircraft, and the like—though it uses the words 'territory', 'possessions', and 'sovereignty' rather than 'property' and 'ownership'. In addition a number of international instruments seek to safeguard the property of individuals. The provisions are usually cast in general terms but broadly speaking they accord to the holding of property the status of a human right to be respected by the relevant State. At the same time, however, they acknowledge the State's right, under certain conditions, to take and to tax private property. For instance, the Universal Declaration of Rights adopted in 1948 by the General Assembly of the United Nations Organization states, in terms broader than most international instruments, that 'Everyone has the right to own property alone as well as in association with others. No one shall be arbitrarily deprived of his property' (art.17). The European Convention on Human Rights has a provision entitled 'Protection of Property' which states that every natural or legal person is entitled to the peaceful enjoyment of his possessions and that no one is to be deprived of them except in the public interest and subject to the conditions provided for by law and by the general principles of international law (Protocol 1).

Constitutional provisions

Similar safeguards are found entrenched in the constitutions of many States. In article 17 of the 1789 Declaration of the Rights of Man and Citizen, the French declared property to be an 'inviolable and sacred right', while the Fifth Amendment to the US constitution says that no one is to be deprived of property without due process of law, nor shall private property be taken for public use without just compensation. In the United Kingdom, the ECHR text cited above is now part of our native constitution under our Human Rights Act 1988.[4]

States are thus restrained from seizing private property, though they can and do take it by taxation, and may confiscate the profits of crime. They also intervene in the use made of property, since that may impose hardships on third parties and involve serious issues of public policy— health, security, and so on. So far as movables are concerned, consumer protection statutes affect usually the law of obligations, that is contract and tort. It is the law of property in land which has most felt the impact

---

[4] Sched. I, Part II, art.1.

of legislative intervention enacted in the public interest. On the one hand this reflects the need for control in the interests of public health, public amenities, wildlife, access to the countryside, and the environment generally so that no longer can we do what we like with our land.[5] On the other hand much legislation has been prompted by the fact of shortage, above all of affordable housing. This takes two main forms: it may compel public authorities to provide accommodation for those in need; and it may prevent private landlords from increasing rent or evicting occupants.

European Union law

The Treaty setting up the European Community provides that it 'shall in no way prejudice the rules in Member States governing the system of property ownership' (art.295, ex art.222). Thus the basic law of property is still entirely within the competence of the Member States and is subject to their national law. But inevitably membership has consequences in some areas. An example is intellectual property where the Union is the source of some important provisions in the law of patents and copyright; another, deriving from the Common Agricultural Policy is the creation of the milk quota as an asset.[6] The most striking, however, is the introduction of the euro which means that the most common form of property—money—is no longer subject to national jurisdiction in those States which have accepted monetary union.

Public law

Leaving the international and constitutional protection of private property, we turn briefly to the general scheme for what belongs to the State, at the levels of both central and local government. There is a vast array of things which may be used for public purposes, or which serve as amenities for private citizens but do not belong to them. They belong to the State acting through both central and local government, both of which collect by taxing and borrowing and invest or disburse for the public benefit. Both have also 'inherited' much property from their predecessors.

'Crown property'. In relation to central government, the phrase 'Crown property' is often used. A very recent study at the highest levels has commented on the 'complex and arcane nature of the law' which governs

---

[5] The topic is well discussed in Kevin Gray, *Equitable Property*, 47(2) CLP (1994) 157 at 188 ff.

[6] A milk quota is basically the right to produce and market a given quantity of milk without having to pay a levy.

this field, especially in relation to land.[7] There are several categories of 'Crown property', and they are not always discrete. But here it is enough to say that the phrase covers property held by the monarch as Head of State, and property held by government departments. So, for instance, treasure which is found is said to 'vest in the Crown', but this means that it is State property and may be disposed of as directed by the Secretary of State, i.e. a government minister.[8] Similarly if an owner dies intestate without close kin, statute says that 'the residuary estate shall belong to the Crown'.[9] This means that it goes to central government funds, managed and administered by the Treasury. Thus most so-called 'Crown' property is in fact vested in and administered by various government departments, some of which, such as the Ministry of Defence, hold a great deal of land. The National Asset Register lists most of the tangible property and intangible assets of the central government departments ranging from Defence through Transport to Forestry.[10]

Other public entities. A great deal of property belongs to other public entities of various sorts ranging from local authorities to the National Health Service, the Post Office, and so on. The detailed picture is bewildering, and it is complicated further by the privatization of such things as the railways, which involves transferring property from a public entity (British Rail) to a private entity (Railtrack plc). The main principles, however, seem to be the following. Firstly, all are subject to specific parliamentary legislation and to ministerial regulation under the particular statute. Secondly, the statutes make each entity 'a body corporate', i.e. a legal person. Thirdly, the statutes empower the authority, in order to carry out its particular functions, to acquire, hold, and transfer property of all types. In many ways, then, they act at least in formal terms like anyone else; if a local council buys land by agreement it will follow the ritual of contract and conveyance, just as if it were a private citizen. But the public entities' right to hold property is limited by the functions they are to serve: for instance, a body within the National Health Service could not buy land to build a prison or an airport. Furthermore—and this is the greatest difference from private ownership—they are not free to neglect

---

[7] Law Commission (No. 271) and HM Land Registry: *Land Registration for the Twenty-First Century: A Conveyancing Revolution*, para.11.2 (2001). Since 1760, at the beginning of each monarch's reign there is enacted a Civil List Act which in effect transfers to the State the hereditary revenues of the monarch, in exchange for an annual stipend granted by Parliament. At the time of writing the sum transferred to the State is some £133m. a year.

[8] Treasure Act 1996, ss.4(1)(b), 6 (1)–(2).

[9] Administration of Estates Act 1925, s.47(1)(vi).

[10] For details go to http://www.hm-treasury.gov.uk/pub/html/docs/nar/main.html.

their belongings. The reason, of course, is that property is acquired by local and other authorities out of public funds and is vested in them for a public purpose and for no other reason. Thus the very fact that something belongs to a public authority will subject it to strict bureaucratic control, especially in relation to its use and disposal. This may be one reason why the equipment in public offices tends to be operational but out-of-date.[11]

SOURCES OF PROPERTY LAW

After this sketch of the context and background of the subject, the rest of this book is mainly about private law which, in a way, provides the basic pattern for the control and handling of all types of assets by all sectors. There is no simple source of the law of property. Like much, if not most, of the common law its structure comes from case law, common sense, and legislation; two other sources—of less importance now—are local custom and certain treatises. It should also be said that there are, so to speak, layers of law. The most fundamental principles governing the acquisition and protection of property seem to be similar in most legal systems. Of these, all the members of the common-law family tend to use much the same set of concepts and techniques.[12] Finally, and building on this base, in relation to the registration and disposition of interests in land, the law of England and Wales has in the last hundred years adopted its own system.[13]

The first thing to be understood about the common law is that, while there are basic principles covering all property, these are not to be found in an authoritative general statement comparable to that of the Civil Codes of many countries. The interplay of legislative and judicial sources in England and Wales may well amount to a coherent system, but it is very difficult to describe it simply. The very word 'property' turns up in a variety of senses. It is often, and quite correctly, used by both Parliament and the people to indicate our belongings; but it is also, equally correctly, used to denote our rights in or entitlement to those belongings. The legislature in fact uses the word in both ways: when the Partnership Act 1890 speaks of 'partnership property' it means the objects used in the partnership (s.20); when the Sale of Goods Act 1979 speaks of the

---

[11] The point is made in Ugo Mattei, *Basic Principles of Property Law: a comparative legal and economic introduction* (Greenwood Press, Westport, Conn. and London, 2000), 94.

[12] See Chapter 5.

[13] See Chapter 7.

'property in the goods' (s.16), it means what civil lawyers call ownership of, and American lawyers call title to, the goods. In other interpretation sections, the English legislator—perhaps wisely—gives merely inclusive definitions covering both objects and interests in them. For instance the Theft Act 1968 says: 'Property includes money and all other property, real or personal, including things in action and other intangible property,' while the Law of Property Act 1925 itself says only that 'property includes any thing in action and any interest in real or personal property'.[14] The Trustee Act 1925 is even wider: 'Property includes real and personal property, and any estate share or interest in any property, real or personal, and any debt, and any thing in action, and any other right and interest, whether in possession or not' (s.68(11)). As far as possible this book will use the word property as we ordinarily do, to mean belongings, possessions, assets, and the like.

Case law

Many of the key tenets of the English law of property were laid down in decisions of the old courts of common law, the King's Bench, Exchequer, and Common Pleas, and, to this day, several important issues of property law, especially between domestic partners, are still left for decision by the courts. Most of the earlier crucial litigation concerned land, since this was the important and enduring form of wealth. But other great cases wrestled with the problems of the newer forms of property such as copyrights and shares. The two main failings of the common law were that many issues were left to a jury and that—until 1850—the parties to the lawsuit could not give evidence. These and other shortcomings led many litigants to another jurisdiction, that of the Chancery. Here the Lord Chancellor took affidavit evidence from the parties and sat without a jury. He thus began a supplementary jurisdiction which assumed at every point the existence of the common-law structures and rules but made good, as far as possible, its deficiencies by doing the right thing in particular cases, otherwise called 'administering equity'. From small beginnings the role of the Chancery developed into a body of technical rules based, like the common law, on precedent and in places modified or restated by statute. Much of it deals one way or the other with property—trademarks, patents, shares, security interests and, above all, with the trust. Although the two jurisdictions of common law and equity were united in England in 1873, the habit of distinguishing the two sources of

---

[14] Theft Act 1968 s.4(1). Law of Property Act 1925 s.205(1)(xx).

law has proved inveterate.[15] The distinction between them occurs in the very first section of the Law of Property Act 1925, and to this day the reader will find judges, counsel, and writers describing the position 'at law' and contrasting it with the situation 'in Equity'.

Legislation

A number of important, if elderly, statutes have, so to speak, been absorbed into the general system of property law whether or not they are still technically in force. For instance the statute of Quia Emptores 1290 acts on every freehold land transfer taking effect today, ensuring that the seller cannot make the buyer his vassal. The Tudor period saw the statutes which permit us to dispose of our land on our death (Statute of Wills 1540), and endeavoured (unsuccessfully) to outlaw the trust (Statute of Uses 1535). Patents were regulated by the Statute of Monopolies 1623, and copyrights by an Act of 1707; they are now of course the subject of modern legislation (and international conventions and EU law). The Statute of Frauds of 1677 laid down formal requirements for the validity of several different types of disposition of property, and many of its key provisions have been re-enacted. The late seventeenth and eighteenth centuries saw the statutory creation of new types of property in government stock and the shares of the great trading and utility companies, while mid-nineteenth-century legislation created a general company law.

At this time the land law still bore the marks of feudalism and differed widely from that affecting personal property. The machinery for reconciling this with the needs of a free market was set up by legislation of 1882, and was streamlined by a set of statutes of 1925 and by the Trusts of Land and Appointment of Trustees Act of 1996. For our purposes, the most important of these statutes is called the Law of Property Act 1925 (LPA), but the beginner should be warned here and now that it does not set out the law of property, and anyone who begins to read it thinking that it does will be disappointed, if not despairing. It does not attempt to state the basic principles of a law of property applicable to all our belongings, possessions, and assets. Its purpose was to modernize bits and pieces of the law, and it cannot be understood without some prior knowledge of basic principle and vocabulary.[16] Land registration, providing public information on proprietorship and other rights in land was begun in the

---

[15] See Chapter 5.
[16] For a full account see J. Stuart Anderson, *Lawyers and the Making of English Land Law 1832–1940* (OUP, 1992).

nineteenth century and by now is almost complete; at the time of writing the Land Registration Bill 2001 is introducing the on-line transfer and registration of interests in land. During the twentieth century there was much legislation protecting the tenants of dwellings, business premises, and farms.

As we shall see in later chapters it has been the land which has attracted most of the attention of property lawyers. One reason for this is that, for centuries, it was by far the most important form of wealth. Another reason is that, since land is relatively limited in supply, the last thousand years have seen, not the creation of new property rights, but the repackaging and redistribution of existing rights. Details of the law dealing with things other than land (which, in total value, far exceed that of land) are scattered in statutes and case law dealing with the particular object concerned, from ships to shares and from goods to goodwill. There is no general enactment that a person's property can be taken in execution to meet that person's obligations, but the matter is dealt with in a series of statutes and regulations.

Sources in general

The interrelation of the major sources may be sketched as follows. The fundamental system of ownership, possession, servitudes, and security is laid down in the case law of the common law courts. To this are added corrections and refinements stemming from equity, so that it is frequently possible, by means, for instance, of the trust, to achieve results unobtainable at common law. Statutes have built on this system, sometimes restating, sometimes extending them, and sometimes amending its rules and techniques. The legislature has never attempted to set them out in a coherent structure. In particular the system tolerates large distinctions between its treatment of land and its treatment of other property, and this despite the fact that the Law of Property Act 1922 described itself as 'an Act to assimilate . . . the law of real and personal estate'.

Vocabulary

This last phrase exemplifies another problem confronting the beginner: the language used by property law is not easy. A mixture of Latin, Norman-French, and Anglo-Saxon, the jargon is thick with fossils ('incorporeal hereditament', 'fee simple') or—what is more confusing— uses in a special sense key words with common and quite different meanings in ordinary English. Worse still, it may employ them in several distinct but unusual senses. This introductory chapter concludes by explaining some of the more important words, while others will be dealt with in the appropriate section.

Legal/equitable. The first is the word 'legal'. In everyday speech this means something that is not illegal, but in English property law it is used to mean a right or interest of a type which, if formally created, will prevail against everyone else whether they know about it or not: the kind of interest enforced by the old courts of common law. The word 'legal' in this usage is contrasted with 'equitable', which here does not mean 'fair and decent'. It is employed in a technical sense to denote two different kinds of proprietary right or interest. One type will not bind a buyer of the property, even if the buyer knows all about it; it will instead be shifted to the price paid and to any investment of that money. The other type will bind only those purchasers who know or ought to know about it.

Real/personal. The next frequently recurring opposition is that between '*real*' property (or 'realty') and '*personal*' property ('personalty'), the former being interests in land other than leases, the latter being everything else.[17] The distinction has nothing to do with reality and unreality. History is the reason for this choice of words, which relates to the way in which the law protected someone whose property was wrongfully taken. If the property was land, the law (by force if necessary) enabled the evicted holder to get it back from whoever had it: to recover the thing itself. The Latin for thing is *res*, hence land was called real property. If the thing taken was a chattel, the legal remedy was against the *person* who had it, who could be forced to come to court and be ordered, not to give it back, but to pay its value. Hence things which could not be recovered themselves were called personalty. As to land, realty was used to describe the entitlement of a freeholder, i.e. someone whose possession of the land had no fixed term. If the land were held on lease, the lease itself was technically personalty (hence avoiding the medieval rule that realty could not be left by will but had to descend to the heir who then paid a kind of tax to take it). However, the lessee, like the freeholder, came to be able to recover the land itself to enjoy for the remainder of the term of the lease. So this interest came to bear the odd title of chattel real. The reasons for this strange nomenclature have long gone, but the names live on. They are mentioned here only because the student is sure to encounter them later. Indeed, common-law authors in this field commonly produce separate books on real property (immovables) and on personal property (everything else). There is something to be said for

---

[17] In American English an estate agent is a 'realtor'.

such a division of labour in writing specialist and detailed treatments of the law. This book is not such a work.

Real, or property, rights. At this juncture, however, a further complication of terminology needs to be explained. '*Real property*' means land. But the expression '*real right*' can be used with regard to *any* type of property (movable or immovable). It is used to describe those interests which, broadly speaking, (a) can be alienated; (b) die when their object perishes or is lost without trace; (c) until then can be asserted against an indefinite number of people; (d) if the holder of the thing itself is bankrupt, enable the holder of the real right to take out of the bankruptcy the interest protected by the real right.

This apparently complicated statement can be illustrated quite simply. If you own this book you have a real right. As to point (a), you can give away or sell both the book and ownership of the book. As to point (b) if the book is destroyed in a fire, it is no longer yours and you bear the loss.[18] As to (c) if you lend the book to a friend, of course you can claim it (or its value) back from him or her. But if your friend lends it to someone else you can claim it from them; indeed, in English law, you can claim it from someone to whom your friend sells it—your right is enforceable against an indefinite number of persons. Finally, as to (d), if your friend goes bankrupt while reading the book, you do not have to prove as a creditor in the bankruptcy proceedings. The book does not vest in the trustee in bankruptcy, since your friend cannot pay off his or her creditors with your book.

Other ways of referring to these features of a 'real right' are to speak of a '*property* right' or '*proprietary* right'.[19] We have used the simple example of ownership, but as we shall see later there is a limited number of other interests which can be described as 'real' or 'proprietary'. This can be illustrated by considering your right to leave your car in next door's yard. Probably at the moment you have no such right. If your neighbour lets you, you can park but you have no right to stay. If you pay for parking, say by the month, you have a contractual right to leave your car, enforceable by an action for damages and possibly an injunction, but enforceable against your neighbour only. If, however, you have an easement—a recognized real right—your claim to park will prevail against whoever owns

---

[18] You might have a claim for its value against your insurance company or against the person who burned it, but that claim stems from a contract with the insurer or from a tort committed by the arsonist.

[19] 'Copyright is a *property* right . . .' says s. 1(1) of the Copyright, Designs and Patents Act 1988.

next door. But before the common law will recognize it as a property interest, the right to park must comply with certain requirements both of substance and form: you must own the freehold or leasehold of your house; the parking must not be a claim to possession of your neighbour's entire yard; it must be intended to add to the value of the house and not just to confer a personal benefit on you; and it must be created by deed and be entered on the Land Register, or else have been acquired by over twenty years open user.

Two other words should be added which are used in a number of different technical meanings.

Estate. The word 'estate' is used in four quite different ways: it may mean a piece of land ('the Osborne estate'). It may refer to both land and other things ('real and personal estate'). It may refer to the totality of assets and liabilities left on death—the deceased's 'estate', solvent or insolvent. Fourthly, it is used to describe an entitlement to property in terms of the time for which it will last: so a leasehold is an estate whose end is fixed (or can be fixed); a life estate lasts for someone's life, and so on.[20]

Equity. The second word of many meanings is 'equity'. In ordinary English this means something like 'fairness'. It came to describe the activity of a particular tribunal, the Chancery, which administered 'equity' in order, in the name of fairness, to correct or supplement some of the rigours of the common law. From this it became used to mean a correction or remedy available in that court. In particular the borrower on mortgage was allowed to repay the loan and redeem the mortgage even after the date specified in the deed: this was called the equitable right to redeem. From this there developed the phrase 'equity of redemption' to mean the amount by which a mortgaged property's value exceeds the loan secured on it. The latter figure is fixed: it is the amount lent plus interest. The 'equity' is not fixed, its amount depending on, and varying with, the market value of the property.[21] From its use in this context, the word 'equity' comes to mean the interest of an ordinary shareholder as contrasted with that of a creditor of a company. Creditors recover their debt plus interests and costs but no more. If these debts equal or exceed the company's assets, the shareholders will get nothing. But if assets exceed liabilities, the residual value will be divided among the shareholders. So, unlike the creditors, they have an interest whose value is uncertain until

---

[20] This is explained more fully in Chapter 5.
[21] Explained more fully in Chapter 9.

the last moment. One sees in the financial pages of the press reports that the creditors of a company are going to 'swap debt for equity', meaning that they will exchange their bonds for shares.

Holder. It comes as a relief to end with one simple word, which is much used and avoids the problems of the word 'owner'. Domesday Book 1086 constantly says '*Rex tenet*'—the King *holds* such-and-such a farm, a mill, and so on. To this day, property law uses the noun either in its French form—'tenant'—or in its Teutonic—freeholder, leaseholder, householder, shareholder, bondholder, 'holder in due course', and so on.

Part 2

Property in General

This part offers an introduction to the private law of property. Chapter 2 explains the main types of property and the means by which they are classified. Chapter 3 deals with the principal ways in which we acquire these various types of property (though succession on death is treated in Chapter 11). Chapter 4 outlines the ways in which the law protects the entitlements so acquired.

2

The Classification of Things

This chapter explains the main legal categories of the things we own. First, however, we should note that lawyers need to distinguish the thing from an interest in the thing. Thus if you own a horse you can say so. But if you and your brother own equal shares in the horse, this does not mean that one owns the forelegs and one the hindlegs, nor can you truthfully say 'I own the horse'. You have to describe your interest in the thing and say 'I own a half share in the horse'. A later chapter will describe these and other interests. This chapter is about the things themselves. It is not, of course, the kind of taxonomy that would appeal to a natural scientist, both because it is crude, and more importantly because it classifies things in their relation to humans.

The things that make up property may be perceived and treated in various ways. Clearly there are physical differences between them. There are also different ways in which we regard them. We can treat things as important for their own sake, and for the satisfaction of our wants (home, food, and clothing are the obvious examples); we can treat them as a store of value (money, current and deposit accounts, life insurance, shares, and so on); or as part of the process of adding value (where finished products are being manufactured out of raw materials). The law deals with our property in all these aspects, covering not just the stuff we can touch and handle, but also our wealth in general. As noted above, it says what we can do with our things—anything we like, if we like; and it says what others can do with them: nothing, unless we let them. More particularly, it defines and classifies particular types of property, and then, depending on their most significant features, it lays down the formalities needed for their transfer or acquisition, and provides certain procedures for their protection.

The physical and economic characteristics of particular things naturally exert an influence on their legal treatment, especially when the thing comes to be transferred or when our rights in it are challenged and require protection. This section, however, aims only to depict the main sets of things 'at rest', so to speak, i.e. neither in transfer nor under threat. Furthermore its divisions are generalizations, that is to say in terms of features which are usually, if not always, true; sometimes there are grey areas and sometimes overlaps, but most of the criteria are simple matters of observation, with which anyone can agree.

First of all not every thing is property. For something to be *property* in the eyes of the law it must be capable of being *appropriated*. So the air, the clouds, the high seas, are not, for legal purposes, property. Furthermore, some things which could conceivably be appropriated are held not to be objects of private property. For instance, in England and Wales, the foreshore cannot be owned privately; this ensures that, in practice, the public can use the beach for bathing, fishing, and navigation. Another, quite different, example concerns the human body, alive or dead, which as such is not the object of property at all.[1]

The English law of property is not limited to material things—as we shall see there are assets which cannot themselves be perceived by the senses (such as copyright, goodwill, shares, milk quotas) yet which are recognized by the law as being property which can be transferred or inherited, and which will be protected against *misappropriation*.

That said, the law has to take notice of the important distinctions among types of property, although the common law (unlike, say, that of Germany) does not do so in any general systematic way. It is worth repeating that, while some of these distinctions are physical, others depend on the use to which the things are put or the way in which we treat them.

GENERAL DISTINCTIONS

An obvious overall division is into tangible (or material) objects and intangible assets. The first class can then be divided into things that, to our eyes, do not move (such as land) and those that do; in this last subset we find things that can move themselves, like animals and insects, and those which cannot, such as goods and crops. Another common distinction is between a tangible thing and its components (a clock and its works), and between a principal thing and the accessories that go with it (a car and its keys). In practice this last distinction causes most problems where movables are fixed to buildings, and will be dealt with later. In the

---

[1] Various statutes deal with the control and use of human tissue for medical purposes. For an interesting discussion of the ethical and other problems arising in this area see J. W. Harris, *Property and Justice* (OUP, 1996), 351 ff.

set of movables we find things that we consume, like milk, and things we do not, like cups; and we find things which are specific, like a Vermeer painting and things which we often treat generically, like needles and nails (this set is called 'fungible' by lawyers).

Intangible assets are a little less obvious at first. In general terms they include those *embodied in* a document (such as a promissory note), which we shall call documentary intangibles; those commonly *evidenced by* a document (such as a share certificate), which we shall call documented intangibles; and those which need have no such piece of paper, such as a credit balance with a bank. It must be added that this scheme is now obscured by the 'dematerialization' of shares, bonds, and investment securities generally and the replacement of paper by database entries.

Another useful division in this set of intangibles is between those assets which are claims to money (cheques etc.) and those which are not (copyrights, goodwill etc.). A further classification much used by English law is one which distinguishes a set of things (such as a flock or an investment portfolio) from individual members of the set (a sheep, a National Savings certificate). Another division is between capital and income; and then there is cash money, which deserves a paragraph to itself.

As we said earlier, one of the main difficulties which the student of property law encounters at the very beginning is the presence of, indeed the preference for, abstractions. English property law is particularly devoted to them, and not just out of historical inertia. The reason why it treats intangible interests as objects, as things, is because people are willing to buy them; and any thing which is the object of commerce may be treated as an asset, just as much if it is an abstraction like a share in a company as if it is a physical object like a house or a car. Many of these abstractions are simply the law's recognition of economic realities; indeed (outside land law) it is commerce which has devised the innovations, leaving it to lawyers to fit them, belatedly, into some scheme of recognition and protection. As was explained earlier, Parliament has not attempted to produce any overall principled structure of property law, and so the system which emerges is the product of custom, case law, and commentary. It is also untidy.

The most obvious distinction among tangible objects is between those which are (more or less) immovable and those which are (more or less) movable. But this simple scheme is not exactly the one used by common-law systems. As explained in the previous chapter, the class of immovables is called real property or realty; everything else is called

personal property or personalty; if it is tangible personalty it is called a
chattel (from the same root as the word cattle).

For many purposes it is still useful to keep land apart from other types
of property since it has a number of important features which the others
do not share. It is permanent, almost indestructible, will produce an
income in crops or in cash, and is capable of almost infinite division and
subdivision into concurrent and successive interests. Accordingly, from
the earliest periods of English law it has been common to make the same
piece of land serve the needs of several persons whose interests may
conflict.

Remembering always that no classification is perfect, and remembering
also that property includes our wealth as well as our belongings, the main
characteristics of the different types of property will be discussed under
the following headings: (1) land; (2) living creatures; (3) goods, i.e.
tangible movables; (4) documentary intangibles such as a cheque; (5)
documented intangibles like shares and other investment securities;
(6) undocumented intangibles such as credit balances; (7) intellectual
property; (8) money; (9) funds; (10) capital and income.

TANGIBLE OBJECTS

1. LAND

Definition. In English law the word 'land' includes the works of nature
and of humans within a particular space on the earth. It consists of any
definite portion of the planet's surface with the natural resources on or
under the surface—trees, waters, and mineral deposits for instance. In
general, whatever attaches to the soil is treated as part of it. This means
that individual movable objects such as seeds or seedlings lose their identity when sown or planted in the ground and become part of the land.
Similarly, objects such as crops or trees which are ordinarily thought of as
things in themselves, and which will become individual movable things
once detached from the soil, are at present part of it. An interest in land
confers rights above and below the surface itself, whereas an interest in a
chattel is bounded by its physical exterior.

The word 'land' also includes what humans have added to the earth,
buildings, structures, and so on. These are part of the land, for a house
has no identity of its own until built on it, and the materials have become
merged in the house. However, although a building is part of the land on
which it is built, it is possible to divide it, not only vertically, for instance

into two semi-detached houses, but also horizontally into flats each of which is a separate piece of landed property. Thus the owner of a top-floor flat owns land, although it is not directly fixed to the earth.

Earlier we mentioned the distinction between principals and accessories. In relation to land, the most difficult questions here arise in connection with what are called fixtures, that is chattels which have become part of the land and so belong to its owner. The primary question is, what is a fixture? It is often raised when one person buys a house and takes a transfer of it from another, or where one person lends money by mortgage on the security of another's land. Clearly, the chairs and tables are not part of the land but the front door is. In between, and in the absence of express agreement, doubts may arise as to whether with the house go the rose trees in the garden, the waste-disposal unit, fitted carpets, and so on. It is impossible in advance to lay down a rule that will apply without hesitation to every object. What can be said is that, generally speaking, anything is a fixture that is not merely placed on the land but is attached to it with the purpose of making it part of the land. Whatever meets this test will pass with the land to a buyer, or will be subject to a mortgage.

The second question is, granted that a thing is a fixture, may it be removed at the end of his term by a lessee (or life tenant) who has affixed it to the land? If the law said no, there would be little incentive for a shop tenant to fit shelving, or for the lessee of a restaurant to install a built-in oven. So the answer is that it may be removed if any damage is made good. This does not mean that, while affixed, the fixtures are not part of the land; it means only that, at the wish of the tenant, they may cease to be so.

Features. By 'land' then, the law understands all immovable property—fields, farms, houses, shops, factories, and so on. It is worth reflecting on the ten most obvious characteristics of this species of property because, as will be seen, they have determined the uses to which land can be put and the concepts which English lawyers long ago devised to give effect to those uses. Furthermore—and this is very important—we shall see later that most of these concepts can now be readily applied to other species of property—particularly stock, shares, and government bonds—which, as investments, share some of the features of land.

(i) *Permanence.* The most obvious feature of land as distinct from movables is that it endures. Of course there may be natural calamities, earthquakes, landslides, and so on, but it would be absurd, for fear of these exceptional events, to treat land as essentially evanescent. The permanence of land has several consequences. First of all it is well suited to long-term and heavy investment in improvements, from land drainage to the construction of a cathedral or a shopping mall. Second, since it and our investment in it will be here when we are gone, it can be used to provide for the next generation and even the one after that.

(ii) *Safety*. Land is not the only thing of permanence—diamonds are forever. But, unlike them, land cannot readily be stolen; in fact the current English Theft Act, while conceding that land is property, provides that as a general rule 'land cannot be stolen'. It is, as we shall see, better protected than are movables by other branches of the law.

(iii) *Limited supply*. While fields may be built on and skyscrapers soar, there is, none the less, a finite amount of land available. Furthermore, this country—relatively speaking—has a large population in proportion to its area. The limit in supply leads to problems in resolving conflicting demands on the use of such land as is available.

(iv) *Externalities*. Since we live in a relatively crowded island, the way in which we use our own land is very likely to affect others. We may confer a benefit on them for which they do not pay, if for instance we fashion a beautiful garden readily visible from their house. But (and this is more noticeable) we may, without any malice or carelessness, impose unpleasantness on them for which we do not pay by, say, operating a licensed slaughter-house. To some extent such problems can be resolved by private bargaining (the imposition of restrictive covenants) or by the law of nuisance, but they are also an area of extensive public-law involvement. Planning and environmental protection legislation are the two obvious examples.

(v) *Fruits/income*. An important feature of land from the point of view of our legal system is that, without depletion, it will produce an income. Apple trees will produce fruit, fields will yield crops and, provided some of the profits are ploughed back into maintenance, the flow will continue. For an office-block, factory, or shop, the rents fulfil the same function. What is perhaps a little more difficult to see at first is that a house has an income value for its owner-occupiers. Admittedly it produces no cash for them, but they are not paying rent or hotel bills to live elsewhere. They are benefiting from what economists call the 'quasi-rent'.

Land is not, of course, the only thing to produce a yield; cattle have calves and humans, children. More will be said of this under the general heading, later, of capital and income.[2]

---

[2] Meanwhile we might add that, under EU law, dairy farm-land may benefit from a 'milk quota' which is, within limits, alienable and may be transferred to other land.

(vi) *Capital value*. Meanwhile, it is obvious that, with reasonable management, land will produce an income without depletion of its capital value—the amount it would fetch on sale. Indeed, given the limited supply mentioned above and the growth of demand for land, its capital value may not only keep pace with inflation but may increase in real terms.

(vii) *Necessity*. Land is necessary to us all. We are born on it and buried in it. In the interval between those two events we need somewhere to live and work, something to eat, and something to wear. Our home is land, and our food and clothes are produced, made, stored, and sold to us on land. Some fraction of its cost at each of these stages enters into the price we pay for the things we buy.

(viii) *Investment*. The combination of the features just described has meant for centuries that land is an attractive investment. People (or corporations) who have wealth beyond what they need to survive will find in it something that is permanent, safe, limited in supply, income-producing, and appreciating in capital value. When to this is added the fact of necessity its attraction becomes paramount: where better to put one's money than in something everyone needs. This feature can give rise to conflicts between the wealthy few and the rest of us, and some countries have sought to resolve these conflicts by simply forbidding private investment in land—this was the case in the Soviet Union for most of the last century. Our system has not attempted this, but has intervened in particular areas; the impact of public law will be described later.

(ix) *Endowment*. As an investment, land may form part of the balanced portfolio of any wealthy person, company, or pension fund. But it has certain features which take it outside the purely commercial calculus and recommend it as a family endowment. The fact that it is permanent, safe, and fruitful makes it suitable as a provision for more than one future generation. The law's response to this has, for centuries, been a system which enables ownership of the income to be split from that of the capital, so that one generation may be given the income but only the income, while the capital is reserved for their children. It is in fulfilling this function that the concept of the 'estate' in land has proved so useful.[3]

(x) *Public power*. Finally, and as a historical note, it should be recalled that the private ownership of this attractive investment (or 'means of production') conferred public power. Along with the ownership of a county, say Norfolk, went the public honour of a peerage and the political

---

[3] See Chapter 5.

power of a seat in the upper chamber of the legislature. The peerage and the power were inheritable until almost the end of the twentieth century, while at a more modest level, the right to vote for a member of the lower house of Parliament was confined to (male) landowners until early in the twentieth century.

2. LIVING CREATURES

Animals, fish, and fowl, whether wild as prey or domesticated as a source of food and motive power, have long been of great importance to human survival. Furthermore those which are farmed are the source of both income and capital development. For instance a flock of sheep will produce lambs, milk, wool, and meat all of which in turn can form the basis for some wealth-creating activity other than farming, such as the production and sale of cheese or chops or clothing. As objects of property, the law has been mainly concerned with the acquisition of animals, as explained in a later chapter. But our powers over them are subject to increasing limitations. Many 'protected species' may not be taken at all. And even for ordinary domestic animals, although they are ours, we may not do what we like with them: it is a crime to cause them unnecessary pain.

3. GOODS

Goods are defined by the Sale of Goods Act as personal chattels other than things in action and money. For the purposes of the law of sale, the category also includes growing crops produced by the labour of the cultivator, and things forming part of the land which are to be severed and sold. That means that the law of goods and not the much more formal law of real property applies to crops and the like which are sold before being harvested or removed, though they are actually part of the land and therefore not goods, until they are severed from it.

Many of the features discussed above in relation to land do not, on the whole, apply to goods. A few may be permanent, but the overwhelming majority are in the process of being manufactured, or of moving down the chain of suppliers to the end-user, in whose hands they will be consumed (food and drink), will wear out (clothing, cars), or will become relatively useless (horseshoes). On the whole goods are readily transferable from hand to hand with no need for formal documents, may be difficult to trace and find, and are often quite indistinguishable from others of the same type. And goods are the subject matter of large-scale transactions in a wholesale market in a way that land is not; most land is bought at retail, in single lots.

For these and other reasons the law's treatment of them frequently differs from that of land. The most obvious difference is in its protection of our claims to particular goods—as we shall see later, the normal rule is that, if we sue because our goods are wrongly taken and withheld, and are successful, the defendant will be ordered, not to return the goods, but to pay us compensation in money so that if we want to we can go and buy some more.[4] The reasons for this approach (apart from the features just mentioned) have to do with the problems and costs of enforcing the order. If the defendant is ordered to return the goods and refuses to do so, it may be difficult for the law to find and return them to us; and so the law is tempted to use the weapon of contempt of court—to imprison the defendant until he or she obeys. This means jailing, for an indeterminate sentence, someone who has not been charged with, let alone convicted of, a crime. If instead, however, the court orders the payment of money compensation ('damages'), then this order can be enforced against the defendant's property, not his or her person: objects can be seized and sold, bank accounts can be reached, and so on.

As mentioned above, a distinction is often made, when we are buying or selling, between goods which are mutually interchangeable (fungible) and those which are not. With goods of the former class, the specific identity of each object is not an issue: it does not matter which nails or milk are delivered, provided they are of the right size, quality, and quantity. Fungibles can be replaced by equal quantities of the same type, and are usually traded by weight, number, or measure. Typical fungibles are raw materials, cereals, coins and the like; and, as we shall see, some documentary intangibles such as shares and bonds form an important class of fungibles. Perhaps there are some goods which are not capable of being fungible—there are certainly many which are never traded as such: think of the great works of art. But even goods normally fungible can be treated as individuals: thus coins, if valued for their rarity or aesthetic or archaeological interest, are not fungible, because they cannot be replaced by others. In other words, goods are fungible if they are treated as such in a particular transaction.

A distinction which overlaps with this, is that between generic and specific, between 'bread' and 'this loaf', between £10 and 'this banknote', between 'my books' and 'this book of mine'. As we shall see later the distinction is important when considering the transfer of ownership in things, because, while we can own things which we can describe only

---

[4] See Chapter 4.

generically ('my books'), and can contract to transfer ownership of the genus ('I will sell you all my books'), we can actually transfer ownership only of the specific books (or other asset). Similarly, if the subject matter of a sale is expressed as so many articles of a class or kind or so many units of weight of a raw material, the goods are at that moment both fungible and unascertained. When so many articles or so much weight of raw material are set aside for the buyer, the goods become ascertained. Yet there are obviously not two different classes of goods; the same goods were unascertained until human selection intervened. Of course for people to be willing to buy goods which are to be ascertained later, they must regard them as fungible, that is to say as not depending for their value or utility on their qualities as individuals.

Yet another distinction is made between existing and future goods, the latter being often the expected produce of agriculture or industry. As such they are unascertained, fungible, and generic, yet they are incessantly bought and sold. Indeed it is the market in future goods that makes possible the whole existing chain of manufacture and distribution. Next year's cotton crop has already been sold, and many of its buyers will sell on: to see how much you will have to pay for a given quantity and quality, consult the commodity prices in the financial pages of the newspaper.

Of course, strictly speaking, future goods are not yet goods and a so-called 'sale' cannot make the buyer owner of them. But a seller's promise to deliver them vests in the buyer a specific claim, and the buyer's undertaking to pay the price vests a money claim in the seller. As will be explained later, such claims are often symbolized by a document and are treated as themselves objects of property to be traded in the commodity and money markets.

Some articles have a value so great and so dependent on their individual characteristics that some sure and permanent means are required of identifying them and the persons entitled to them. This often leads to the formation of registers, sometimes private such as that of racehorses, often public such as the registers of ships and of aircraft mortgages. Ships, indeed, have long been governed by special rules of law and are for some purposes treated almost as if they were floating plots of land.

INTANGIBLE ASSETS

In general

It is natural when we think of property to look first to tangible things. But in fact a great part of the world's wealth is not tangible. At the time of writing, this country owes some £325,000,000,000 borrowed by the issue of government bonds.[5] Debts, by definition, must be owed to someone, so there must be creditors (human or corporate, British, foreign, or international). Their claims are so safe that they are called 'gilt-edged' or just 'gilts', and they form part of the creditors' fortune. Even more modest savers may well hold National Savings certificates. When to all this are added the billions invested in stocks and shares, and the billions in bank accounts, it will be seen that intangibles are a very large segment of wealth. Indeed, at the beginning of this century, those who were said to be the richest people in the world were thought to be so because of the market value of their holdings, not of land and other tangible objects, but of shares in cyberspace companies—the 'dot.com millionaires'.

All this means that the category of intangibles is very disparate and is difficult to characterize in general terms. It is made up of quite different kinds of asset whose nomenclature is by no means as settled as that of the physical world of land and goods. Furthermore, the law seems always to lag behind commerce, so that the new types of asset which are developed and eagerly traded (such as financial derivatives) take on a dynamic of their own before the legal system catches up.

The most general name which the common law gives to the class of intangibles is 'things in action' or 'choses in action', using the French word for 'thing'. To the modern reader this is not a very helpful or informative designation. It is given here only because it is still used in modern legislation such as the Sale of Goods Act and the Theft Act and (in the USA) the Uniform Commercial Code. The phrase was coined to convey two notions, one positive and one negative. The word 'thing' catches the idea that, whatever it is, it is an asset; it has value, it can be inherited and traded, and can be reached by its holder's creditors. The phrase 'in action' is meant to convey the idea that this asset is not tangible and can be transformed into a tangible object only (if at all) by successfully suing someone. If someone owes you £100, your claim is certainly

---

[5] A somewhat greater sum is owing on non-government bonds denominated in sterling and issued by companies and supranational borrowers such as the European Investment Bank.

an asset which would pass on your death and which you could give away or sell. But to get the money you would, as a last resort, have to go to law. The older books use the phrase as one of a pair: there are 'choses in possession' which you can touch; and 'choses in action' which are yours but which you cannot take hold of.

Over the last few hundred years, as new types of intangible property interests have come into being, common lawyers have tended to shovel them into the general category of 'things in action' until it becomes so large as to be of little use. Great judges have disagreed as to whether a share in a company is a 'chose in action'. Parliament in 1945 classified patents as a chose in action and then in 1977 said that they were not.

Further complications are caused by the vocabulary of the financial markets. An official publication tells us that 'the Government finances its borrowing requirement by *selling debt* to the private sector'.[6] By this strange phrase is meant the issue of bonds whereby the government borrows money and the lenders in return get a marketable claim. Private business, also, has its own jargon. This is particularly so in one of the most common of commercial relationships: if L, a lender, lends money to B, a borrower, we have a word to describe the borrower's position: B is in *debt*. L is in credit, but what do we call L's claim? We can say that the lender *owns* and the borrower B *owes* the debt, but the use of the same noun to describe both ends of the relation may well cause confusion. The international bond markets nowadays tend to use the word 'credits' to denote the assets held as a result of a loan. Business, on the other hand, uses a different word to describe L's chose in action: a *receivable*. Suppose a firm has sold goods or supplied services to its customers and is owed money by them. Instead of chasing each account it may, in exchange for cash, transfer its claims against its customers to a firm (called a 'factor'), which specializes in collecting payment. The standard contract document between the firm and its factor provides that 'the ownership of each Receivable shall vest in the Factor'.

Another difficulty in explaining this general category is the role of documents. Some widespread obligations are commonly embodied in a document; the obligation may be to deliver goods (such as a bill of lading issued by a carrier) or to pay money (such as a promissory note). The claim to performance of the obligation is enshrined in the document; it passes with delivery of the document (with intent to transfer and with indorsement if necessary); the debtor need pay the money (or deliver

---

[6] *Britain 2001*, 405, col.2 (Office of National Statistics, Stationery Office, 2001).

the goods) only on production of the document, and discharges the obligation by doing so whether or not the person who produced the document was actually entitled to it.

Other types of intangible are commonly, but not necessarily, evidenced by written documents. This is the case, for instance, with company shares; or rather it was the case before the computerization and 'dematerialization' of many securities.

A third category is the intangible which may or may not be accompanied by a document (such as arises from an ordinary loan of money), but whose validity and enforceability are in no way dependent on the document.

1. DOCUMENTARY INTANGIBLES: COMMERCIAL PAPER

There are excellent works on commercial law where the reader can find detailed information on this topic.[7] We need give only an outline here, emphasizing the part played by the paper itself in the law of property.

Certain types of written undertakings to pay money or deliver goods have become so standardized and accepted by the world of commerce that the paper represents almost completely the money or the goods. On a commercial contract for the sale of goods, one that is not to be performed for some time, each party has the benefit of the other's promise. This benefit is an asset which each owns and can transfer, but in itself it is merely a claim by which the buyer can require the seller to deliver the goods and the seller can require the buyer to pay the price agreed. If, however, each party's obligation is embodied in a certain written form, the documents themselves can be traded almost as if they were the money or the goods. For instance, the seller can take to the bank the instrument containing the buyer's obligation to pay the price at a certain time in the future (say, a post-dated cheque).[8] The bank will pay for it (i.e. credit his account) in a sum which represents the present value of the future payment by the buyer. The actual process of 'discounting' is explained later. Thus the obligation of each party can be traded by the other, and there are global commodity and money markets where this happens constantly.

Monetary obligations: negotiable instruments. Normally if you transfer something you cannot pass a better title than the one you have. But certain species of documentary intangible are not merely tradable but

---

[7] See above all Sir Roy Goode, *Commercial Law* (2nd edn., Penguin, 1995).
[8] Since the Cheques Act 1992, a cheque crossed a/c payee is not even transferable, let alone negotiable.

negotiable, in the sense that any 'holder in due course' (i.e. one who takes in good faith an instrument for which value has been given) obtains a good title despite any defect in the title of the transferor.[9] Thus if, in good faith, you buy books or a car from someone who has stolen them, you must return them to their owner and are left, for what it is worth, with an action against the thief. But a thief can pass to an innocent purchaser a good title to a negotiable instrument. Such a purchaser owns, and can trade, the instrument itself and is entitled to payment on presentation at the due time. The best-known negotiable instruments are the bill of exchange, the promissory note, and the cheque. For the law of property the essential feature of a bill of exchange is that it represents in documentary form a debt which is owed. Its holder can deal with this asset just as if it were a physical thing like a book or a motor car. Indeed a negotiable instrument is even more suitable to commerce than either of these things. Being an entitlement to money, it has an abstract value which is detached from, but can be exchanged for, any particular physical object.

Goods obligations: documents of title. The obligations of sellers, carriers, and custodians of goods are often—above all in international trade— embodied in standard documents. Sellers issue a contract of sale, for instance 'f.o.b.', which means 'free on board' and contains the seller's undertaking to get the goods on a nominated vessel, at which point they belong to the buyer. The carrier, for its part, gives the seller two copies of a document called a 'bill of lading' which functions as a receipt for the goods and an undertaking to deliver them to the person who is the then holder of the bill of lading. The seller sends a copy to the buyer who can then sell the goods before they arrive by indorsing and delivering the bill of lading. The ultimate holder can call for delivery on surrendering the bill, and the carrier's obligation is discharged by delivery to such a person. To that extent the bill of lading represents the goods; but the document is not quite so powerful as a negotiable instrument because, although the carrier must deliver to the person who presents the bill, if it has been lost by or stolen from anyone properly entitled to it, that person can recover the goods from the person who has taken delivery, or indeed from anyone who has acquired them since. The same rules apply to other documents of title unless in some way, by custom or otherwise (especially in the USA), they have been made fully negotiable.

---

[9] Cash is the most obvious example of this, but money deserves a section to itself.

2. INVESTMENT SECURITIES: STOCKS, SHARES, BONDS ETC.

The word 'security' is ambiguous. In one usage it covers the devices developed to ensure payment of a debt: a watch, left with a pawnbroker, is the lender's 'security', since return of the watch is conditional on repayment of the loan. In this section, however, the word means investments such as bonds and shares. Their description as 'documented' and not 'documentary', conveys the notion that, while documents such as share certificates are (or were) common, they are merely evidence of, and are not essential to, entitlement to the security. Transfer of a share certificate may entitle the transferee to be registered as owner of the share, but does not itself transfer ownership.[10] And nowadays, for many companies, share certificates have given way to entries in a computer database.

Bonds is the general name for instruments which acknowledge the loans made to central government, other public authorities, and commercial entities—we have already seen that at the time of writing, investors hold UK government bonds to the tune of about £325 billion. They bear interest at a fixed rate on their nominal value, and may provide that the capital is redeemable, or irredeemable. After their issue, they are assets which are traded in the bond market at prices which may be less or more than their nominal value.

As to shares issued by companies, one can begin by saying that each represents a stake in the net capital of the company proportionate to the sum contributed on its issue—for companies are not allowed to give their shares away for nothing. Now a person may have shares, for the time being undivided, in other things such as land, or a collection of pictures, or a heap of coal, and in all such cases a majority may insist on having the property divided and so convert the shares in the whole into sole ownership of a specific part or quantity. But a company shareholder cannot force a division of the company's assets, nor sue the company for the value of the share. True, a share confers membership of the company together—though not necessarily—with voting rights and thus with some power to participate in the corporate governance. So a majority of shareholders' votes can bring the company to an end by 'winding-up'. We can say in general terms that a company share gives its holder, apart from the right to participate in the governance of the company, the right to income—if the company makes a profit and its directors decide to 'divide'

---

[10] That is the general position in English (unlike US) law.

it—hence the word 'dividends'. Each share also embodies the entitlement to a proportionate amount of the capital fund represented by the company's (ever-changing) assets, minus the amount owing on its (ever-changing) obligations. The current value of that entitlement, as compared with other possible investments, is determined by the market price of a share. Of course if a company is wound up when its liabilities exceed its assets, its creditors have the first claim, and the shareholders may get nothing. But that latent uncertainty is one of the common marks of 'ownership'. It applies to our own belongings, for, if we are insolvent, our creditors can take them from us (except for necessaries such as our clothes and bedding). So shares represent a kind of deferred residual right to a fund of property. Meanwhile, during the life of the company, a share is an asset of its holder which can be bought and sold, will pass on death, and may be reached by its holder's creditors.

Uncertificated units. Traditionally, shareholding was denoted by entry of the holder's name in the company's register of shareholders, while the investor received a certificate evidencing her title. To alienate her share she would sign a transfer (usually printed on the back of the certificate) and hand it to the transferee who would forward it to the company, which was then obliged to amend the register accordingly and issue a new certificate to the new holder. This is a labour-intensive process which, towards the end of the last century, threatened to bury itself under mountains of paperwork.

The solution which developed bears the daunting name of 'dematerialization'. This means that the securities of many public companies are nowadays held and dealt in, not by documents, but by a computer system. Legislation and regulations are in place to achieve two aims: first of all to enable title to securities to be evidenced otherwise than by a certificate and to be transferred otherwise than by a written document; and secondly to ensure that the holders' property rights remain secure, although they have no piece of paper and the object of their entitlement is no longer particular shares but the requisite number of uncertificated units denoted by some entry on a database.

Intermediation. This second novel name is given to the modern method of indirect holding of investments (which themselves may or may not be dematerialized). In the traditional system, each investor usually holds directly from the company, with his or her name on the register of shareholders. On transfer of the share the register is altered so that the new holder's name replaces that of the old. The new system—developed by the market, not the lawyers—interposes between the investor and the company a number of intermediaries. Securities such as shares and bonds of any given company are issued to a custodian or depositary, which is the holder of record in the books or database of the issuer: the securities themselves are said to be 'immobilized'. The depositary holds them for the benefit of other financial institutions such as banks and registered brokers who, in turn, hold for their clients. At each level the books (or database) maintained by the higher of the two indicate that the appropriate investment asset has been credited to the account of the lower. For instance, the register of shareholders of Widgets plc may show that 90 per cent of its securities are held by the Custodian Trust Company. The latter's books will break down this figure and indicate, for instance, that it holds in equal shares for the accounts of nine brokers. Each broker's records will show the clients for whom the firm holds its Widgets asset. This eliminates the need for the brokers to hand share certificates back and forth as they buy and sell for their clients. Furthermore the number of entries made in each broker's account with the Custodian Trust Company is greatly reduced by the process known as 'netting'. Thus if, on a given day, a broker's customer A sells his entitlement to 100 shares of Widgets plc and another customer B buys an entitlement equivalent to 100 shares in the same company, the broker's account with the depositary does not change at all. Similar procedures higher up the chain ensure that the company's register of shareholders needs few amendments. Nowadays virtually all institutional investors such as pension funds hold their investment securities through arrangements with banks which act as intermediaries.

Under this new system, then, investors have no share certificates and are not named in the company's register. Yet they paid good money for a stake in the company and so it is important that their entitlement be a property interest which gives them all the rights and risks of ownership. Here, English law uses (in addition to financial services regulations) concepts developed in the law of trusts to ensure that each client's entitlement in the asset held by the intermediary is freely alienable by the investor, and that it cannot be reached by the creditors of the intermediary. Intermediaries must always hold enough of the relevant assets to meet their clients' claims. In this they resemble trustees who must conserve the trust fund, and they differ from banks, who are not required to keep enough cash in their vaults to meet the claims of all their customers. Thus the investor's entitlement comprises both personal, contractual, claims against the intermediary broker, and a property interest consisting of a pro rata claim (in common with other investors) to the pool of fungible security assets held by the broker. This pattern is repeated at each level of holding. One might add that the chain of property relations from the company to the main depositary down through intermediate custodians to the banks and brokers and ultimately to the investor looks rather like the system of feudal tenure, applied here, not to land, but to investment securities.[11]

3. UNDOCUMENTED INTANGIBLES

This description is used to cover property interests which, although they may be recorded in writing, have never needed documentary embodiment. It is a large and rather imprecise category, which may roughly be divided into those which are directly about money and those which are not. As explained earlier, the first class is nowadays often called 'receivables'.

Receivables. To take a very simple example: a lender (L) makes an unsecured loan of a £100 note to a borrower (B), repayable on demand (this is the essential structure of a current bank account which is in credit). The loan may be recorded in writing, but this is not necessary. The effect of the loan is that B owns the banknote and owes £100. If L calls for repayment and then has to sue, L will win; but of course the action can be brought only against B—no one else owes L that £100. For this reason L's claim is often called personal, to denote that the right is good against only one person. But in fact he can do nothing to B's *person*. The judgment will not be enforced by imprisoning B, or by forcing B to work for L. It will be enforced, if at all, only against B's *property*, which public officers will take and sell. If B has other debts which are due, and if their total exceeds the value of his assets, then B is insolvent, and may be made bankrupt (or 'liquidated' if B is a company). In those proceedings L is entitled, in competition with other unsecured creditors, to repayment in whatever proportion B's assets are to B's debts.

This situation is often summed up by saying that L has only a personal right—a money claim—against B, and has no property right over any specific object, which might be enforced against an indefinite number of people. This is an accurate description of the relation between L and B (although it does not quite capture the fact that the 'personal' claim is enforceable only against B's property overall). But there is more to be said

---

[11] It resembles the system of subinfeudation forbidden for land by a statute, *Quia Emptores*, of 1290, with fees replacing the feudal services. The trust concept is explained in Chapter 5. In the USA the revised Title 8 of the Uniform Commercial Code sets out a flexible legislative framework for this system.

about L's rights to the receivable. One simple way of doing so is to say that L owns the receivable, just as he owned the £100 note before handing it to B; that amount of cash in his assets has been replaced by a claim for the same sum. L owns this claim because it has value and because he can do anything he likes with it, and the law provides formalities to help him. He can give it to charity, sell it, mortgage it, declare himself a trustee of it, or leave it by his will. If, say, he does the first, and B goes bankrupt, then the charity will have only the same personal claim against B that L had. But if B stays solvent and *L goes bankrupt*, then the charity can take out of his assets the full claim: they can say to L's other creditors, you cannot use our property (the claim against B) to pay your debts.

The treatment of the receivable as an object of property in the hands of L does not depend at all on the fact that the loan is repayable on demand. If it were repayable in, say, one year, the lender's claim would at once have a present value. The figure would, of course, be less than £100, but not much less: it would be that sum which, at current interest rates, will amount to £100 in a year (at a rate of 5 per cent, that is £95.20). And as the date for repayment grows nearer, so the value of the claim rises until, on that date, it amounts to £100.[12]

To sum up: between the creditor and debtor, the receivable is a right to be paid, not an interest in any specific asset of the debtor: all that the creditor can do is compete with others for a rateable share in the body of assets belonging to the debtor. But as between the creditor and the creditor's assignees, the receivable is an asset, the subject of property rights. And if the creditor is insolvent, that receivable may belong to his assignee and thus not be within the reach of the creditor's creditors.

Contracts as assets. The point we have been trying to make in the preceding paragraphs can be generalized by saying that a right arising out of an obligation is the property of the person to whom it is due and may be transferred as such. Admittedly, this goes too far—it does not apply to family obligations, nor to others which bind the obligor to some personal service. But in many cases *non-monetary* obligations arise out of a commercial contract and involve no personal element: so if you buy a ticket to the theatre you can give it to a friend, i.e. you treat the right to see the show as your property, to be disposed of as you choose. On a much larger scale, a company which has entered into a contract to have a ship built, or a shopping mall, can, in principle, transfer the benefit of the builder's obligations.

---

[12] See below Capital and income.

Furthermore the claim to performance of a non-monetary obligation may be protected against interference by outsiders. A theatre manager engages a popular musician to appear for a season, but a rival manager tries to lure the artist elsewhere. The original manager could, of course, sue the artist for breach of contract. But he may well secure an injunction (backed by the threat of jail for contempt) against the rival to prevent this form of poaching. The manager cannot compel performance of the contract by the musician but can ensure its protection from unjustified interference. Furthermore, as far as the manager is concerned the protection is against all the world—that is to say against all the world that matters—that of show-business rivals. It is interesting to note that entrepreneurs in the popular music industry use the language, not of contract, but of property. They do not say 'I have signed a contract with such-and-such a singer' but 'I have a piece of that boy'.

4. INTELLECTUAL PROPERTY

We turn now to a very important category of intangible property. The receivables described above give their holder the right to require someone to do something—usually, but not necessarily, to pay money. Intellectual property is different: it confers the right to require everyone *not* to do something, and to make him or her pay compensation if they do. In that way, intellectual property rights are similar to the rights of a landowner against trespassers. But of course they are very dissimilar in that there need be no tangible object: they protect the products, not of nature but of the human mind.

The national statutes dealing with intellectual property apply to the whole of the UK, and it is also subject to an important body of EU law and international conventions. The oldest and best-known types are patents, copyright, trademarks, and trade names, although other varieties (e.g. design rights and plant breeder rights) are also recognized. They are really monopolies, protected by the law for a limited, and in some cases for an unlimited, time. The law governing them has become complex with the advent of developments such as computers, the Internet, and biotechnology. Therefore all that will be attempted here is an elementary account of their nature and purpose.

Patents and copyright. The main temporary monopolies are patents and copyright. Both are governed by statute, and both deal with specific human creations, patents with inventions, copyright with literary, dramatic, musical, and artistic works. The law does not usually require the inventor or author to make, use, publish, or sell the product. It simply forbids others to do so without consent. Again, in this respect it is like the law of property in tangible things, which does not require you to cultivate, or even to visit, your own garden, but which stops others from doing either without your permission. There is an interesting exception, however, because your neglect of your garden does not stop others from tending theirs. But a failure to make use of one's patent may be considered an abuse of the *monopoly* right involved—imagine a deliberate refusal to exploit a cancer cure which, if patented, prevents everyone else from making use of it. The Patent Office may grant a compulsory licence to some other applicant to use the breakthrough, paying the patent owner reasonable compensation.

The reason for this grant of monopoly is to induce the investment of mental time and skill in the production of something new. But on the whole monopolies tend to stifle competition, and that is why the grant is not permanent. Yet during their lifetime, patents and copyrights are treated as assets, and are described by Parliament as being personal property. They are bought and sold; their use is licensed; they may be charged to secure the performance of an obligation; on the breakdown of a marriage they may be available to their holder's spouse; they descend on death; and they may be taken to pay their holder's debts.

Beyond this, the two systems diverge. Patents must be applied for in a Patent Office, such as the European or UK office, and are granted only if on examination they reveal a new and unobvious invention. The patent is then registered so that details of the invention or process are disclosed to the public. In return, their holder has a twenty-year period from the date the application was filed, during which, without consent, no one may use the invention or process even if they thought it up themselves without ever knowing of the registered patent. After the period everyone is free to act as if the monopoly had never existed.

In this country there is no general register of copyright, as there is of patents. Copyright is a statutory property right to prevent anyone, without the author's consent, from making copies, adapting into other formats or other media, translating, or performing the author's work. The work need not be especially creative—the writer of an everyday family letter owns the copyright, although the recipient will own the piece of paper. That is why, if this book is yours, you may do anything you like with it *except copy it*. You own the copy, you do not own the right to copy; you may be given the right to set it to music, but the result must not then be given public performance without the copyright holder's authority. In most cases copyright vests in the author or his or her employer automatically when the work is created, and lasts for the author's lifetime plus seventy years. So in contrast to patents, which belong to only a few, copyright is an indiscriminate, unregistered, long-lived, and manifold asset bestowed on all of us as soon as we learn to hold a pencil.

In addition to these commercial rights, copyright confers 'moral rights' which cannot be traded. The moral rights of the author or creator, as distinct from those of whoever owns the copyright, include the right to be identified as author, and to object to derogatory treatment or false attribution of the work. The rights can be waived but are not property and cannot be alienated; indeed the right to be identified as author must be expressly asserted (and will be found at the beginning of this book). Under the influence of EU law, artists have also been given the *droit de suite*, the right, for a certain period, to claim a percentage of the price for which their work is resold.[13]

The law of intellectual property is territorial: that is to say it forbids unauthorized acts only within the borders of, or imports into, the State concerned. This leads to two problems. Firstly, patents and copyright would have a very limited efficacy if they gave protection only within the United Kingdom. Hence every attempt is made to extend their effect to foreign countries.[14] For instance, for patents there is machinery whereby a single application to the European Patents Office in Munich may give the applicants a bundle of national patents for each of the participating countries designated. But for well over a century, international conventions have striven to make copyright genuinely international so that any work published in a member country will enjoy protection in all States parties to the convention.

The second problem with the territorial ambit of intellectual property is that different jurisdictions may have different notions as to what can be patented or given copyright protection. Recent developments in biotechnology have led to the patenting in the USA of genes, and of a cancerous mouse. Equally rapid innovations in cybernetics have led to attempts to patent 'one-click shopping', and to the extension of copyright protection to computer programs, and of a similar protection for databases.

Much standardization has occurred under the aegis of the World Intellectual Property Organization (an arm of the UN) and the World

---

[13] This right comes into effect throughout the EU in 2006 for living artists and in 2012 for artists who died in the preceding 70 years.

[14] There is an international Patents Co-operation Treaty of 1970 and a European Patents Convention of 1973.

Trade Organization, and through EU Directives and Regulations. Pressure continues for the recognition of new rights, e.g. over traditional or indigenous knowledge which is said to be sometimes exploited by the developed world at the expense of poorer countries. The World Trade Organization is working on a standardization of the trade-related aspects of intellectual property, but details have no place in an introductory general book such as this.

Trademarks. Trademarks and trade names are perpetual monopolies. That is why, for instance, so many lifts still bear the name 'Otis', even though the patent for the process which made possible the safe elevator (and hence the skyscraper) granted to Elisha Graves Otis in 1852 has long since expired. Essentially, trade names and marks are a way of identifying one's business and its products and services, and so building up customer loyalty and goodwill generally. Indeed in the late twentieth century customers were persuaded to buy and wear garments displaying a trade name in big letters.

The exclusive right to one's trade name is protected at common law by 'passing-off' actions in which the plaintiff must prove that the public may be misled by the similarity between the plaintiff's name and that of the defendant, and that this confusion has caused or is likely to cause injury to the plaintiff's goodwill. Much more important, however, is the statutory safeguard of registration, now the subject of both UK and EU law.

A trademark is some sign, symbol, shape, or the like which is capable of being represented graphically and is used to indicate a connection in the course of trade between the provision of specified goods or services and the person entitled to use the mark. If registered, it gives protection free from the difficulties of proof which sometimes face a plaintiff in a common-law action for 'passing-off'. Registration is in the first instance for ten years, but it may be renewed indefinitely for successive periods of ten years. Like other forms of intellectual property a registered mark is territorial. It is personal property which can be transferred outright, or licensed, for instance as part of a franchise operation or of a character merchandizing project. Unlike other objects of property, however, the exclusive right to use it may be lost if the mark is not used for five years, or if the product is so successful that its name becomes generic: aspirin, thermos, vaseline.

There are two main reasons why the law grants an exclusive right to a particular trade name or mark. One is to protect customers, for whom it is an indication of provenance, and also perhaps a reassurance that they are getting what they want. The second is to protect the owner's investment of time, skill, funds, and so on in building up a brand which is known and preferred. This is particularly important where the item in question is just another variety of some commonplace product, such as a soft drink or a pair of jeans. Of late, however, some internationally known names and marks seem to have acquired a life of their own. They no longer exist merely to protect the goodwill of a particular manufacturer or supplier, but have become desirable in themselves.

Fame. This seems an appropriate place to mention briefly a type of property which is essentially the exclusive right to profit from one's celebrity. It is just beginning to develop in English law, but other systems point the way. It originates in an attempt by the law to protect *privacy* by putting limits on the extent to which our name, likeness, lifestyle, and so on can be brought to public attention. But there are people whose livelihood depends on being in the public eye. Their business is *show*-business, and what they want is the *exclusive* right to profit from their own celebrity. They want a monopoly of their own fame, but their name cannot be protected by the UK law of copyright. It could be registered as a trademark, but there are then problems with its connection with particular goods or services.

At the moment, English law does not make it easy for a celebrity to turn his or her personality into property. But other common-law jurisdictions may point the way—for instance Tennessee, which has no little experience of the problem, since it was the home of a famous popular singer of the mid-twentieth century, Elvis Presley. In addition to recognizing (in common with several other US states) a common-law property right in a celebrity's name, Tennessee has enacted a Personal Rights Protection Act 1984, which provides that every individual has a *property* right in the use of his name, photograph, or likeness in any medium in any manner. These rights can be sold and licensed, and descend on death whether or not they were commercially exploited during the individual's lifetime. The exclusive protection lasts for the individual's lifetime and ten years, but then continues indefinitely until commercial exploitation ceases for a period of two years. After that, the name, likeness, and so on fall into the public domain. Thus in theory the exclusive monopoly could last for longer even than the seventy years after death granted by the law of copyright.

Goodwill. A more general and widespread version of the types of property just described is business goodwill. One does not have to be a celebrity to build up a business or, more precisely, *repeat* business, meaning that customers are likely to come back. They may return because of the locality of the business, because of the product or service it provides, or because of the personal qualities of its owner or staff. We may not know the precise reasons impelling customer loyalty, but it is a recognised component of a successful business, evaluated by accountants, and taxed by the State. Yet it is a peculiar kind of property, since its protection is an issue only when it is transferred. The person who takes over, for instance, a shop will pay the seller for the premises, equipment, stock, and goodwill. But if the seller opens an identical shop next door, customers of the old business may well switch to the new. Consequently, when buying the business the new owner will take from the seller a promise (usually called a 'covenant') not to compete within a reasonable area for a reasonable time. The buyer's asset is thus protected against the one person most likely to do it harm. It is not protected against any other independent competitor.

5. MONEY

Cash money consists of both coins struck by the Mint and notes issued by the Bank of England (and certain Scottish banks). English banknotes bear on their face a promise to pay the bearer a certain sum, and so still look like the promissory notes they once were. If and when the United Kingdom becomes part of the European Monetary Union, its power to issue money will pass to the European Central Bank.

At one level, then, money is a tangible, movable, and anonymous, object. In at least one respect it is like other tangible objects: if it is destroyed, its owner loses the right of property. (There may be some claim in tort against the person who deliberately or carelessly destroyed the cash, or in contract against one who had guaranteed to keep it safe, but these are personal actions which, on the defendant's insolvency, must compete with other unsecured claims.) The risk of loss by destruction is obviously true of coins. It seems to be also true of banknotes even though they appear to be promissory notes, which are usually replaceable if destroyed or lost. But the Bank of England's statutory obligation is only to exchange notes, so if your savings are destroyed in a fire, even if you have photocopies of the notes, you lose their value just as you do that of your other burnt belongings.

In many other ways, however, cash is quite different from other objects. First of all, its value is not that of the metal or paper but of the sum which it denominates. Second, it can be used as money only by being handed over. You can keep your coins and banknotes and use them as ornaments and wallpaper, but to use them as money you must give them up. Third, cash money (unlike most bank credits) can be instantly reused, and at no extra cost—you can spend your wages as soon as you open your pay packet. Fourth, money is a generic good: when used as money, and not as collectibles, coins and notes are fungible, one is as good as another. Thus debts are expressed in terms of a quantity of abstract monetary units, so many pounds and pence: any will do. Fifth, money is the thing with which everything else is bought and is not in itself the object of sale. Sixth, since it is meant to serve as a universal and trustworthy means of exchange, the law must not weaken confidence in it. This means that if, in good faith, you take money in exchange for something, the money is yours—it does not matter that the person who gave it you had stolen it. If the previous owner finds you, and is able to prove that those very notes were stolen, you can still keep them, free of all claims. Seventh, money is legal tender: in the absence of some prior agreement, a creditor can insist on payment, and a debtor can insist on paying, in money. Eighth, money seems to be the only object which entitles its owner to a fixed amount; the complete ownership (as distinct from, say, a secured loan) of anything else includes the prospect of loss or gain as the value of the thing (expressed in money) rises or falls. But we must add that, because of inflation, money may gradually lose its purchasing power. Ninth, the preceding eight propositions are true only within the jurisdiction whose currency is in issue. Foreign currency does not have these attributes of money and is bought and sold by money changers. Euronotes, by the way, may have national signs on them, but circulate freely, and of course are treated as the money of all the jurisdictions in the European Monetary Union.

Finally, it may be worth stating the obvious: the word 'money' is used to mean more than coins and notes. We often use the word to describe what we are owed, as when we speak of 'our' money in the bank. Parliament does the same, describing the debt owed to a secured lender as 'the mortgage money'.[15] And to economists anything constitutes money which is generally accepted as a medium of exchange.

6. FUNDS

The essential nature of a fund is that it preserves its identity as the object of property rights, even though its contents change. In a pension fund, for instance, employees and pensioners have certain rights which can be

---

[15] Land Registration Act 1925, s.32.

enforced over the fund, although the objects in which it is invested may change from day to day, or even from minute to minute. This example alerts us to the fact that, in most funds, control and management are separated from enjoyment and entitlement.

Another common example of a fund is the capital of a manufacturing company. The form taken by that capital is constantly changing, as debts due to the company are paid and others contracted, as out-of-date machinery is written off and replaced, and as stock-in-trade is sold and new goods manufactured; yet the capital is regarded as a continuing entity over which lenders may have security in the form of a floating charge and in which shareholders may have shares producing dividends.

The capital of a company is a fund of a specialized character, for it is the property of an abstract person, the company (while the company is still in existence). The power of managing the business, and therefore of varying the composition of the capital, is vested in a board of directors who are merely officers of the company, but have very wide powers—which must not be used for their personal benefit. The shareholders, as members of the company, share in the profits produced by managing the fund, but they are not brought into immediate contact with either the objects composing the fund or the fund as an abstract entity.

However, it is by no means necessary to interpose an abstract person between human beings and a fund: it can be vested in human beings for the benefit of other human beings. In the common law this is done by means of the trust.

Property may be given to trustees for the benefit of persons or for purposes, usually charitable. Trusteeship is an office of private law, conferring on the holder powers of control and management of the property, including usually the power to sell the items composing it; the things so disposed of are replaced within the trust fund by the price (or other object) received for them. As trustees, the managers may not take anything for their personal benefit (except that it is usually agreed that they may charge for their services). A most important element of the structure of the trust is that the personal creditors of a trustee cannot reach the trust fund. The fund is held for the benefit of others, whose creditors can ultimately, through court proceedings, reach the assets comprised in it. Thus, since a key criterion of entitlement to property is its availability to its owner's creditors, the fund belongs to the beneficiaries, although it is controlled and managed by trustees. Another indication of this feature is the fact that if the fund is lost or destroyed through no one's fault, it is the beneficiaries, and not the trustees, who bear the loss. In addition to their property rights, beneficiaries have personal rights against trustees guilty of breach of trust enforceable if necessary by execution on the private property of the trustees.

So far we have looked at funds in which control is separate from enjoyment. If we look at our own property, for a moment, it may appear at first that there is no need for the notion of a fund, since we alone both control and enjoy our own possessions. Yet the idea that everyone has a fund is widespread in many legal systems, which speak of a person's *patrimony*. This is a term of Scots law, but it helpfully expresses a number of important legal propositions, all of which are true for English law.

First, all that we can really call our own is our false teeth (if any), our clothing, bedding, and the tools of our trade. Everything else, the law will, if necessary, take away from us to pay our creditors. In other words, our property—our patrimony—is our net worth. Secondly, we need draw no distinction between ourselves and our patrimony *only while we are sane, solvent, and alive*. If we lose our mind, control of our assets (after the appropriate precautions and formalities) goes to someone else: our property is still in our name, and we benefit from it, but its management—including the power to sell particular items and the duty to pay our debts—will fall to our guardian. If we are bankrupt, our property vests in our trustee in bankruptcy who controls and manages it, not for our benefit but for that of our creditors. And when we die, our property—called our 'estate'—vests in our personal representatives who pay our debts and distribute what is left according to the law of succession.

7. CAPITAL AND INCOME

Some things bring forth other things. Fruits grow naturally, animals have young, cows give milk, fields can be cultivated to produce crops. In normal circumstances, the arrival of these new things causes little diminution of the old. Apart from such natural events, things like land, machines, motor cars can be the source of income by the interposition of a contract between their owner and the person who leases or hires them: in return for possession and use of the object, a rent is paid. In all the above cases the person with the first right to the income is generally the person who owns the object producing the income.[16]

Interest on loans is technically different, since a lender does not own the money that he or she lent. We may, on first impression, think of the interest as payment for 'the use of' the money, but money cannot be used

---

[16] For the situation where the income-producing object is leased, see below Chapter 3.

in the same way that a car is used. The hirer of a car does not need to own the vehicle, merely to have lawful possession of it. But money is the ultimate consumable, for it can be used only by handing it to others, so a loan of money must pass ownership of that money. The borrower is gaining (and the lender relinquishing) the instant purchasing power inherent in that sum of money, and may have to pay for this in interest (though this is not inevitable, a loan could be interest-free).

Despite this technical point, we may say that for practical purposes income includes the fruits of agriculture, the rent of land or machinery, the dividends on shares, royalties on patents and copyright, and interest on money lent.

Though the line may sometimes be difficult to draw, the distinction between capital and income is prevalent in the law—first of all because income tax is not a tax on capital. But it is also important because entitlement to income can be, and often is, exchanged for, or separated from, entitlement to capital. If you subscribe for shares in a company, you part with capital in return for the hope of income in the shape of dividends. If you take out an insurance policy on your house, you pay income in the form of premiums in order, if your house is burned down, to receive the capital to rebuild. If you take out an annuity, you pay over capital in return for an annual income. Furthermore, as we shall see later, if, say, a testator wishes to provide for children and grandchildren, this can be done by dividing the capital at once among them. But it can also be done by a scheme which invests the capital, gives the children the right to only the income produced thereby, and provides that later on the grandchildren will take the capital.

A final, important, point needs to be explained in this section: the right to a future income stream has a present *capital* value. This may not be immediately obvious, but it must be grasped since it lies at the heart of both traditional property law and the operation of all asset markets.[17] We start with the obvious: a sum of money today is worth more than the same sum to be received a year from now. Given a choice between a gift of £100 today and a gift of the same sum in one year, we would prefer the first. This is so even if there is no risk that we will not get the gift next year, and even if we do not plan to spend the money this year. The reason we would take the money today is that it can at once be invested at a positive rate of return (say by putting it in a bank deposit account) and in one year's time

---

[17] See Jonathan R. Macey, *Introduction to Modern Financial Theory* (2nd edn., American College of Estates and Trust Counsel Foundation, Los Angeles, Ca., 1998).

will have grown to some amount greater than £100. How much it will grow depends on the rate of interest. If that is 5 per cent then, on the day we would receive £100 had we chosen to wait for our gift, we shall instead have £105.

A similar calculation can be done in reverse to give us the present value of a future payment. To keep the arithmetic simple, take as an example a government bond for £105 which matures in one year's time. There is no risk that the government will not keep its promise, so we are certain that in one year it will pay the bondholder £105. How much is that worth today—i.e. what price should we pay for the bond? Well, there is another way to obtain the present certainty of getting £105 a year from now—by depositing in the bank the sum that, with interest, would reach £105 in a year. If current rates are 5 per cent; we need to deposit £100 today, so we would not pay more than that amount in order to buy the bond.

We work out the greater future value of a present sum from the current *interest* rates. We work out the lesser present value of a future sum by the current *discount* rates—the same figures used for a different calculation. Of course, tables or computer programs will do our sums for us, and will work to more decimal places than those used here.

At a 5 per cent discount rate, the present value of £100 payable in a year is £95.24 (i.e. 100 divided by 1.05). If the payment of £100 is to be made in two years, rather than one, and if we assume that interest is compounded annually, then its present value is £90.70. If it is not to be made until ten years from now, its present value is £61.39; if twenty years from now it is today worth only £37.69. (Another way of understanding this last figure is to think of investing it now at 5 per cent compound interest. In twenty years it will grow to £100.)

Now suppose that we are entitled to the income produced by a given asset *every year for a number of years*. £2,000 is deposited today in a bank account paying 5 per cent interest, and the bank is told to send us the income at the end of each year for twenty years and then to close the account and pay the capital to a charity. That future income stream lasting twenty years has a present capital value, i.e. the sum total of the present values of each annual payment. Assuming an annual payment of £100 each year for twenty years at a discount rate of 5 per cent, we can find out how much we are worth today by adding together the present value of next year's payment (£95.24), of the second year's payment (£90.70), and so on down to the present value of the £100 we shall get twenty years hence (£37.69). The total of these figures gives us the present value of the twenty-year income stream—£1,256.

The charity's entitlement is what is called a 'future interest'—that is to say a present right to receive in the future an income-producing capital sum. This present right to £2,000 at the end of twenty years is today worth £744. This sum and the present capital value of the twenty-year income stream, £1,256, add up of course to £2,000, the amount that has just been deposited with the bank. Looking at it from the end of the period, we shall have received £100 x 20 = £2,000. The charity will then get £2,000. This makes a total of £4,000, made up of the capital originally deposited plus the total of the interest it has produced over the period.

In an attempt at simplicity, these examples use money and interest on money. The same principles apply, however, to other forms of capital and income—for instance to an orchard and its fruit, a farm and its crops, an office and its rent, a patent and its royalties, or a fund of varying assets and its annual return. And as we shall see later, they are a vital step in calculating the present market value of both a life interest—that is, an entitlement to income, not for a fixed term, but for a human life—and of a future interest (also called a 'reversionary interest'), being the present right to the capital, with its income, at the end of that human life. So if a wealthy testator leaves the income of his fortune to his daughter, and the capital, after her death, to her son we can begin to work out the value, at the testator's death, of each gift. Though we need to ask her how old she is.

3

The Acquisition of Property Interests

As we shall see in a later chapter, there are a number of different interests which can exist or be created in property. For the moment, however, we shall deal with the most general type of entitlement which enables us to say 'this is mine'. Most things (or at least their components) already exist and their acquisition involves some form of transfer from one person to another; the obvious exception is intellectual property such as copyright, in which the acquisition of the right occurs on creation of the work. There are a few other situations where property interests arise anew, and they will be described first.

ORIGINAL INTERESTS

First titles

New tangible objects are made by nature or by humans. If the latter, they will come within the law of property at the moment of creation and someone will be their first owner, usually the maker or his or her employer. If the former, they will come within the legal system at the moment of creation if their source is already within it: so the apple when picked and the lamb when born belong to the owner or tenant of the orchard and the sheep.[1] This simple solution conceals the fact that it answers two separate questions. The first is: who possesses the thing? the second is, who owns it? Taking first possession of the apple or lamb (even wrongfully) gives the possessor some sort of right to it: the fact that he stole it from the farmer would not entitle us to steal it from him. So any possessor, by the fact of taking possession, acquires a real right in the thing possessed, an interest which will prevail against an indefinite number of persons, and which can be alienated by its holder and reached by his creditors.

This does not, of course, mean that a thief's claim will prevail against a

---

[1] Earth which, by the action of river or sea, accrues to land belongs to the landowner.

person who, both ethically and legally, has a stronger right. Normally this would be the owner of the tree and the sheep. This means that in the overwhelming majority of cases, first possession and ownership will coincide since in the normal course of events apples will be picked and lambs delivered by the person entitled to the tree and the sheep, or that person's employees. It is also much easier to prove that you own a tree or a sheep than to prove that you own an apple or a stray lamb; the law saves time and money by simply presuming that if you own the source you own the product. The owner may, however, have leased the land and the flock in which case the parties intend that, when the tenant takes possession of their produce, he or she is to acquire ownership of it: it may make sense to take a lease of an orchard, but no one would take a lease of an apple. The law, of course, gives effect to the parties' intention so that the tenant becomes owner of the produce.

Wild animals belong to no one, though many species are now protected by special legislation. As to the unprotected species, the law gives the primary title to the person who first takes possession; that person will be owner so long as possession is retained. If the animal escapes and resumes its wild character, no one owns it, though the person who had it is allowed to retake it so long as he or she keeps it in sight and has the right to chase it.

Later titles

The example of wild animals in the preceding paragraph dealt with the situation where an object comes for the first time within the law of property, which says that it belongs to the first possessor. After that, later possessors of any tangible object whatever also acquire a title, one which will yield to that conferred by earlier, but prevail over that conferred by later, possession. If, without consent, B takes over the land and wheelbarrow of a neighbour, A, the mere fact of taking possession gives B an (alienable) interest which the law will protect, not of course, against A or persons claiming through A, but against everyone else. In this way B's possession—though not the first—gives rise to an entitlement. Furthermore, at the end of the limitation periods within which A can bring an action to recover the land (twelve years) and the wheelbarrow (six), A's title dies, together with any interests dependent thereon, such as a mortgage.[2]

---

[2] The Law Commission proposes that the periods be changed to three and ten years: Law Com No. 270, Limitation of Actions (2001). The acquisition by adverse possession of registered land is also to be changed, since if registration is conclusive as to entitlement, mere possession, however lengthy, should not confer ownership. See Land Registration Bill 2001, Part 9.

A's title is not transferred to B, who continues to hold the interest conferred by taking possession but now strengthened by the disappearance of the earlier, stronger, title. If the limitation period is not a bar (because it has not expired or is not pleaded) and if A claims and B pays damages ordered as compensation for the land and the wheelbarrow, A's title is similarly extinguished. Here again it is not transferred to B.

Finding. A common example of the importance of later possession as a root of title is that of the finder of a chattel. Taking possession gives the finder an alienable interest which will be protected by the law. If the previous owner has lost the thing, the finder is open to a claim by him or her; but if the previous holder has *abandoned* the thing, the finder ought to be safe. If the previous owner is unknown, there may be a conflict between the finder and the owner of the land on which the thing was found. If it was buried, the courts tend to hold in favour of the landowner; if lying on the surface, in favour of the finder.

Possession. What we see from the above examples is the importance attached by the law to the act of taking possession, whether first possession of something belonging to no one, or adverse possession of something already owned. In both cases it confers on the possessor a property interest which is protected, can be alienated, and can be reached by the possessor's creditors. But this is not true of treasure.

Treasure. Statute now gives a precise definition of treasure. A loose description would say that it covers old and valuable things whose owner is unknown. When found, treasure vests in the 'Crown', i.e. the State. The finder of anything that might reasonably be treasure must report to the local coroner. In deciding whether it is treasure, the coroner notifies the British Museum or National Museum of Wales, the finder, and whoever occupied the land where it was found. If held to be indeed treasure, and if the relevant minister decides that it is to go to a museum, the museum can be instructed to pay a reward to the finder. Payment of the reward is not enforceable at law.[3]

Accession and alteration

Property rights end when their object or its proceeds cease to exist as such. If B feeds his horse with A's hay, A owns neither the hay nor a share in the horse. A may have a claim against B for the value of the hay, but that is a personal claim, and unsecured. Similarly if B paints his wall with

---

[3] For details see Treasure Act 1996.

A's paint, although the paint (unlike the hay) can still be seen, A no longer owns it, nor any share in the wall; it belongs to B, though once again he may well owe its value to A. We may say, therefore, that once a chattel has become annexed to land, it belongs with the land, regardless of what the parties intended.

But the same does not necessarily apply when one person's goods are mixed with those of another in such a way as to lose their separate identity: A's nails are mixed with B's, A's petroleum is added to a tank containing B's. Here, if possible, the law looks to intention and consent rather than to physical form. If that enquiry fails, the default rule will hold that the parties have concurrent property interests in the mass.

DERIVATIVE INTERESTS

Most property already belongs to someone, so its lawful acquisition requires its transfer. This may be effected under the general law, as with the intestacy and bankruptcy regimes, or the confiscation of the proceeds of certain crimes. Here, however, we shall focus on the normal case, where the current holder wants to transfer and the recipient wants to get the property.

Consensual acquisition. The holder's consent can be given *inter vivos* or by will, but succession on death will be dealt with in a later chapter. This section deals, therefore, with transfer by way of gift, by way of sale, and by loan of fungibles. Furthermore—to state the obvious—for anything to be transferred it must exist and be identifiable. Although an enforceable contract can be made to transfer a non-existent object ('a copy of next Friday's *Times* newspaper') this can result in only a personal obligation until the object exists and is identified as that copy which is to be transferred.

The modes of transferring property vary with the different kinds of thing transferred. Moreover, sometimes the actual transfer is and sometimes it is not preceded by preliminaries which are almost as important as the transfer itself. Gifts rarely need preliminaries—you do not look a gift horse in the mouth. But the actual transfer of land on a sale is almost always preceded by a contract, and the contract is preceded by enquiries about the property itself and about the seller's title thereto. On the other hand, when goods are bought for cash in a shop, contract and transfer are rolled into one, there are usually no negotiations, there is nothing in writing, and there is certainly no investigation of title. The acquisition of shares and other securities lies somewhere between the two; the transfer is preceded by a contract but there is nothing like the same ritual as in the purchase of land.

Form. A final preliminary remark must be made about legal formalities. Certain common types of transaction must, to be fully effective as such, comply with statutory requirements as to form; and this is particularly the case where their subject matter is land. Contracts for the sale or other disposition of an interest in land can be made only in writing signed by or on behalf of each party. Declarations of trust respecting land must be evidenced in writing signed by the person able to declare the trust. To convey or create a legal estate in land, a deed is necessary: a deed is a document which describes itself as such and is duly signed by the person making it and attested by a witness. Where the title to land is registered— now by far the larger part of England and Wales—the transferee must be registered as proprietor to acquire the legal (i.e. formal) estate.

The requirement of writing or of a deed involves, of course, the use of paper. In the near future it is probable that dispositions of land will be effected electronically. This has the following implications. First, it applies to interests which are, or are required to be, recorded in the Land Registry. Second, the electronic form must itself comply with certain requirements as to time and date, 'electronic signature' and its certification. Third, the electronic method if correctly used will be deemed to have complied with the relevant common-law or statutory requirements as to form. Fourthly, if dematerialized conveyancing is made compulsory, use of the electronic form will be mandatory. Fifth, its effect will be that dispositions are registered at the same instant that they are made. Sixth, failure to use the correct electronic form will invalidate the entire disposition even as between the parties.[4]

Outside the case of land, it should be noted that, to be fully effective, the transfer of a debt or other chose in action must be in writing and written notice must be given to the obligor. Commercial paper can be transferred only by endorsement, unless it is payable to bearer; shares require a proper instrument of transfer to be delivered to the company and alteration of the register of shareholders, unless exempted from these formalities by compliance with those of an authorized computer-based system.[5] The transfer of patents requires writing, the signature of both parties, and entry in the Patents Register; that of copyrights requires a signed assignment by or on behalf of the assignor.

---

[4] Electronic Communications Act 2000; Land Registration Bill 2001, Part 8.
[5] Stock Transfer Act 1982.

The preceding paragraphs describe the main situations where, to have its full intended force, the transaction must comply with certain formal requirements. On the other hand the deed is so respected by the law that in the case of chattels (where it is not necessary) its use will operate to transfer title.

Gifts. On the whole the law relating to gifts operates to ensure that not only do the parties know that the object now belongs to the donee, but so can everyone else. For a gift to be effective, the donor must of course intend to make a present to the donee, but then the requisite formalities must be met. It is not necessary for the donee expressly to consent to the gift, but of course he or she can reject it. If the object is land, the donor must execute a deed of conveyance and the transferee must apply to be entered on the register as proprietor. A roughly similar procedure (or its electronic equivalent) must be followed in the case of shares. A debt owed to the donor can be given by assignment. To make a present of the donor's whole interest in a chattel, the object must be handed over or otherwise delivered to the donee (unnecessary if it is already in the donee's possession) or else the donor must execute a deed of gift (dangerous because if the donor keeps possession the Bills of Sale Acts may give priority to his or her creditors). If the donor wishes to give, not the whole interest but a share in a chattel—say a half share in a live horse—it is difficult to see how delivery can be effected, and the donor must use either a deed of gift or declaration of trust. In the latter case the donor declares that he or she now holds the horse in trust for the donee and himself in equal shares; strictly speaking, that is sufficient, but its informality makes it unadvisable.

In the normal gift the donor's entire interest is transferred to the donee: you give away money or a book, shares, or your estate in land. The donor may, however, wish to make a gift that is to operate over time by giving the income of property only for a period—say for the costs of a child's education. Or, in the case of a gift to charity, the donor may wish to give only the income for ever, without giving the charity the right to spend the capital. In these situations the capital will have to be conserved, invested, managed for the appropriate period and the gift can hardly be effected by an out-and-out transfer. Instead the trust is used, either by transfer of the property to trustees or by the donor's declaring himself a trustee. More will be said about this in later chapters.[6]

Promises. The law distinguishes sharply between *making* a present and

[6] See Chapters 5 and 12.

promising a present. Making a present has been described above: if the correct ritual has been observed—delivery (chattels), conveyance (land), registration (land, shares, patents)—and if the donor stays solvent (so there is no risk of a fraud on creditors or transaction at an undervalue), then the law just leaves the property with the donee. Unlike the position in many countries, the donor's heirs or family cannot claw back the gift. But the common law treats quite differently a *promise* to make a present. This will not be enforced at all unless made by deed, and even then the remedy is damages as compensation for breach of the formal promise. Equity would not compel the donor to keep the promise. The result is that neither an informal promise to make a present, nor the gift itself, is thought of as a contract in the common law, because neither gives rise to any legal obligation. The former is not enforceable at all. The latter—an out-and-out gift—is a once-and-for-all disposition which need not have been carried out and which, once made, gives rise to no legal obligations on anyone's part.[7]

Transfer on sale

The most common way to get something is, of course, to buy it. For the law of property, there is an important difference between a transaction which makes something yours and a promise to make it yours, even though the latter will normally be readily enforceable. When you telephone a bookshop and place an order for a copy of the latest bestseller, from that moment each party has rights against and obligations towards the other. But you do not yet own their book any more than the shop owns your money. It is fairly easy to see when ownership of money passes from buyer to seller—when the currency is handed over, or the cheque cashed, or the credit transfer effected.[8] It is not so easy to determine when ownership of the book passes from seller to buyer. First of all, we need to know which book, i.e. which one of the pile of copies of the bestseller is to be that particular buyer's. Second, will the copy selected become the buyer's when it is picked out; or packed; or sent off; or delivered; or finally paid for? This example shows that it is not uncommon for a seller to have for a while possession of a thing which already belongs to the buyer, or for the buyer to get the thing before owning it.

The answer to the question of when ownership passes may be important because various legal consequences then ensue. First of all,

---

[7] Unless the gift is effected by means of a trust, in which case the trustees incur obligations: see Chapters 5 and 12.

[8] Technically in this last case the money itself belongs to the seller's bank.

the seller's main obligation is to make the buyer owner of the thing (it is this which distinguishes buying from hiring) and that obligation is performed once and for all when ownership passes. The buyer must then pay the price and not merely damages, even though the price be higher than the market value of the thing. On the other hand the fact that the seller is no longer owner binds the seller's trustee in bankruptcy, so even if the price is lower than the market value the trustee must surrender the thing in return for the money. A further consequence is that risk normally falls on the owner, so if the thing becomes the buyer's on despatch and is destroyed in transit, the seller has performed his or her part of the contract and the buyer must do likewise, i.e. pay the price. Next, the thing itself is available only to the creditors of its owner. Finally, it is possible that a seller who has sold, but still retains possession of the thing may dispose of it to a third party; as may a buyer who has the thing but is not yet its owner.

The law on this subject is complicated by the use of varying terminology, by the living relics of the distinction between law and equity, and by differing formal requirements for the transfer of goods, land, ships, shares, intellectual property, and so on. There is also an important distinction between cases concerning only the two parties (and their creditors) and the transfer of ownership as between them; and cases where some third-party acquirer is involved and the question is as to the general effect of the apparent transfer on an indefinite number of persons.

Goods. So far we have referred to the passing of 'ownership'. Where goods are concerned 'ownership' is called 'the property in the goods' (in Britain) and 'title to goods' in the USA. Where an interest in land is concerned, both countries tend to use the old technical words like 'estate', 'fee simple', 'life estate', and so on. As to the formal mandatory requirements, there are none as regards goods; the formal transfer of interests in land requires the use of deeds and entry on the Land Register; changes in shareholding and the proprietorship of patents and trademarks must be registered; transfers of receivables should be notified to the debtor, and of interests in funds to the trustees of the funds.

If the law were easy, it would say that ownership of goods and money passes only when they themselves are handed over by their owner with the intent to transfer ownership; and that ownership of other things passes when, with the like intent, the correct register entry is effected or the appropriate person notified. It is not so easy, presumably because such simplicity would be attained at the cost of a desirable flexibility. Instead, the law says, first and obviously, that the ownership of unspecific or inexistent things cannot be transferred. A bookshop can promise to make the buyer owner of an advertised bestseller, a farmer can promise the next barley crop, but the buyer cannot become owner until it is clear exactly which copy or what barley is involved; and of course the seller cannot own the money until it is paid. Assuming that the particular thing is ascertained, the law then says that as between the contracting parties (and their creditors) ownership passes when they intend it to pass; but that as against others, the transfer must be made public in the appropriate way—by delivery of the goods, registration of the transaction, and so on.

Having stated that, as between seller and buyer, ownership passes when they intend it to pass, the law has to face the common situation where the parties never say what they intend. In other words it has to lay down a default system which will operate—and so become mandatory—unless the parties choose to set it aside by agreeing their own terms. As far as goods are concerned, the Sale of Goods Act says that the property in specific goods in a deliverable state passes to the buyer when the contract is made, even though they are still with the seller and have not been paid for.[9] So the seller's principal obligation is performed by being incurred: the promise to make the buyer owner has the effect (as between the parties) of making the buyer owner. But the buyer's promise to pay the price does not make the seller owner of the buyer's money, because of course it relates to an arithmetical amount of a generic entity—money—ownership in which can pass only when specific cash is handed over, a cheque issued and met, or some credit operation performed.

This default provision of the Sale of Goods Act, if not modified by the parties, makes the buyer owner of specific goods even before they are delivered, and so liable to pay the price and run the risk of their destruction. A buyer who does not like this result needs to stipulate in the contract for some other system. Commercial buyers can easily do this. The ordinary consumer can not, but even so the default rule no doubt works smoothly in the vast majority of cases and its existence saves the cost of individual negotiation in every purchase.

Third parties, however, may be misled: goods which are with the seller may already belong to some buyer, but there is no cheap and easy way of discovering this. Consequently the Act provides that, in this situation, a good faith third party who gets delivery of the goods is as protected as if the transfer had been authorized by the owner.

While the original buyer could of course sue the seller for breach of

---

[9] The Act applies also to Scotland.

contract and for converting his property, he cannot claim against the third party. In other words, as regards the rest of the world, the important thing is not who owns the goods but who has them: possession is as good as title.

Land. The law's treatment of the sale of land is, in the last analysis, not dissimilar to that applied to the sale of goods and described above. However, its historical development and vocabulary make it look quite different. We are concerned here with the sale of either of the two formal 'legal' interests in land: the freehold ('fee simple absolute in possession') and leasehold ('term of years absolute').[10] For ease of explanation we shall concentrate on the freehold sale. Furthermore the practice of 'conveyancing' has long been a routine in the hands of solicitors; most matters are dealt with in great detail by means of standard forms and conditions, but in what follows we shall deal only with basics.

To be valid the full contract of sale must be in writing signed by or on behalf of both parties. It will, of course, contain a promise by the seller to convey his interest in the specific property and by the buyer to pay the agreed price. At that stage the buyer is not formally and for all purposes the owner of the land because there has been neither deed nor registration. Yet *as between seller and buyer* this contract has an effect similar to the default status enacted for the sale of goods—the land at once belongs to the buyer, the money does not yet belong to the seller. This result is attained because historically, disputes concerning land contracts came most frequently before the Chancery which was prepared, at the request of the buyer and on tender of the price, to order the seller to carry out the formalities necessary to make the buyer owner *erga omnes*, that is to execute the appropriate deed and yield possession (sellers who refused were jailed). In effect, the court regarded the buyer as already the owner of the land and would protect that entitlement against the seller, his creditors, any donee, and any other buyer who knew or ought to know of the contract. Nowadays, after making the contract, buyers can take the precaution of registering notice thereof in the Land Register.[11] They are thus protected *against the whole world* and registration does for land what possession does for goods. If a third party were to take a transfer of the land, the buyer could recover it from him on paying the price. In the normal case, of course, the buyer does not bother to enter notice of the

---

[10] See Chapter 7.
[11] If the title itself is not yet registered, notice is given by an entry against the owner's name at the Land Charges Registry.

contract on the register and the seller does not transfer to some third party. Instead the seller's promise is performed by the execution of a deed of transfer which makes the buyer the formal 'legal' owner and, on payment of the price, this is handed over. The buyer then applies to the Land Registry to be entered as proprietor of the fee simple (or of the 'term of years' if a leasehold interest is transferred).

The basic principles—and complexities—of the system may be illustrated by an example. A agrees by word of mouth to sell her house to B at a price of £100,000 and the furniture for £10,000. At that moment (in the absence of any special terms) the furniture belongs to B who is obliged to pay the price for it. But the house does not belong to B nor does B have even an enforceable claim: contracts for the sale of land are void unless in signed writing.[12] A and B then record their full agreement in a duly signed contract. A is still, of course, the apparent owner; her name is on the Land Register and she is still in possession of the house and furniture. As between her and B, however, the furniture—as we have seen—already belongs to B and now so does the house, since the court would if necessary order specific performance of A's obligation to convey her estate to B. The price does not belong to A; she has only the benefit of a claim to payment by B. In breach of her contract with B, A sells and transfers the furnished house to C for £150,000 for the house and £15,000 for the furniture. C acts in good faith. A moves out and C moves in. The furniture belongs to C. B's only remedy for its loss is an action for damages against A where he will be awarded the amount by which its value exceeds the price he was to have paid. As to the house, the position is the same unless B entered a notice of the contract on the Land (or Land Charges) Register. If he did, he can compel C to effect a formal transfer of the house to him in return for payment of £100,000. He can thus obtain specific performance of a contract against someone with whom he never made a contract but who bought a house which he knew, or could have known, really belonged to B. C will have to look to A to recover the £50,000 he has lost.

Securities. Like the conveyance of land, the transfer of shares was traditionally effected by a contract followed by the registration of the buyer as shareholder. Nowadays, in the case of companies listed on the Stock Exchange the seller sells to the exchange which sells to the buyer,

---

[12] If, against an unwilling buyer, the seller tried to enforce the sale of the furniture but deny the sale of the flat, it would no doubt be argued that the two should stand or fall together. But perhaps the buyer would be happy not to buy the flat and yet want the furniture.

the whole process being effected by computer and through regulated intermediaries. A 'dematerialized instruction' from the system operator obliges the company to register the transfer of title to the requisite number of uncertificated shares; further details are beyond the scope of this work.

Other assets. Commercial paper is transferred by delivery (if payable to bearer) otherwise by indorsement and delivery.[13] Choses in action such as receivables or debts are subject to yet another regime. For the transferee of a receivable to be able to sue the debtor in his own name the formalities of the Law of Property Act must be fulfilled: the assignment must be in writing and written notice must be given to the debtor. If the debtor pays the assignor before receiving such notice, he cannot be made to pay again. If, after assigning the receivable, the assignor makes a second assignment to a good faith transferee who succeeds in giving notice to the debtor first, he will take priority. Notice to the debtor thus has the effect of conveying information to the person mainly concerned—the debtor—and so functions rather like a register in ensuring that necessary information is made public. Yet in spite of all this, the assignee who has not given notice to the debtor will be preferred to the trustee in bankruptcy of the assignor. In other words the transfer may be good as between the assignor and his creditors and the assignee before it is good against others.

Beneficial interests in a fund held by trustees are subject to similar rules. Between the parties and their creditors assignments may be valid, but to bind others the assignee must give notice to the trustees of the fund. Thus the trust instrument, on which notice of the transfer may be entered, acts as a kind of private register of dealings in the beneficial interests in the fund just as the public Registers do for dealings in formal legal ownership of land, shares and so on.

Loans of fungibles. In describing the transfer of ownership a final brief word should be said about those loans which have the effect of making the borrower the owner of the thing, subject to an obligation to return an equivalent. The points can be made by means of a trivial example. If you go next door and ask to borrow a cup of sugar and your neighbour takes a cup from her shelf, fills it with sugar and hands it to you, you do not own the cup, you merely possess it. But you do own the sugar and owe an obligation to return a similar quantity. The usual consequences follow. You can sell or throw away the sugar, but not the cup: if you attempt to

---

[13] Indorsement is also an undertaking to pay if the maker or acceptor does not; an indorsement 'without recourse' effects the transfer without incurring the obligation.

sell the cup you cannot pass ownership, and your neighbour can sue the buyer. But as you do not own the cup your creditors cannot levy execution against it, nor do you bear the risk of its destruction by a natural calamity and in that event are not liable to restore its value to your friend. Your creditors can, for what it is worth, enforce their claims against your sugar and, if the sugar is lost along with the cup, it was your sugar which perished and an equivalent quantity is still owed the lender.

This example is trivial but should remind us of two things. First of all, money: where money is lent the borrower becomes owner of that money and owes its equivalent. Thus if you open a bank account and pay in cash, the cash belongs to the bank and you are an unsecured creditor for the corresponding amount. Second, investment strategy: if you invest in tangible things, you risk their destruction; if you invest by making loans (of money or other fungibles), you are spared this hazard, but run the risk of the borrower's insolvency.

4

Protection of Property Interests

IN GENERAL

The law of property imposes no positive duties on anyone. The owner, in principle, need do nothing at all with her belongings, and neither need anyone else. What the rest of us must do is abstain: the law does not bid us act, it forbids us to act. Without the owner's consent we must not trespass on, damage, take, or in any way interfere with her property. This is a negative obligation, a duty not to act, and so can bind everyone, child or adult, sane or insane.[1]

Self-help. We are of course entitled ourselves to protect our property rights. We can resist trespass on or interference with our tangible things; if, without our consent, we are excluded from our land, or our goods are taken, we can physically recover possession. If, in doing so, we use more force than was necessary we may be subject to criminal prosecution and civil suit, but the property we have recovered will not be taken from us and handed back to our victim.

Judicial protection. If self-help does not avail us, we have to go to law, and one of the law's tasks is to protect our entitlement to and enjoyment of our property.[2] The criminal law attempts this by defining and penalizing such offences as theft and wanton damage. Other branches of law provide means to rebuff trespass, to recover our possessions, and to claim compensation by an award of damages.

In approaching this complex area, the following matters need to be considered: the type of property involved; the kind of infringement committed; who is protected; against whom; how; and for how long.

---

[1] There are, of course, exceptions. First, there is the State's power of eminent domain, or compulsory purchase. Second, many statutes authorize what would otherwise be acts of trespass: utility companies may be allowed to lay pipes through private land and so on. Third, the common law (like other systems) has evolved exceptions to deal with emergencies (hostilities, fire, flood, shipwreck, and the like) where the trespass would be trivial in comparison with the benefits obtained thereby.

[2] The European Convention on Human Rights, art.13 obliges the States to provide an effective remedy.

TYPE OF PROPERTY

The law's protection of interests in property varies with the nature of the asset involved. Some kinds of property can be possessed, others cannot. The former type can come into the hands of a person not the owner, and protection means the return of the thing or payment of its value together, where appropriate, with compensation for the loss sustained and income forgone by its detention. Of the other types of property, some, such as patents or copyrights, can be infringed, and protection is afforded by a suit to restrain infringement and perhaps to obtain damages or a recovery of the profits made by the infringer. The interests of beneficiaries in a trust fund are protected in various ways: for instance by ordering a defaulting trustee to restore the fund; by ordering a transferee from the trustee to return the asset or its proceeds; or by removing and replacing the trustee. Here we shall concentrate on the protection given to interests in tangible objects. The protection of security interests and servitudes is dealt with in the relevant chapters.

WHO IS PROTECTED?

The owner. Obviously the law protects someone whose belongings are taken from her. But how does she prove they are hers? In some cases this can be done by pointing to a register, of land, shipping, or shares. But there is no register of the ownership of ordinary movables, nor do we normally keep documents such as receipts relating to every item in our household. Consequently, all that the law can do is to start by assuming that if we have something in our possession then it is ours.[3] The Theft Act 1968, for instance, treats property as belonging to 'any person having possession or control of it' (s.5(1)). The law's approach seems sensible since most movables belong to the person who has them. One cannot, however, make quite the same generalization about land, ships, or aircraft, since many non-owners—tenants, lodgers, visitors in the one case, charterers in the other—may have control of them.

Where chattels are concerned, the law's approach reduces costs in the resolution of disputes by protecting possession without requiring the person so protected to prove ownership. It is up to the defendant to justify the taking or detention of the thing. The presumption also imposes a respect for possession, however it was obtained. If someone finds a ring, or a thief steals a bicycle, each is protected against anyone

---

[3] There are sensible exceptions for the kind of situation where employees are using their employer's things or guests their host's or lodgers their landlord's.

who takes it without consent—except, of course, the person who had prior possession and who lost the ring or had the bicycle stolen and so on.

In more technical language, we may say that there are rights to possess and rights which flow from having acquired possession. For the first phrase English (and American) law tends to use the word 'title': your title to some asset indicates your right to possess it. It is possible for there to be two or more titles to a thing, one being stronger than another. If you make a ring from your own hair, there is no doubt whatever that it is yours and that you have a better right to it than anyone else. If you lose it, you can claim it from the finder. But in the absence of any claim by you, the finder is treated as having a title good against everyone. You have a better right to possess the thing than does the finder, but the finder has a better right to possess it than does anyone else.

Furthermore the acquisition of possession confers other rights, and risks. A finder can leave the thing by will, give it away, settle it and so on; and it can be taken in execution by the finder's creditors. Of course if the 'true owner' (or person who can prove prior possession) makes a timely claim, her entitlement will prevail over any right derived from a title weaker than hers.

In general then, where the thing itself is tangible, possession is protected. But the law must also sometimes protect an owner who is not in possession. If you lend your book to a friend, the friend's rights are protected against everyone except you; you, of course, can reclaim the book. Furthermore you can reclaim it from anyone who has taken it from the borrower since, although you did not have possession of the book when they took it, you can show that you had the right to immediate possession. We can sum up by saying that the possessor of a thing is protected because he or she has possession; the owner is also protected because he or she ought to have possession.

AGAINST WHOM?

Indefinite number. It is a characteristic of proprietary (or 'real') interests that they are protected against an indefinite number of persons. Most are protected against everyone who comes by the thing without the consent of the person entitled. In the case of registered land, the State guarantees the title of the person registered as proprietor, and assumes liability to pay an indemnity to anyone who, without carelessness on his part, has been injured by the state of the register. In the same way a person who has been registered as a holder of shares in a company is a shareholder for all purposes.

The persons entitled to interests in a trust fund are protected against everyone except those who acquired trust assets for value and without notice that they were being transferred in breach of trust.

In the case of movables, their owner is, in general, protected against a wider range of persons than is the case in many legal systems. First, she is of course protected against anyone who takes it or comes by it without her consent—thieves if it is stolen, finders if it is lost. Secondly, she may claim against any transferee from such a person. Thirdly, she may claim against any person who has it with consent if that consent has been lawfully withdrawn: so if she lends a book to a friend she can ask for it back and sue if it is not returned. Fourthly, she is protected against anyone who, in good faith, bought and took delivery of the thing from someone who was not the owner but was in possession with the owner's consent. In the example just given, if the friend to whom she lent the book sold and delivered it to some innocent buyer, the buyer must return the book to the owner or pay compensation in damages: the innocent act of buying the book from someone who is not its owner is an infringement of the owner's rights. Furthermore, the innocent buyer cannot defend the owner's action by pleading her negligence in trusting her friend.

Having surrendered the book, or paid its value, to its owner, the buyer can then sue the seller for breach of the contract of sale (and perhaps also for deceit). But it was the owner who trusted the friend with the book in the first place; the buyer acted perfectly sensibly and honestly in assuming that the person in possession of the book was its owner and that he was safe in handing over money in return for delivery of the book. The common-law's approach protects ownership as against commerce and is usually justified by repeating, in Latin, that no one can transfer what they do not have (*nemo dat quod non habet*).

Exceptions. But this maxim is subject to the following exceptions which protect the innocent recipient in certain common situations.

(a) Money. The good-faith recipient of coins or notes who has given something in return for the money, can keep it: so if a thief pays for his haircut with stolen money and the barber does not know this, the victim of the theft can recover nothing from the barber. This result is mandated by the very function of money.

(b) Negotiable instruments. Commercial paper such as bills of exchange and promissory notes, once issued, are treated like currency. A holder in due course—that is to say the person who takes in good faith an

instrument for which value has at some time been given—gets a good title and the right to claim payment.[4]

(c) Dealers. Owners often employ agents to sell for them—the professional mercantile agents are often called 'factors' in the older lawbooks. Of course such a person can pass a good title in anything he is employed to sell. But he may also have goods which he is not authorized to sell—their owner may have instructed him to display the goods and report offers which the owner could then decide whether to accept. The ordinary customer would not know which the dealer could sell and which not. Consequently nineteenth-century statutes protect the good-faith buyer who buys in the ordinary course of business by providing that the transaction is as valid as if it were authorized by the owner.

(d) Sellers in possession. A similar problem arose where a person had sold goods (so that they were no longer his) but remained in possession of them. It is very difficult to know which of the goods have been sold and which are still for sale, and so statute—now the Sale of Goods Act—provides that the sale and delivery of the goods to a good-faith buyer passes a good title. A similar provision protects the person who purchases from someone who has agreed to buy the goods from their owner and has got possession of them but has not yet acquired ownership.

(e) Hire purchase of motor vehicles. The person who acquires goods on hire purchase has an option to buy them but has not agreed to do so, i.e. is not bound to buy. Consequently, although the hire-purchaser has possession of the goods, a sale by him or her during the period of hire would not fall under the Sale of Goods Act provisions described in the preceding paragraph and the buyer, however innocent, would not prevail in an action by the person or finance company which was selling the goods on hire purchase. In the case of motor cars this gave rise to frequent problems where the customer 'sold' the car as his or her own and then vanished leaving the buyer vulnerable to an action by the finance company and with little hope of successfully suing the fraudulent seller. Consequently, a statute of 1964 protects a private citizen, i.e. not a trade or finance purchaser, who buys in good faith a vehicle which the seller in fact holds on hire purchase.

The general rule recalled. But the narrowness of this exception, confined as it is in terms of object—motor vehicles—and person—consumers—illustrates the importance which the common law attaches to its general

---

[4] Cheques payable to order fall into this category, but the common printed cheque crossed a/c only is now not even transferable, let alone negotiable (Cheques Act 1992).

protection of ownership. Disputes over title to movables usually involve three persons, two of whom are innocent: the owner entrusts possession of her property to someone; that someone swindles an innocent citizen by pretending to be owner, sells him the goods and then disappears with the money (or is not worth suing). The owner sues the buyer. Unlike other systems, in this situation the common-law's general rule favours the owner, and judgment will be entered against the innocent buyer. Exactly what type of judgment is appropriate will be explained in the next section.

METHODS OF PROTECTION

The types of judgment which may be entered, or orders made, differ according to a number of factors. The most important question to be asked is: who now has the thing—the claimant; the defendant; a third person; no one? As to this last possibility, if the thing has perished or disappeared the court can award only a money judgment. Furthermore and in practice it will do the same where the thing is perfectly fungible like a litre of milk, otherwise the cost of compliance might well exceed the value of the interest protected. And if the thing in question is money, there is generally no way of compelling the return of that very money. All that the court will do is order payment of the same amount.

Claimant still has the thing

If the object is tangible and the infringement does not deprive the owner of possession, but consists in intrusion on or damage to the object, then the remedies are an action for compensation (an action for trespass) and a suit for an injunction to restrain likely future infringements. If the object is an immaterial monopoly right such as that bestowed by the law of patents or copyright, then the only possible infringement is some breach of the monopoly. The appropriate remedies are an injunction to restrain further infringements plus an order for damages or an account of the profits made by the breach; the court may also order the destruction of infringing articles. Where the object is a trust fund and the infringer is a trustee, the appropriate protection compels the trustee to make good the fund out of her own assets or, in the last resort, provides for the trustee's removal and replacement.

Claimant does not have the thing

A more complex picture unfolds when the claimant no longer has the object: a landowner has been evicted, or her goods have been stolen and transferred to a third party. In principle, the claimant does *not* have to show that the defendant knew or ought to have known that there was something wrong with the title to the object or with the transaction by which the defendant obtained it. So long as the claimant can show that her entitlement is the stronger, the defendant will lose, no matter how innocent, how honest, or how careful his conduct. The exceptions to this rule, such as money and commercial paper, were explained in the preceding section.

The modes of protection available here are entirely different according to whether or not the defendant still has the object (or its identifiable proceeds).

Defendant has the thing or its proceeds

If the thing is tangible the claimant can, in theory, get it back by taking it. This form of protection—'self-help'—has the advantages of speed and low cost, but in order for it to work the claimant must locate the thing, there must be no dispute as to her entitlement, and no risk of force or violence. In practice, therefore, the claimant must often go to law. In an action to recover land, the claimant can insist on its return. She can bring proceedings to recover possession (the old name for it is 'ejectment') and, if she succeeds, will obtain a judgment for the return of the land plus damages to compensate for being deprived of possession and its fruits. If the defendant refuses to comply, state officials (the sheriff) will be ordered to proceed to an eviction. The important point to notice about this procedure is that it is unaffected by the insolvency of the defendant: whatever other possessions may be claimed by his creditors, the land is safe from them. The defendant cannot pay his debts with the claimant's property.

This crucial feature is the same if the object in the defendant's possession is not land but goods. However, the legal procedure differs in that it is a matter for the discretion of the judge, who has three options: to order the return of the goods; to order payment of damages by reference to their value; or to allow the defendant to choose whether to return the goods or pay for them. If the article is unique, the judge will usually order its return without giving the defendant any choice in the matter; on the other hand, if it is not, it is thought to be more efficient to order monetary compensation with which the claimant can, if she so wishes, acquire a similar object, though this is a sort of forced sale of the claimant's property at a price fixed by the court. But even if the claimant is only to be compensated in money, the claim still takes priority over the defendant's other creditors, and is therefore a real, a proprietary, claim. The reason for this is that the claimant's title to the goods is not extinguished until the money is in her hands; until then, of course, her property cannot be used to pay the defendant's creditors.[5]

Where the object in question is trust property which has been transferred in breach of trust and the defendant has that property or its identifiable proceeds and either got it for nothing or, if he paid for it, *knew or ought to have known* of the breach of trust, the beneficiaries can claim that the property or proceeds be restored to the trust fund. As in the instances above, the property cannot be reached by the defendant's own creditors. If, however, the recipient of trust property transferred in breach of trust has paid for it without any notice of the breach, then that person is safe from any claim by the beneficiary. But by definition the recipient paid for it: and the price in the hands of the defaulting trustee is the property of the beneficiaries, and is not available to the trustee's creditors.

If the object is money, it is usually impossible to secure the return of those particular coins or notes. Instead the claim is for repayment of an equivalent sum, and, as we have seen, it will never prevail against one who took the money in good faith and for value. But if someone, without your consent (whether a thief or your trustee), gives 'your' money as a present to an innocent recipient, and if the donee still has a sum representing the original amount, you, as the true owner, ought to be protected. Thus if, for instance, the donee pays it into a bank account which is in credit, you may be given a charge on that account so as to ensure repayment ahead of other creditors. If, however, the account is or becomes overdrawn, then the object of your property entitlement has gone.

Defendant has neither the thing nor its proceeds

A defendant who no longer has the object or its identifiable proceeds will still be liable if at some stage he appropriated the claimant's property. This is so even though he acted in the utmost good faith and took every possible care. If, in all innocence, you buy a stolen car, then, as explained above, if you still have it you must return it or its value to its owner (leaving you with a personal claim against the seller). If you have sold it and the proceeds can be traced (into, for instance, your bank account), then the owner can claim those proceeds in priority to your other creditors. But if you have neither the car nor its traceable proceeds—because

---

[5] The rule is not new, but is now stated in the Torts (Interference with Goods) Act 1977, ss.3(2), 5(1)(b).

you have given it away, written it off, had it stolen from you—then the claimant can point to nothing in your possession which is, or which represents, her property, and can claim from you only damages by reference to the car's value, *in competition with your other unsecured creditors*.

To sum up: in an action against someone who still has her land or her goods or the traceable proceeds, the owner has a proprietary claim enabling her to take the asset (or its value) out of the defendant's patrimony. But as against a defendant who has appropriated the property but no longer has it or its identifiable proceeds, the owner must be content with a personal unsecured claim for damages.

THE PERIOD OF PROTECTION: LIMITATION OF ACTIONS AND RIGHTS

Ownership is protected for ever against a thief or fraudulent trustee. If, for instance, a work of art is stolen and is kept for hundreds of years in the thief's family home, the owner's heirs or successors can still recover it. Again, the statutory limitation periods do not protect trustees who cheat or take trust property for themselves (though equity may exercise a discretion to penalize the lazy beneficiary).

Apart from these cases, however, the period of protection has been curtailed by the Limitation Acts (currently dated 1980).[6] We have only a certain number of years in which to bring an action to recover property and if we do not sue in time, and if the defendant pleads the statute, we lose both the right to sue and our right to the object. In the case of goods the general period is six years; in the case of land it is twelve.

Several reasons are given for this type of legislation (which is found in many countries). The first is that it encourages owners to enforce their rights; the second is that, after a long time, evidentiary problems become very difficult to resolve; the third is that, in the old jargon, it 'quiets title' and enables the possessor, after a time, to rest easy. A final reason is to afford some eventual protection to others, since the person in possession of something is usually its owner. On acquiring the thing they take the benefit of any period that has run in favour of the transferor.

The existence of the limitation periods does not mean we have to sue our good friends; that is to say, time runs against us only if our property is

---

[6] The Law Commission has recently produced a Report and Draft Bill on Limitation of Actions: Law Com No. 270 (2001). It proposes two main periods of three and ten years, and makes other important changes. Go to http://www.lawcom.gov.uk.

being held adversely to us and we know (or could know) about it. If we lend a book to a friend, time does not start to run until we ask for it back. If the friend then says falsely that it has been stolen, time does not start to run until we find out that he still has it. Furthermore, any signed acknowledgement of our right starts time running again.

Where time does run and the period has expired, the effect of the legislation is extinctive, not acquisitive. That is to say, the expiry of that period does not transfer title to the possessor, nor does the statute confer some new title on him or her at that moment. So there is no requirement that the adverse possessor be in good faith. As to the *right to sue*, the Act says only that 'no action shall be brought' after the expiry of a certain time. As to the *right to the object*, land or chattel, the Act says only that, after the expiry of the period, the title of the person who could have sued 'shall be extinguished'.[7] The point of having both provisions is this: suppose A when visiting B finds his book which he lost seven years ago on B's table. If he sues, and B is not a thief and pleads the statute, then A will lose the case. If, instead of suing, A puts the book in his pocket, since the statute also bars his title, he must give the book back to B, and will lose in an action by B to recover possession.

A similar approach is taken in the case of land, but it runs into complications. Suppose A is the registered proprietor of a piece of land and, while he is away, B (a 'squatter') takes possession of it. At that moment B, by the fact of possession, acquires a title to the land which enables him to leave it by will or give it away, which can be reached by his creditors, and which will prevail against anyone except A or A's successors. After twelve years A's right of action is barred and his title expires, so B's title is now the best. But A still appears in the Land Register as proprietor. B can apply to have himself registered as proprietor in place of A, but until the register is amended the Land Registration Act 1925 says that A's 'estate shall not be extinguished but shall be deemed to be held by the proprietor . . . in trust for' B. Thus B's enemy is made his trustee.

This was an unhappy solution and the Land Registration Bill 2001 proposes major changes. Time will never run in favour of a squatter on land the title to which is registered. However, after ten years in adverse possession, the squatter can apply to be registered as proprietor. There are then two years during which the registered proprietor can take steps

---

[7] The Land Registration Act 1925, s.75(1) uses the word 'estate', not 'title'. The current Limitation Act extinguishes the title only to tangible things (except money), as does the Law Commission's draft Bill. The title to money is normally lost by mingling or by payment to a good faith recipient for value.

to object, evict the possessor, or otherwise regularize the position. A person still in adverse possession after the two years will be entitled to be registered as the new proprietor of the estate, but the onus is on the squatter to take the initiative. Doing so will extinguish the title acquired by adverse *possession* and replace it with an estate vested by *registration*. This estate will normally be free of any registered charge which affected the estate in the hands of the previous proprietor.

Part 3

Common-Law Techniques

This Part focuses on the particular features of the common law's treatment of the law of property. Chapter 5 explains the main concepts used. Chapter 6 deals with the common figures of ownership, concurrent ownership, and life interests. Chapter 7 outlines the main features of the scheme adopted by legislation for land in England and Wales.

5

Concepts and Categories

Much of the basic law described in the preceding chapters is similar to that found in other legal systems which recognize private property. But, for reasons which are largely historical, common-law countries make great use of a number of concepts, techniques, habits of thought, and simple jargon which have no counterparts elsewhere. Some have already been alluded to, but we need to give here a fuller, if still brief, description of their basic features. Their use in combination with each other will be examined in a later chapter on Wealth.

The topics to be discussed are: tenure; estate; bailment; the persistent reification of relations; the apparently ineradicable distinction between 'law' and 'equity'; the trust; and 'tracing' (or real subrogation). Some of these concepts and categories persist although the reason for them has long gone, others remain because they are still useful.

TENURE

The institution of tenure is of little practical importance today. It must be briefly mentioned, however, since it gave rise to a number of concepts and technical terms which are still in use throughout the common-law world—even in the USA, which broke with the monarchy long ago. The word itself means 'holding' (Latin *tenere*, French *tenir*) and is found in such forms as 'tenancy' and 'tenant'. The Middle Ages used these forms where nowadays we would say 'own' and 'owner'.

In relation to land, tenure is historically a product of the feudal system which reached its strongest form in England after 1066. In a society short of the precious metals and unable to pay for services in money, land was the most convenient medium with which the monarch could both reward his chief supporters and at the same time bind them to provide further services. Politically, the most important of such services were military. The king therefore granted parcels of land to men of substance or status (so-called tenants-in-chief) upon the terms that they would provide a certain number of knights to serve for forty days a year. The tenants-in-chief would procure the services of the knights by giving each a portion of the land to hold by the service of serving in the army. A knight might replicate the process by granting some of the land which he held of his lord to the Church in return for the provision of religious services. Economically, the most important services were agricultural, performed at the lower levels of society. This is only the core of what was a most complicated pyramid of landholding but it gives sufficient information to explain what is meant by tenure.

Tenure is a relation which looks two ways, to a parcel of land, and towards the lord of whom it is held: the abbot might hold the abbey farm of the local squire who held it within a larger terrain of the local duke who held the county of the king. Tenure is a relation between lord and vassal, but with regard to the land itself—the abbey farm in our example—it involves four layers of entitlement, of the abbot, the lord, the duke, and the king. As a means of organizing the economy, the system itself died out long ago, leaving a few picturesque and some profitable relics, a number of legal terms, and certain entrenched ways of thought.[1]

The student needs to be aware of the notion, for a number of reasons. First of all the Crown still holds some land—for instance, the foreshore— as sovereign, as lord paramount, by an entitlement which is at the root of property relations in land. The technical term for this Crown (i.e. State) property is 'demesne land' and its existence has awkward consequences for the Land Registry, which was set up to record only the entitlements of private landowners.[2] Secondly, something very similar to the old notion of tenure operates nowadays, not in its old terrain of freehold land but in the law of leases, where the words 'tenancy' and 'tenant' are part of ordinary English. A modern counterpart to the abbot just mentioned might be the firm which leases one office from the person who has a sub-lease of the whole floor from the company which has a lease of the whole office block whose landlord is the freeholder.

The third reason for having some grasp of the old notion of tenure is that it was not applied to movables, thus causing a sharp difference in treatment between realty and other property. Goods and cattle seem to have always been the object of direct and absolute ownership. From the earliest times they could be left by will, a privilege accorded to

[1] Lordships of the Manor are picturesque; the exclusive right to hold a market may be profitable.

[2] The word 'demesne' is pronounced 'demean' or 'demain' and is the same as 'domain', deriving via French from the Latin word *'dominium'*. Modern Australian courts use the phrase 'radical title' to denote something similar in the Crown's entitlement on their territory. The Land Registry problems are outlined in Chapter 7.

landowners only gradually after 1540. Goods could be taken to pay their owner's debts after his death as well as in his lifetime, a liability not fully imposed on realty until the nineteenth century. Until 1926 succession on intestacy to realty differed from that applied to personalty. Thus in strict terminology, it is said that the doctrines of tenure and that of estates (see below) do not apply to movables. In fact, as we shall see, very similar techniques seem to operate

THE 'ESTATE CONCEPT'

A final reason to remember tenure is that it gave rise to the habit of classifying entitlement to land in terms of the time for which it could be enjoyed. Where land was given in return for the performance of personal services, it might well be granted only for the life of the tenant, so that on his death possession reverted to his lord: the tenant's entitlement came to be called a 'life estate', the word being a version of *status*. If land is given to endow a family, it could be granted for the tenant's life and that of his children, grandchildren, and so on. Finally it could be granted so as to be inheritable by the person who was heir (not necessarily lineal heir) on the death of the current holder. Each of these latter two entitlements was called a 'fee' (from the word *feodum*) to denote that it was inheritable. If the range of permitted heirs was limited to lineal descendants, there was a 'fee tail' from the French word '*tailler*' meaning to cut (or to tailor). If the land could descend to any heir the fee was 'simple', that is not limited in any way.

These three estates endured. The fee tail was not abolished until 1996. The life estate still flourishes, not tied to a particular piece of land, but as an interest in a fund, as explained in the chapter on Wealth. The 'fee simple' in any given land—nowadays often called simply 'the freehold'— is the basis of modern land law, and is the interest title to which is recorded in the Land Register.[3]

Thus English lawyers have always been accustomed to classifying interests in land in terms of the time for which they could endure. Leases were easily fitted into this perception, although they grew up outside the feudal system. Furthermore, the co-existence of these estates was common. Land might be let on a yearly farming lease by A who was entitled to the land for his life; on his death B or B's lineal descendants might be entitled to the land while the family line endured; and when it died out, C or his successor would be entitled. Thus four people had at the same time

---

[3] See Chapter 7.

an interest in the land. It is very difficult to say that any one of them *owns* the land, and the common law instead said that each holds an estate in the land (respectively a lease, a life estate, a fee tail (entail), and a fee simple). These estates coexist, but each can be treated as the object of property, since each can be sold, mortgaged, given away, reached by creditors, and so on. Indeed at the present time, where title to land is registered and guaranteed by the State, if you buy a house you will be registered as proprietor, not of the land, but of the 'fee simple absolute in possession' if it is freehold and of a 'legal term of years absolute' if it is leasehold.

The largest and most valuable estate is the fee simple absolute in possession, an entitlement that may last for ever. It has outlived feudalism and is a useful concept because it does not necessarily denote that its holder is the true owner of the land. Usually, of course, that will be the case: but the estate notion does not include the element of title in the sense of the best right to the land. If a person occupies another's land adversely, then the occupant's title is weak since she may readily be evicted. Meanwhile, however, in relation to the rest of the world it makes good sense to say that she has an estate in the land—a fee simple since it may last for ever—which she can alienate during her lifetime, which may descend on her death, and which can be reached by her creditors.[4] There is another reason why the estate concept has outgrown its feudal roots: it does not necessarily entail the notion of benefit. It is perfectly possible, and very common, for the holder of an estate (the 'tenant in fee simple') to be a trustee of it for other persons or charitable purposes. The holder may lawfully exercise only those powers of an owner which are needed to carry out the functions of the office of trustee: thus she cannot neglect the estate, nor give it away (except to a beneficiary under the terms of the trust) and it cannot be reached by her creditors.

A final warning is needed. In England and Wales, in relation to *land*, the word 'legal estate' is now used in relation to the normal fee simple, to the lease, and to certain other rights (such as mortgages and rights of way) which, if created with the requisite formality, will bind the land.[5] But the estate *concept*, which classifies assets by reference to the time for which an income stream may be enjoyed, is still very useful in the world of wealth.[6]

---

[4] A similar doctrine of relativity of title applies to chattels. See Chapter 3 above.
[5] Law of Property Act 1925, s.1(4); Land Registration Bill 2001, s.129(1). See Chapter 7.
[6] See Chapter 12.

BAILMENT

We are not supposed to use the estate concept in relation to movable things. Yet in the case of chattels, an analogy to the relation of landlord and tenant is to be found in the notion of bailment. Whenever a tangible movable is delivered by one person to another for a time or for a purpose and on the understanding that the object is to be returned at the end of that time or on the accomplishment of the purpose, there is a bailment. The person who hands over the thing is the bailor, the recipient the bailee.

Someone who takes a lease of a furnished flat is technically 'tenant' of the land but 'bailee' of the furniture. Just as the lessee of a flat must, at the end of the lease, give back possession of the flat, so the bailee of a chattel must in due course return it to, or deliver it as designated by, the bailor. Furthermore while the bailee has the object, he or she must take reasonable care of it (and must often comply with detailed contractual terms, as in a furnished letting, or the rental of a television set). Just as the lessee of a flat is treated as having a property interest, so the bailee is said to have a 'special property' in the chattel, while the bailor has 'the general property'.

Bailment for a period confers possession of the object on the bailee, to the exclusion of the bailor. Thus the bailee, not the bailor, can bring an action of trespass against an intruder and can alone recover the object (or its value) from a dispossessor (see the chapter on the protection of property). If the bailment is at will, as where you lend a friend something on the understanding that you can have it back when you need it, the bailee's position is the same, though it seems that the bailor also has possession with the rights it confers. So far there is little to differentiate in principle a bailment of a chattel for a period from a lease of land. Moreover, such interest as the bailee has in the chattels is derived from that of the bailor, as is shown by the rule that, just as a lessee cannot be heard to deny the lessor's title, so a bailee cannot deny that of the bailor's. Thus (although the matter is not free of controversy) bailment presents a similar sort of mingling of personal and property relations as is found in a lease of land. Indeed, in modern commerce the words 'lease' and 'rental' are commonly used in relation to a range of chattels.

REIFICATION

Unfortunately there is no simple word for this process, which in this context means treating rights as if they were things. The account of ownership given in the previous chapter began by assuming that the thing owned was a single tangible object. But a characteristic of the common-law approach is to apply, as far as possible, the same principles and the same verb to intangible assets. The technique has a long history. The great legal historian Maitland says 'any right or group of rights that is of a permanent kind can be thought of as a thing. . . . medieval law is rich with incorporeal things'.[7] This approach has persisted to this day so that it is natural to speak of the *owner* of a patent and our legislation refers to 'the *owner* of a mortgage', or an 'estate owner'. A standard form by which a business assigns to a finance house the debts due from its customers warrants, not that the borrower is the creditor of its customers, but that it is 'the legal and beneficial *owner* of the receivables'. A clear statement of this technique is to be found in California, where legislation dating from 1872 provides that 'There may be ownership of all inanimate things which are capable of appropriation or of manual delivery; of all domestic animals; of all obligations; of such products of labor and skill as the composition of an author, the good-will of a business, trademarks and signs, and of rights created or granted by statute'.[8]

LAW AND EQUITY

It is an ingrained habit of common lawyers everywhere to distinguish between rights and remedies which exist at law and those which exist or operate only in equity. This is a distinction which is hard to grasp and which has nothing to do with the popular meanings of law and of equity. As mentioned in Chapter 1, historically it is a distinction between rights recognized and remedies afforded by courts exercising different jurisdictions, on the one hand the old courts of common law, and on the other the Chancellor. The Chancellor exercised what was in effect a supplementary jurisdiction, assuming at every point the existence of the common law but making good, as far as possible, its deficiencies. In this he was greatly assisted by the fact that the parties to a dispute could themselves give him testimony on oath, by affidavit. The common-law courts, by contrast, refused to hear the parties themselves until the mid-nineteenth century. But equity remained a supplementary system, though it may fairly be said that common law and equity taken together make up a coherent, if complex, system. This is

---

[7] Pollock and Maitland, *History of English Law*, ii, 3–4, 124–49 (2nd edn., CUP, 1968).
[8] California Civil Code, s.655.

more evident now in that both are administered in the same courts and both common law and equitable remedies can be obtained in the same proceedings.

Equity is in no way synonymous with natural law or natural justice though, like all good law, it aims at justice. It is now a body of technical rules and principles based, like the common law, on precedent and in places re-stated or modified by statute. Most of it deals in one way or the other with the law of property, but only the most important principles and characteristics need to be discussed in an elementary work. They are the following.

Curing informality. Before the common law will enforce rights it often insists that they be created by some particular formality. To this day, a transfer of land or a lease of it exceeding three years, must be effected by deed before it will be 'legal' in the sense of being recognized by the common law (even after the parties have acted on it). But equity was, and is, prepared to enforce informal transactions such as a contract to transfer land or an unsealed long lease of land, provided that the claimant has given value and that it would be unconscionable of the defendant not to give effect to the transaction. The frequently cited maxim is that 'Equity looks on that as done which ought to be done.'

If the common law recognizes a property right or transaction, then it is enforced against everyone, whether they know about it or not.[9] This is still the law, and a simple example is an easement such as a right of way over one piece of land for the benefit of the land next door. If the right has been formally granted by a deed executed by the owner of the burdened land, then it binds everyone who takes that land. It does not matter that they were not told, and could see no traces of it.[10] A property right (such as a right of way) which is recognized 'at law' will also be accepted, and enforced by injunction if necessary, 'in equity'.

Equity, however, is wider in its acknowledgement of property rights but narrower in their enforcement. On the one hand it will not refuse to recognize transactions simply because they do not comply with strict formality. But on the other hand it will not enforce such rights against a blameless defendant who has paid for their property, complied with all formalities, acted prudently, and yet has no knowledge of the adverse

---

[9] Exceptions, such as money, were explained in Chapter 4.

[10] Though this might give them a personal claim against their vendor for compensation for breach of the covenant implied in the conveyance: see now the Law of Property (Miscellaneous Provisions) Act 1994, s.3(1).

right.[11] Such a person's conscience is clear and equity has no jurisdiction over them. In the technical jargon which developed it is said that an equitable right will bind only those who paid nothing for the property, and those who paid but had notice of the equitable claim. Nowadays such notice is usually provided by registration of one sort or another, as explained in a later chapter.[12]

Specific performance of contract obligations. The common law readily compels performance of the most common type of contractual obligation: the obligation to pay a specific sum of money. If you promise £100 to anyone who uses your medicine and yet catches influenza, then, in an action by someone who meets those conditions, the common law will ensure that you (or your assets) keep that promise. But the common law does not compel performance of other obligations. The reason for this difference of treatment is presumably that it is much easier to compel performance of a monetary obligation, by seizing and selling the defendant's goods, than it is to make the defendant perform some other promise. Equity, however, would if necessary compel performance of other obligations by ordering the defendant to perform and threatening imprisonment for contempt of court if he refused to obey. The courts are still prepared to imprison people for failure to obey injunctions, even though they have not been and could not be charged with, let alone convicted of, any crime at all.

The importance of all this for the law of property lies in the fact that an obligation to convey or make a lease of land can be enforced in this way— the promisor can be ordered to carry out the necessary formalities and to deliver possession. And since these obligations can be enforced, equity acts as if they have been: equity treats as already done that which ought to be done. So once a promise to convey property has come into existence that a court of equity will enforce specifically (and above all, this means a promise to sell and convey land), then in the eyes of equity the buyer is the owner and the seller is not, although, for purposes of the common law, formal (or 'legal') ownership does not pass until the deed of conveyance (and registration of the buyer as proprietor).[13] The practical importance

---

[11] Between two blameless persons each of whom has an informal, and so 'equitable' claim, the first has priority, though this may be modified by registration or the giving of notice, depending on the type of interest involved.

[12] And a number of valuable interests are called 'equitable' although they do not bind a purchaser who knows all about them, because they are shifted to the price paid and any investment thereof: see Chapter 7.

[13] Equity thus treats contracts to sell land in the same way that the common law treats contracts for the sale of specific goods in a deliverable state.

of equity's attitude becomes evident if, between contract and conveyance, the value of the property changes and one of the parties becomes insolvent. If, for instance, the value goes up and the seller is insolvent, then the buyer can insist that the land is his and is not available for distribution among the seller's creditors. What they get is the price which, *ex hypothesi*, is of lower value. The buyer is also protected if, between contract and formal conveyance, the seller sells to someone else. If the new buyer has notice of the prior contract (which nowadays means that it was protected by entry on a register), then he can be compelled to convey the property to the original promisee who pays him the price due to the original seller.

Specific performance will be decreed only if three conditions are satisfied. The first is that money would not be an adequate remedy: thus, in the area of sales, only contracts for the transfer of unique objects will be enforced, since, if the subject matter is not unique, the buyer can take the damages awarded and, if he choose, buy an equivalent elsewhere. Land is almost always treated as unique for, even if the particular house is identical to many others, the neighbours are different. The second condition is that the obligation sought to be enforced is not one for personal services, since to force one person to work for another would be too near slavery. The third condition is that the claimant must have given value for the promise: an informal promise to make a present is enforceable neither at law nor in equity.

Dealing with unconscionable conduct. The equitable jurisdiction arose in order to deal with situations where, in purely formal terms, a person's conduct might be unimpeachable, but in the given situation before the court, reliance on it would offend conscience. To this day the courts will, in such situations, protect certain interests that do not fit the standard pattern. Since they have no names of their own they are called 'an equity' or even 'a mere equity'.[14] By the nature of the case they arise in uncommon situations, and details have no place in a work such as this.

We may sum up by saying that the equitable remedies have had profound effects on English law and on those systems to which it gave birth. For they have been extended to protect claimants against increasing classes of persons, as is shown in the example above of the person who signs a contract to buy land and enters notice of this in the appropriate register. Thus rights which begin as claims against one person, the seller, become effective against an indefinite class of people, and a personal right

---

[14] See for instance Land Registration Bill 2001, cl.108(4); 114.

grows into a real right. But it must be repeated that this operates first, only in favour of a person who has given consideration, that is to say money or money's worth, or has been treated unconscionably by the defendant; and secondly, they will not prevail against a person who has given consideration and acquired the property without notice of the other's right. Finally, the property affected must be identifiable and specific; but a trust fund and a particular bank account are identifiable and specific enough.

Of all the various interests protected by these equitable remedies the most permanent is that enjoyed by the beneficiary of a trust fund.

THE TRUST

The trust is equity's greatest contribution to the law of property. Originating in the England of the early fifteenth century, the institution has now spread to many countries, not only of the common law, but also of other legal traditions. Indeed in the last decade of the twentieth century a dozen tax havens enthusiastically enacted their own Trusts Acts.[15]

By the institution of trust one or more persons (called trustees) hold property for the benefit of someone else, or for charity. As we have said—but it bears repetition—the trustees always hold jointly, so that when one dies he or she simply drops out and the survivors hold the property. Any kind of property can form the subject matter of a trust—land, chattels, shares, receivables, patents, and so on. The property is vested in the trustees by whatever formalities are appropriate to its particular type. Thus if it is land they will be registered as 'proprietors', if chattels they will have possession, if shares they will be registered as the shareholders, a bank account will be in their name, and so on.

By an unfortunate historical convention, trustees are often called the 'legal owners'. The adjective is not meant to indicate that they are not illegal; it is used to mean that they hold the property by the kind of formal title that would be recognized by the common law. To call the trustees 'legal owners' is both inaccurate and misleading. The adjective is wrong since any property interest (however 'equitable') can be held on trust. The word 'owners' indicates that very often they will have the powers of sale and management that go with ownership. But they are not really owners because they cannot treat the property as their own. They

---

[15] Perhaps it should be said at once that the American 'anti-trust' has nothing whatever to do with trusts—they are not like matter and anti-matter. 'Anti-trust' comes from nineteenth-century US business history and refers to the law against cartels and agreements in restraint of trade.

cannot even neglect, let alone destroy, it. They cannot give it away for nothing (except to a beneficiary and in compliance with the terms of the trust). They cannot leave it to their family on their death. And, most important of all, *their own creditors cannot reach the trust property*. If the trustees hold for the benefit of other persons, it is the latter who are rich; it is their creditors who can reach the assets. So it is probably best to think of trusteeship as an office, created by private law.[16]

Very often a trust is established by a person (the 'settlor') who transfers property to the trustees, observing the formalities of transfer requisite for the particular asset involved, but making it clear that this is not a present, nor even a loan, to them. They are to hold and manage the property for the benefit of others. It is not a present to the trustees but to the beneficiaries, though it is to be managed by the trustees. As such it is particularly suited for a gift that will take effect over a period of time. The trustees might, for instance, be told to invest and manage the trust property, pay the income to A until she dies, and then divide the capital among her children. The mechanics of this are explained in the chapter on Wealth. Meanwhile it is enough to emphasize that this is not a *promise* for the benefit of A and her children, it is a *present*, given to them behind a trust. In fact perhaps the best way to understand the peculiar nature of the trust is to look at what it is not.

A trust is not a legal person. It is not like a company. The trust itself cannot hold property or make contracts.[17] This must be done by the trustee. The advantage of this is that, not being a legal person, the trust (unlike a company) needs no approval by the State, and need not register or file accounts.[18]

The trustee is not the agent of the settlor. In principle the settlor cannot remove the trustee, nor revoke the trust, nor need it end when the settlor dies, though these can be altered by express provisions in the trust instrument. Nor is the trustee an agent for the beneficiaries. If a trustee contracts in a way authorized by the trust (say by insuring a building which is one of the trust assets), neither the settlor nor the beneficiaries are liable for the premiums. That liability falls only on the trustee, though he or she can claim an indemnity from the trust property.

---

[16] That most perceptive outsider Max Weber called trusteeship 'ein Surrogat des Amtsbegriffs'—a substitute for officialdom. See his *Rechtssoziologie*, 162 (ed. J. Winkelmann, Luchterhand, 1967).

[17] There are statutory exceptions such as the National Trust.

[18] Many trusts for charitable purposes are subject to a form of registration with and supervision by the Charity Commissioners.

A trust is not the same thing as a contract, although it may involve agreement between the settlor and the trustee, since the trustee can always decline the office. Furthermore if the trustee is a professional, such as a bank or a Trust Company, they will insist on contractual terms of remuneration, restrictions on their liability, and the like. But the trust need not involve a contract. It may be created by will. It may be created unilaterally *inter vivos* if the owner of property declares himself a trustee for certain beneficiaries or for charity. And even where there is a contract between the settlor and professional trustees, the settlor cannot sue for breach of contract unless he is also a beneficiary and has suffered loss (in which case he sues as beneficiary). Furthermore the court may remove a bad trustee and appoint another, but no court could remove and replace your co-contractor. So, as it is not essentially a contract at all, it is not a contract for the benefit of third parties, i.e. the beneficiaries.

The relationship between the trustee and the beneficiaries is not that of debtor and creditors. For one thing, they never make a contract. For another, the trustee's obligation is only to do his or her best. If, through no fault of the trustee, all the trust property is lost, the beneficiaries' interests come to an end. There is no property in which their rights subsist, and the trustee has performed his obligation by doing his best. If, however, the trustee's fault causes loss to the trust property, then the beneficiaries have an unsecured claim against the trustee's private assets.

TRACING

When you buy something you part with money and acquire the object. Among your possessions, you no longer have the cash but you have the thing you bought. It is possible to see the object as a replacement of, or substitute for, the money. If the money was yours to spend, the object is yours to keep. If the money was mine, the thing should be mine. This is obviously so if I gave you the money to buy it for me. But it ought to be so if you stole my money. I cannot get the money back from the seller (assuming she acted in good faith), but I ought to be able to get what you bought with it, not as a mere creditor—who will lose if you are insolvent—but as its owner.

That, put very simply, is the technique to which English lawyers give the name 'tracing'. It involves the following requirements. First, one thing must be exchanged for another; second, the replacement must be identifiable; third, the replacement must still exist—it will not, for instance, if a thief buys beer with the stolen money and drinks it all. If these conditions are met, then possibly (but not inevitably) certain proprietary rights to or claims over the original thing may be asserted over the substitute.[19] In the simple example just given, if my money is stolen and spent on an identifiable object still in the thief's possession, I can claim that object as my own.

This replacement and recovery technique is widely used in English law. It extends beyond tangible things: so if I can prove that the money stolen from me was paid into the thief's bank account, and if that account is in credit, then I have a proprietary claim over the account in priority to the thief's other creditors. It is employed for purposes both placid and contentious. It is the basis of the operation of a fund: particular objects in which the fund is invested will change continually but the beneficiaries' entitlements persist. It is also the basis for the operation of a type of security interest over the undertaking of a business—particular items may be freely sold in the ordinary course of business but the proceeds form part of the security, whether they are cash, a credit balance in the seller's bank, or a debt owed by the customer.[20] As to its contentious applications, it has been much litigated recently in attempts to trace and recover the proceeds of corporate fraud, often on a global scale.[21]

---

[19] There is a fine account in Lionel Smith, *The Law of Tracing* (OUP, 1997). Civil lawyers use the phrase 'real subrogation', to denote the case where one thing (*res*) stands in for another.

[20] See Chapter 9.

[21] Perhaps the very ancient remedy of distress for unpaid rent provides a version of the technique: the landlord has the right, in priority to other creditors of the tenant, to seize whatever goods happen to be on the premises. In modern criminal law the technique is used to confiscate the profits and proceeds of the illegal narcotics trade and the like.

6

Ownership and its Fragmentation

One of the greatest difficulties encountered by students of property law comes from the English habit of splitting what may in a general way be called ownership into its component parts and making each of them an abstract entity. The estate concept developed for realty and outlined in the last chapter is a strong and persistent example of this type of approach. But over-concentration on this somewhat abstract approach may lead to great confusion. Consequently, this chapter attempts first to give a simple and general account of ownership, before turning to its most common types of fragmentation.

OWNERSHIP

The strongest and clearest form of ownership occurs where a tangible thing belongs to, and is in the possession of, a single person, with no one else laying claim to it or to any share in it. It is how most of us own our stuff. The main features of this form of simple ownership are the following:

1. In principle, owners can do anything they like with what they own: use it, use it up, neglect it, destroy it, give it away entirely or for a time, lend it, sell or lease it, pledge it, leave it by will, and so on. Furthermore the owner is perfectly free to do nothing at all with the thing: in principle, the law of property imposes no *positive* duties on an owner. *Negative* duties may arise but, as we have seen, in England they are imposed by other branches of the law and usually fall on anyone who possesses the thing, not merely on its owner. So we must *not* deliberately or carelessly injure our neighbour, *not* cut down a listed tree, *not* cause suffering to animals. Such provisions are not limits on ownership as such: they apply if we happen to own the thing but are forbidden to everyone, and not by the law of property, but by the law of tort, criminal law, environmental law, and so on.

2. As regards the thing owned, without the consent of its owner, no one else may interfere. As we saw in Chapter 4, the owner is protected

against those who trespass on, interfere with, or take the thing owned; and in English law this protection extends to those who are putative owners.

With these two positive features goes a downside.

3. Risk: the owner bears the risk of loss, destruction of, or damage to the thing. Further, the owner bears the risk of changes in value caused by extraneous factors. If the asset is, say, a very rare postage stamp and, by some accident, all the others are destroyed, its owner will benefit from the rise in market value; and, similarly, will lose heavily if a sheet of identical stamps is found somewhere.

4. Debts: the relationship between ownership and debt is very important. The general basic principle is this: *to pay what you owe, the law will take what you own; it will not take what others own*. This means that creditors can invoke legal procedures—distraint on goods, judgment and execution, or bankruptcy or liquidation proceedings—to ensure that your belongings are sold and the proceeds distributed among them.[1] But if you hold assets for other people, your own creditors cannot reach those assets. It is in the context of insolvency that we find a good deal of modern litigation brought in order to determine exactly who owns what. For instance, a man mortgages the family home to secure payment of his business debts. He has family creditors—wife or domestic partner and children—and trade creditors—employees, suppliers, the mortgagee, and so on. So long as he is solvent and can meet their claims, it does not matter much who owns the family home. If he becomes insolvent, then, if the house is all his, the family can eventually be evicted and the house sold to pay his debts. But if it belongs to his wife or domestic partner, or if she is a co-owner, the husband's business creditors cannot reach that interest of hers.

The account of ownership just given assumed that the property was a tangible object. But a characteristic of the common-law approach is to apply, as far as possible, the same principles to intangible assets: intellectual property, securities, and so on. Statute, for instance, speaks of 'the *owner* of a legal *mortgage*', indicating thereby that the person entitled can abandon, transfer, or bequeath the claim and the mortgage which secures it, and that his or her own creditors can reach

---

[1] The law on this subject is technical, piecemeal, and (relatively) recent, but the principle is as stated in the text. For human beings (as opposed to companies) certain things are safe from the creditors, either because they are worth much more to the debtor than to the creditors, or to prevent the debtor from becoming a burden on State provision: examples are personal effects, the tools of the debtor's trade, and an approved pension.

it.[2] A standard form by which a business assigns to a finance house the debts due from its customers warrants that the borrower 'is the legal and beneficial *owner* of the receivables'.[3]

CO-OWNERSHIP

The features outlined above are easy to understand in the simple case of a single owner of a tangible thing. The next step is to look at the position where more than one person is owner. We are not speaking here of a conflict between two claimants, but of the situation where the same thing belongs to two or more persons. Ownership of the same thing at the same time and in the same way by a number of persons has been general from very early times. Indeed, some students of very early law think that ownership by communities such as families, tribes, or households preceded ownership by individuals. Roman law admitted common ownership and it has survived everywhere in one form or another. Everyday examples in English law are found where domestic partners together own their home, its furnishings, and the 'family car', or where commercial partners run a business. In such situations the law regulates both internal and external relations. It must handle the rights of the co-owners among themselves; and at the same time it needs to facilitate transactions so that third parties can simply and safely acquire, or lend money on the security of, the whole thing, or the rights of one of its co-owners.

In English law today there are two kinds of co-ownership, in accordance with which two or more persons enjoy what are called concurrent interests. They are respectively joint ownership and ownership in common. The reader needs to be warned, however, that for historical reasons they are often called 'joint tenancy' and 'tenancy in common'. In this context the expression has nothing to do with leases. As explained in Chapter 1, the word tenancy comes from Latin via French and means 'holding'.

Ownership in common. The difference between joint owners and owners in common is that each of the latter owns an individual asset, a separate but not separated share in the asset held in common. Traditionally it is called an 'undivided' share: this rather puzzling name means that, while the share itself is of course separate from the others, it does not entitle its owner to a particular physical part of the asset. But the 'undivided' share

---

[2] Land Registration Act 1925, s.34(1).
[3] See the form printed in Sir Roy Goode, *Commercial Law*, 809.

can be alienated (without needing the consent of the other co-owners) and will pass by will or on intestacy. The simplest way to grasp the idea is to think of shares in a company. The shareholders each have a separate thing which they can alienate or leave to pass on death, but none of them can go to the company's head office, point at a particular room and say 'I claim my share'.[4] So if there are two owners in common of a house each has a separate, though intangible, asset: it is the house which is not divided into separate shares. There is no need for the co-owners' shares to be equal. Although equality is the default status, other factors—such as agreement, or unequal contribution to the purchase price—may result in their having shares of unequal proportion and value.[5]

Joint ownership. Joint ownership—or joint 'tenancy' to use the common legal name—is distinguished from tenancy in common by the striking rule that 'survivor takes all'. This means that, on death, a joint owner simply drops out: no interest in the asset held jointly descends under the deceased's will or by intestacy. So if something is given as a present to A, B, and C jointly and B dies, A and C between them own the gift. If A then dies, it goes to C who is now the sole owner with, of course, power to dispose of the whole thing while alive or on death.

This right of survivorship at first sight gives such unfair results that it is difficult to see why anyone should want to hold property that way. But there are three factors that ensure the survival of the regime.

1. *Severance.* A co-owner can turn the joint entitlement into a separate, though undivided, share i.e. can become owner in common. This is done most simply by giving notice to the others; and if the joint owner becomes insolvent, the trustee in bankruptcy will certainly take this step. So, in the example above, of a present being given to A, B, and C jointly, if A gives such a notice to B and C, A then holds a one-third separate, though notional, share in the undivided asset. The remainder is held by B and C as joint owners. If B then dies, the rule of survivorship means that C now owns a two-third share which will pass on C's death. So by giving notice, A has avoided the risk of losing everything by dying first, but has also forgone the chance of taking by survivorship if one of the others dies first.

2. *Spouses/domestic partners.* English law has no special category of matrimonial or family property: the default status of its property law

---

[4] All the shareholders acting together would have to wind up the company—the legal person—and pay its debts before they could physically divide its assets among themselves.

[5] The expression 'commonhold' refers to an entirely different issue, namely the proposed recent statutory regime to facilitate the operation of apartment blocks.

applies to spouses the same regime that it does to strangers. So if, on getting married, the wife buys the house and the husband the car, the one is hers, the other his. But spouses and other domestic partners often wish that, on the death of one, most or all of the deceased's property will go to the survivor. This can be done, of course, by making a will, but it can also be achieved if they are joint owners of the home and other family assets. As regards the family home and similar property, including bank accounts, it is quite common for spouses or domestic partners to hold the assets jointly. Indeed, if the asset is transferred into both their names without more, the default rule will ensure that they hold jointly.

3. *Trustees.* Trustees are appointed to their office in order to hold and manage assets for the benefit of someone else. While there may be a single trustee (especially if it is a corporate body) it is common, when human beings are trustees, for there to be more than one (and usually two, three, or four). But of course these persons also have their own private assets, family, creditors, and so on. It would be extremely inconvenient if, on the death of one of them, some share of the trust property devolved on the personal representatives of the deceased and then had to be separated from the private assets. Consequently, they always hold the trust assets jointly. Any attempt to sever and turn their holding into an undivided share would not work, so a trustee who dies simply drops out. If there is only one left, another is commonly appointed so that the trust property never devolves on the death of a trustee. Indeed, by a nineteenth-century statute, a human being can be joint trustee with a company, although it is virtually certain that the latter will outlive the former.

Any property may be held by concurrent owners. Partners, for instance may well be owners in common—that is, have separate shares in—the goodwill of their business, debts due to it, patents, copyrights and the like. Tangible movables may be held in a similar way—racehorses owned by a syndicate are one example. A commercial example is to be found in the ownership of fungibles held in bulk, such as oil or grain aboard ship. By a fairly recent reform of the law on sale of goods, a buyer of goods which form part of an identified bulk owns a share in the bulk proportionate to the amount bought and paid for: so if that is 10 per cent; at the time of purchase and the ship then unloads, for other consignees, half of the bulk, the buyer's share will be 20 per cent of the remainder.

Whether holding jointly or in common, all concurrent owners are entitled to possess and use the property. If it produces an income, say by being leased, they share the rent equally or, if they hold in common, in proportion to their holdings. To alienate the property they must, in principle, all agree, and must all concur in physical division. This is fair treatment among the co-owners, but can give rise to holdout problems and to disputes whose resolution might be very costly in comparison with the value of the thing owned. Consequently, in the case of chattels, the Law of Property Act 1925 (s.188) gives the court power to overcome a deadlock and to override the wishes of a minority interest. For land it laid down a different system, since amended, and explained below.

The two categories of co-ownership outlined above are exhaustive and mutually exclusive. They are exhaustive, in that nowadays they are the only two types which remain, older varieties having been long abolished in England and Wales. They are mutually exclusive, in the sense that the same people cannot at one and the same time have both joint and common entitlements to the enjoyment of property: the rule for joint holding—that the survivors take—is entirely incompatible with the rule for holding in common—that the deceased's estate takes. Because of this, when something is transferred to co-owners, it is important to know whether they are to hold jointly or in common. In most cases, of course, the transfer will make it clear: 'to A and B in equal shares'; or 'to A and B jointly'. But where it is unclear, and the transfer says only 'to A and B', the law needs default rules which, in the absence of any other indication, can be applied to solve the problem. The main ones are as follows:

If A and B are trustees, they take jointly.
If A and B are business partners, they take in common beneficially, though they will be joint managers of the business and joint holders of its assets.
If A and B are buyers who provided the purchase money in unequal shares, they take in common in the same shares.
If A and B fall into none of these three categories, they take jointly.

The first three default rules are perfectly sensible. The fourth, residual, rule may produce unexpected disappointments to the heirs of whichever co-owner dies first, and in some common-law jurisdictions it has been altered, so that they are presumed to be owners in common. However, it is still the rule of English law; an argument in its favour is that it is relatively easy for a joint owner to become an owner in common by simply writing a letter to the others stating that he is severing his interest from theirs.

Concurrent interests in financial assets. In considering the notion of a share in property, the reader is confronted with an intangible. A share in a horse is not the horse: you cannot ride it, nor can anyone tell by looking at the animal that you own a share in it. To sell the horse you would hand over the animal itself. But some other method—typically documentary—has to be used in selling a share in the horse. Yet such intangibles are often very valuable.[6]

The concept proves very useful in the modern world of dematerialized securities. Under this system investors have no separate share certificates or bonds—indeed these do not exist—nor are shares in listed companies numbered. It is thus impossible to say that they own any specific, identified, securities. What each investor has is an account with the custodian of a pool of identical securities, denoting entitlement to a share in the financial asset constituted by the pool. This protects the investment from the custodian's creditors in the event of the custodian's insolvency.[7] Though of course if the financial asset itself becomes worthless (by collapse of the issuer of the securities or squandering by the custodian) the investor's property interest dies and he or she is left to whatever personal unsecured claim may be available.

Concurrent interests in land. A word needs to be said here about the variant of co-ownership which is mandatory in England and Wales for any situation where two or more persons are concurrently entitled to the possession of land. Above it was said that two (or more) persons cannot at the same time *enjoy* property jointly and in common. But it is perfectly possible for the same two or more persons to *manage* property jointly but *enjoy* it in common. It is not unusual to find two or more people holding joint powers of control and management in trust for themselves as owners in common. This means that, among themselves, each has a separate inheritable share as to the enjoyment of the property (its use, rents, and so on). But to the outside world they are joint owners, so a purchaser from the survivors need not concern herself with the estate of any deceased co-owner. So long as, in good faith, she pays the price to the survivors (and, in the case of land, so long as there are two of them) she takes free from any claim. The survivors hold the purchase price 'on trust' for themselves and for the deceased, whose share is fully protected against their insolvency, and largely protected against their dishonesty. This technique is obligatory if the object is land. When two or more persons are concurrently entitled to freehold or leasehold land (whether jointly or in

---

[6] Furthermore, a moment's thought will reveal that interests other than full ownership, such as a lease of land or hire of a car, can be held by two or more persons. And obligations are often concurrent, as in the everyday case of a joint bank account.

[7] This is a very simple account of what is in practice a much more complex series of links from issuer to first-tier global custodian, through a chain of intermediaries to their clients.

common) the title is held by them jointly as trustees with power to sell the land.

TIME

Whether enjoyed by a single person or by co-owners, ownership, in the fullest sense, is potentially eternal, or at least it can last as long as the thing itself; and if the thing is a diamond or a field, that may be a very long time indeed. But it is very common for people to have property rights that are limited in time. There are two main types: in one, the asset itself has a fixed life—for instance twenty years for a patent. In the other, to which we shall now turn, the duration of the asset is unlimited but that of the property interest itself is limited, either by reference to a human life or to a term certain (such as seven years). The two types—life interest and lease (or bailment)—have in common the fact that, since their enjoyment is limited in time, there must at the same time in the same asset exist an interest which is not so limited. In other words, there are two concurrent interests but only one confers the right to present possession. That said, it should be noted that the life interest and the lease arise from different motives and are used for quite different purposes. The first is almost always conferred by way of gift, will, or intestacy as part of a family endowment and is explained in the next section. A lease is paid for and is employed in a wide range of housing, agricultural, manufacturing, and commercial settings. It deserves a chapter to itself.

LIFE INTEREST

We shall first describe the general features of this type of property interest and then explain its use in practice.

In general. A life interest (or life estate) confers the right to enjoy property for the lifetime of a human being; the right ends with the life. Normally the life involved is that of the person entitled, but that is not necessary: property could be given to X (or X Ltd.) for the life of Y.

Life interests can be created in two ways: by statute (in certain cases of intestate succession)[8] and by private disposition, for instance a gift or a will. A private disposition must make quite clear that the donee is to take only a life interest, since the default rule for transfers is that everything passes. However created, a life interest has the following main features. First, it may be conferred over many types of property, tangible such as

---

[8] Administration of Estates Act 1925, s.46(1)(i)(2)(a); s.51(3) as amended.

land or intangible such as shares.[9] Second, a life interest entitles its holder
to possess, use, or take the income of that property. Third, as has been
said, this entitlement lasts only for the life of a particular person or
persons, and comes to an end on their death. Fourth, since the property
itself may be expected to survive the life, there will be someone else to
take it on the death of the relevant life. Fifth, that person may be a minor,
or may not even be born ('to A for life, then to her daughter'). Sixth, the
coexistence of these two interests may hinder the outright sale or other
disposal of any particular asset: whose name, for instance, should appear
on the Land Register or in the company register of shareholders? As we
shall see, English law solves this particular problem by means of the trust.

The fact that the life interest is limited in duration has important
effects on the rights of its holder. Essentially the holder may use, but not
use up, the property: in other words, a life interest confers the right to,
not the capital, but its income or yield, understood in a wide sense: and a
gift of property 'to A for life, then to B' is a gift of the yield of the
property to A for life. Thus if it includes an orchard and shares, the fruits
when picked and the dividends when declared belong to A absolutely. If
the assets include a house, she may choose either to live in it—thereby
saving the rent it would cost to live elsewhere—or to lease it and keep the
rent. It follows that the holder of the life interest must meet expenses
which are properly attributable to income, such as income tax, the maintenance and insurance of the house, or the interest payments on any loan
secured on the property. But expenses properly chargeable to capital,
such as capital gains tax, rebuilding, or the repayment of a mortgage, do
not fall on the life interest. We have explained already that an entitlement
to a future net income stream can be discounted to give the present value
of the life interest.

Since only the yield belongs to the holder of the life interest, she
cannot give away any capital asset, or sell it and keep the money. And yet
she is probably the best person to know the price at which the assets
should be sold since it is that price, once invested, which will provide an
income for her. So, as we shall see, it is perfectly possible, and may be
prudent, for the law to give her the power of alienation to be exercised,

---

[9] As explained in Chapter 12, this is effected by means of a trust. Consumables, such as
milk, would hardly be given to a person for life, but could be so given with an obligation to
restore an equal quantity. This, however, would seem, without more, to create an obligation
rather than a property relation, i.e. on the death of the holder of the life interest, the
claimant would be an unsecured creditor of his estate with a claim amounting to the value of
the consumable.

not for her sole benefit, but as trustee for herself and those with the right to take possession on her death.

Life interests end: at the end of the relevant life; on the entire destruction or disappearance of the property in which they subsist; and by being merged with all other entitlements—if, say, the holder of the life interests takes by will all the property of the person entitled absolutely.

Family endowment

As a means of providing for the generations of a family—children, then grandchildren for instance—many legal systems find it necessary to allow one person to be given property for a limited time and for a second person to be assured during that time that he or his successors will then take. A simple example is a grant of property to a child A for her life and then to B (her son) absolutely. Its important features are the following:

1. The first thing to note is the obvious: A's interest ends on her death and B's interest does not end on his death. As far as A is concerned, this means that when A dies no rights to that property descend to her successors; and if, during her life, she has transferred her interest to C, C's rights end on A's death. But as to B, the property was not given him for his life only; it was given absolutely. So if he dies before A, his interest can pass under his will or on his intestacy. And if, during A's lifetime, he gives away or sells his interest, the transferee will take the property on A's death.

2. The second thing to note is that, on A's death, there must be something left for B or his successors. So the effect of this gift is to limit A to the possession and use of the property, so that it is still there when she dies. If the property is barren—say a diamond necklace—then all she can do is wear it, and keep it safe. But if the property produces fruits or an income, then that belongs to her absolutely and she may do whatever she likes with it. Almost invariably this type of property regime is set up with income-producing assets, so that the capital must be held for B but the income goes to A.

3. The third thing to note is that, since B's right to the property itself is postponed until A's death, in the meantime the assets will need to be managed with some care, and with an even hand between the entitlements of A and B. In the past, English law imposed a particular and highly detailed framework for the management of land, while leaving other assets to a more flexible and freely chosen regime. Nowadays the system is much simplified. At this stage it will suffice to say two things. First, that

while A is alive, management of the assets is done by the machinery of the trust. Second, that the older law has left an enduring technical vocabulary, which is still used because it is still useful.

Its main terms are the following. The regime set up when property is given to A for life then to B absolutely is called a 'settlement'. The person who sets it up is the 'settlor'; A is the 'tenant for life' or 'life tenant'; B is the 'remainderman'. A's entitlement is the 'life interest' or (in the older law) 'life estate'; B's interest is the 'remainder'. Since A is the only person presently entitled to use or take the income of the property her interest is said to be 'vested in possession'. B's entitlement is 'vested in remainder'. This last word is the most confusing, because it seems to mean whatever is left over. But originally the name was used to express the idea that, on A's death, the property does not revert to, but *remains away*, from the settlor. In strict technical terminology, 'remainder' is distinguished from 'reversion', the name given to the interest of a person to whom possession will revert on the ending of the particular limited estate: for example the settlor who has given away only a life estate, or the landlord of a lease.

4. Concurrent entitlements. So far we have assumed that there is only one life tenant and one remainderman. But a life interest or a remainder can be held by two or more persons. This may arise from the initial settlement—as where property is given for life to the settlor's two children—or it may be the result of some later disposition. So if, in the example above, A gives her life interest to C1 and C2, they are concurrently entitled to the enjoyment of the property for A's life. Between themselves they may hold jointly or in common. If C1 dies first and is holding jointly, then C2 is entitled to the whole interest until A dies. If they were holding in common, C1's successors would share with C2 the entitlement to the property during A's life.

5. A will die. This is certain, and when it happens the life interest will end. But B's interest will not end on B's death. His interest—the 'remainder'—was given him absolutely; it is not dependent on his outliving A. This means that, during A's life, B's interest is potentially eternal, or will at least last for the life of the asset: A's rights are bound to end but not so B's. It follows that the value of each interest can be calculated, at least at a general statistical level. An earlier chapter explained how the certainty of acquiring property in the future has a present value. The calculations themselves are the business of accountants and actuaries. But it is very much lawyer's business to understand the related property concepts; they are treated in a later chapter on Wealth.

7

Land Legislation for England and Wales
1925–2001

Although this book aims to cover the law of property generally, it may be useful to devote a brief chapter specifically to the basic principles of the present law governing the normal holding and transfer of land in England and Wales. It has been the subject of major legislation which is still ongoing.

Freehold and leasehold

Virtually every parcel of land in the country is occupied and controlled by some specific legal entity, whether an organ of the State such as the Ministry of Defence, a public institution like the Church of England, local government, a business corporation, or private citizens. In relation to that land these entities are either freeholders or leaseholders. The former hold the land for an unlimited and potentially eternal period and can convey this entitlement to any transferee.[1] The latter hold the land for a period which is certain or capable, by notice to quit, of being made certain, and is a form of landholding which entails the following consequences. First of all, the existence of a lease denotes the existence of a freehold. Every lessee has a landlord: if you are entitled to hold land for only a limited period, someone must have the present right to resume possession at the end of that period. Secondly, as time does not stand still, the lessee's right to possession is always dwindling, while the landlord's is approaching. Thirdly, in practice the lessee will be paying the landlord who has traded occupation for rent. Fourthly, there can be more than two coexisting entitlements to the same piece of land, for instance, sub-lease, head-lease, and freehold. Finally, lessees can transfer only what they have, that is to say the right to possession for the unexpired period of the lease.

---

[1] Crown (i.e. State) land held 'in demesne' is technically not held in fee simple, although the Crown can of course grant a fee simple to anyone else, whether a government department or a private citizen. The ordinary modern use of 'freehold' is a simple way of saying fee simple absolute in possession. In the older law, the word was also applied to other entitlements whose duration, though limited, was uncertain, such as a life interest.

English law treats these two interests—freehold and leasehold—as the key elements in the system covering the holding and transfer of land. The machinery is contained in legislation of 1925 with its amendments, especially the Law of Property Act (LPA) and the Land Registration Act 1925 (LRA).[2] These were part of a package of statutes which took several decades to prepare, met with much opposition both political and practical, and cover a large number of highly technical topics.[3] The legislative approach, and above all its terminology, were determined by the needs of the time and nowadays may seem somewhat obscure; what follows is an attempt to explain the crucial points as simply as possible.

The LPA begins by using technical terms for the two key interests, freehold and leasehold. The first is called 'fee simple absolute in possession'. The purpose of this phrase is to make clear that the interest may last for ever (fee simple), is not subject to some condition which might curtail it (absolute), and includes the right to present possession (as distinct from the present right to future possession). This last point is somewhat complicated by the fact that the Act defines possession as including the right to receive rent, but the point of this is to ensure that the freeholder who leases still holds the 'fee simple absolute in possession'.

The key leasehold interest is described as a 'term of years absolute'. This definition is blurred by the provision that 'years' includes periods of less than a year, or a fraction of a year, but the point of the statute is to cover the ordinary lease, whether for a week, a month, a year, or a number of years.

The first section of the Act lays down the rule that these are the only two estates in land 'capable of subsisting or of being conveyed or created at law' and that all other estates 'take effect as equitable interests'. At first sight this is a somewhat enigmatic provision, harking back as it does to a distinction in jurisdictions abolished in 1873. But the next section makes things somewhat clearer. It says, in effect, that other entitlements such as a life interest, or a reversionary interest ('to A for life, remainder to B') can be overreached on a sale of the legal estate and shifted to the price in the hands of the sellers and any investment of that price. In other words, those property interests which entitle their holder to possession, or the

---

[2] At the time of writing the twentieth-century Land Registration statutes are still in force but should soon be repealed and replaced by the 2001 Act. See Law Commission and HM Land Registry, *Land Registration for the Twenty-First Century: A Conveyancing Revolution* (Law Com No. 271, 2001).

[3] There is an excellent account of the background in J. Stuart Anderson, *Lawyers and the Making of English Land Law 1832–1940* (OUP, 1992).

chance of possession, but which are not the standard freehold and lease-hold are all treated as interests in a fund. More will be said about their acquisition and protection in the chapter on Wealth.

Meanwhile, if we return to the general picture we see that the legisla-tion selects the two main interests which serve the purposes of those who use land for its own sake as farm, factory, office, shop, or home: they do not want merely a life interest or an entitlement in remainder, nor do they need to interpose trustees between themselves and the land, they want to have it absolutely (fee simple absolute in possession) or to take it on lease (term of years absolute). These (and only these) estates can exist 'at law', two tiny words which mean that the holder of such an interest, if granted by the appropriate formalities (usually a deed) and (in most cases) duly entered on the Land Register, has an unassailable right to the freehold or leasehold and one that cannot be shifted without the holder's consent. The Act then deals with the other common property rights such as mort-gages and rights of way and provides that these too, if created in the appropriate way, will subsist 'at law', i.e. will bind everyone.[4]

The problem of concurrent ownership of land (where A and B hold jointly or have shares) is dealt with by imposing a trust under which the legal estate is vested in trustees who have power to sell the land and will then divide the proceeds among the co-owners or invest the money for their benefit. There is no objection to the same persons being trustees and beneficiaries, so in the very common case where husband and wife or domestic partners are co-owners of their house, the legal estate is vested in them jointly in trust for themselves.

Successive entitlements to land occur where one person is entitled for life and someone else thereafter. The traditional regime was known as a 'settlement'. It gave the life tenant the key management powers and vested in him or her the fee simple as trustee. This system is impossible after 1996. Instead the freehold will be held by trustees (with duties to consult beneficiaries and so on) and with power to sell it. The crucial feature of both the old and the new system is that the freehold itself can always be sold, the money paid to trustees, with the investments thereof replacing the land. Thus the life tenant will be entitled to the yield on the investments in place of possession of the land. More is said of this in the chapter on Wealth.

---

[4] So will restrictive covenants but, as they were invented by equity which enforced them only against those who took with notice, they nowadays need to be registered.

Land registration

For the standard case of freehold and leasehold, the Land Registration Act addresses the issue of how the holders of these interests prove their title, something which is of course vital if they wish to sell or mortgage. The older traditional method of 'unregistered conveyancing' is to produce to a prospective transferee the deed or other document under which the holder acquired the interest. If this appears to deal with the right parcel of land, to transfer the appropriate interest, and to contain nothing doubtful, it is known as a 'good root of title', and if at least fifteen years old it is acceptable (remembering that, if anything has gone wrong, the limitation period for bringing an action is only twelve years). If it is less than fifteen years old then (subject to any special term in the contract of sale) the transferor must produce the deed under which the predecessor acquired the land, and so on.

Land registration seeks to do away with this method and replace it by a register of proprietors, just as the entitlement of company shareholders is attested by the register which the company must keep. It was first introduced in 1862, made compulsory for the County of London in 1897, and greatly extended by the Land Registration Act 1925. It proved both technically and politically impossible to force registration of title on all landowners, but since 1990 all of England and Wales is subject to compulsory registration. This means that any land whose title is still not registered (about one-fifth of the whole) must, when it is transferred or mortgaged, be entered on the register.[5]

The entire system is at the moment undergoing a major revision in order both to simplify the existing law and to pave the way for the electronic creation and transfer of interests in registered land. Details of the system must be sought in the many specialist works.[6] Here we give only the basics. The Land Register is organized by property, not by the names of landowners. There is an Index Map, and each interest which is registered is allotted an identifying number. The property register describes the parcel of land and identifies its general boundaries by reference to a

---

[5] Of course there still exist landholdings which do not change hands for centuries (such as those of the Church, or the Oxbridge colleges). Their title could be registered voluntarily.

[6] See Law Commission and HM Land Registry, *Land Registration for the Twenty-First Century: A Conveyancing Revolution* (Law Com No. 271, 2001). The proposed system of electronic conveyancing deals with land, not money. The financial institutions will need to devise an interlocking mechanism for the electronic transfer of the price. No proprietor or mortgagee is likely to permit cancellation of their register entry without the simultaneous receipt of the money due.

map—it does not purport to give the exact line of the boundary. The proprietorship register gives particulars of the proprietor and the nature of his or her interest, freehold or leasehold. The charges section, as its name suggests, relates to burdens such as mortgages. The register is open to public inspection, though not the financial details.

On an application for first registration by a freeholder the title is investigated and, if satisfactory, the title is allotted a number, the applicant is registered as proprietor, not of the land, but of the fee simple in the land, and is sent a Land Certificate which (like a share certificate) is evidence of entitlement at the date it was issued.[7] Similar machinery applies to leases which have over a certain time still to run (currently twenty-one years, but to be reduced to seven years): the applicant is registered as proprietor of the leasehold interest. Shorter leases are perfectly valid but for administrative reasons cannot be registered. If, as is common, there is a simultaneous mortgage of the freehold or lease, the charge is noted on the register, the mortgagee gets a Charge Certificate, and the Registrar keeps (or does not make) the Land Certificate (so that the proprietor cannot readily mislead anyone).[8]

Registration as proprietor of a freehold or leasehold is, in principle, conclusive. Except for a few reasons, such as fraud, a person registered as proprietor normally has a guaranteed title to the freehold or leasehold estate and cannot be disturbed. If, however, some error has been made and the Register needs to be altered, monetary compensation may be made. This makes it possible for the Registrar not to spend unnecessary time or trouble in investigating titles which appear sufficiently sound on their face.

The Register also reveals matters which prevent or restrict the proprietor's freedom to deal with the land. These may pre-date the proprietor's acquisition (such as a restrictive covenant) or be the result of some transaction by the proprietor who may, for instance, have borrowed money on the security of the land or have contracted to sell it. Mortgages, as we have seen, are entered on the Register and the lender is entered as

---

[7] The requirement that even the freehold applicant be registered as proprietor, not of the land, but of a fee simple estate in the land was appropriate when the system began in the nineteenth century. Its persistence to the twenty-first century, however, meant that the Crown (i.e. the State) could not register its proprietorship of its ancient 'demesne', since technically that is held, not in fee simple, but by sovereign title. The Land Registration Bill 2001 will permit the Crown to grant itself a fee simple in its own land and then register its entitlement to that estate.

[8] Under the dematerialized title scheme of the Land Registration Bill 2001 the use of paper certificates will decrease and Charge Certificates will no longer be issued.

proprietor of the charge, so that the charge itself can be sold or otherwise transferred. If the landowner contracts to sell the freehold or leasehold of which he or she is registered proprietor, or enters into a restrictive covenant for the benefit of neighbouring land, the purchaser and the neighbour can protect themselves by entering a notice on the Register. A 'restriction' warns the world that, for instance, the proprietor is a trustee and that, although he or she will have power to sell, the purchaser must pay the price to at least two trustees or a named trust corporation.[9]

When the land is sold—technically when the 'fee simple' or 'term of years absolute' is transferred—the seller's name is deleted and the buyer's name registered as proprietor. Registration confers on the transferee the full formal 'legal' freehold or leasehold interest, good against any claimant, but subject to any burdens appearing on the Register. The usual burdens which do appear relate to things like (a) mortgages; (b) neighbours' rights such as easements and restrictive covenants; (c) restrictions, which indicate that the powers of the registered owner to effect a registered disposition are subject to some limitation: for instance she might be a trustee in which case, although she could sell, the price would have to be paid to at least two trustees or a trust corporation.[10] In principle buyers and secured lenders, who deal in good faith and for value with the registered proprietor can trust the register in two ways: what is there is true; what is not there cannot burden them.[11]

Overriding interests

But, given the complexities of land use, this last proposition cannot be entirely accurate and the system has to accommodate a number of 'overriding interests', that is to say burdens which will affect the land and will bind a transferee although there is no sign of them on the Register. The most obvious example is short leases: these are estates in land—property interests—yet they cannot be registered. However, the tenant or subtenant will almost always be there to be seen by anyone proposing to acquire the registered estate of the landlord. A second, simple, example is

---

[9] In practice there will often be at least two joint registered proprietors, so the same persons will both transfer the land and receive the price.

[10] This is not as complicated as may appear. By one deed a trustee-proprietor appoints a co-trustee, transfers the property, and both trustees acknowledge receipt of the purchase price. Presumably the electronic equivalent is being devised.

[11] This covers the vast majority of cases and protects those who give value (by buying the land, lending money on mortgage, and so on). Those who get the land as a present take subject to any interests binding their donor (such as the claim of someone with a valid but unregistered option to purchase the land).

that of easements burdening the land—it is quite possible that the neighbours' water pipes or electric cables will run over or under the land being transferred. These will usually be legal easements having been created by deed or by long user (prescription) but they may well not appear on the Register. They will 'override' the transfer and bind a buyer.

A third type of interest which conflicts with the Register is that of someone in adverse possession of the land (whether or not the limitation period for its recovery by the proprietor has expired[12]). Such a person—often called 'squatter'—may well not register their claim or their entitlement, but the very fact of their being in possession should be ascertainable by anyone thinking of buying from or lending money to the registered proprietor.[13] Nonetheless, the presence of a squatter poses a challenge to the system: is entitlement to depend on registration or on possession? The Land Registration Bill 2001—which is firmly in favour of registration as the only key to entitlement—proposes that the limitation period will never run against a registered proprietor but that, after ten years, a squatter may apply to be registered in his place.

Apart from short leases and squatters, however, there are other situations where possession and registration may conflict and where the interests of persons who are on the land but not on the register may prevail over a purchaser who has relied on the Register, taken a transfer, and registered himself or herself as proprietor. The category of 'overriding interest' which has caused the most dispute comprises 'the rights of every person in actual occupation of the land' except where they are asked about their rights and fail to explain them.[14]

Much of the litigation concerns dwellings, and arises in situations that in many countries would be dealt with by their law of matrimonial community property. In the absence of any such system in England, the courts have been forced to rely on the technicalities of the 1925 legislation. The problem commonly arises where there are two types of creditor of a defaulting debtor who is the sole registered proprietor of a house. The debtor's general assets are insufficient to meet all the debts, and so there is competition for the house between family 'creditors' and commercial creditors. The first class comprises the spouse, domestic partner, or some family member who has contributed to the acquisition of the house; the second is the bank or building society whose loan is secured on

---

[12] See Chapter 4.
[13] The relation between the dispossessed owner and the squatter is explained in Chapter 4.
[14] LRA 1925, s.70(1)(g); Land Registration Bill 2001, Sched. 3, 2(1)(b).

the house and who has made possible the acquisition or extension of the house or the launch of some business venture. The courts had first to decide what counts as 'actual occupation' by the family member, given that the proprietor will also be living in the house and the claimant may appear to be a visitor, or may be absent at the time the house is inspected. In the end the courts held that the meaning of the phrase in any given situation is a matter of fact and that residence in the premises if not fleeting will usually amount to actual occupation.[15] The second issue is what the statute means by 'the rights' of such a person. Here the courts have held that the word means 'property rights', i.e. those interests which, apart from the statute, have been recognized as capable of binding an indefinite number of persons. In practice the most common such interest is that of a co-owner. This arises where one person is the sole registered proprietor but someone else has put up part of the money needed to buy the property and has done so, not by way of gift or loan, but with a view to acquiring a property interest. In practice if the family creditor shows that, though not registered as joint proprietor, she is an informal but genuine ('equitable') co-owner with the proprietor of the freehold or lease by which the house is held, she will prevail over a subsequent buyer or lender who relied on the Register. If she cannot establish any such entitlement, then, although as against the proprietor she may have a matrimonial or domestic claim to occupy, she has no overriding interest protected against everyone merely by the fact of her occupation.

The principles of the Law of Property Act and the Land Registration Act conflict in one situation. As we have just seen, the latter seeks to protect the unregistered property interest of a person in actual occupation. Typically this interest will be co-ownership which, as its holder is not registered as one of the proprietors, must be informal hence equitable. But section 2 of the other key statute, the LPA, lays down the principle that a conveyance to a purchaser of a legal estate in land overreaches any equitable interest capable of subsisting in money, whether or not the purchaser knows of it, provided that the money is paid to the correct persons, which will be trustees (at least two) or a trust corporation. The need to do this is notified by a restriction on the proprietorship register. So a purchaser who pays the correct number of trustees and

---

[15] The phrase 'actual occupation' has a long statutory history. See, for instance, the Reform Act 1832, s.20 *in fine*; 2 Will. IV, Cap. 45. The Land Registration Bill 2001 preserves this category of overriding interests but makes certain amendments: cll. 11(4)(b), 12(4)(b), Sched. 1; cll. 29(2)(a)(ii), 30(2)(a)(ii), Sched. 3.

then registers himself as proprietor takes the land free of the rights of the co-owner, even though he knows all about them and even though the co-owner was living in the property: far from overriding, the interest is overreached. In theory the co-owner will not suffer because her entitlement to a share in the money takes the place of and is as good as her rights in the land. In practice this may well not be the case.

Part 4

Standard Patterns

This Part takes four types of property interest that are found in many legal systems and explains the English version of them. Chapter 8 deals with the situation where one person is allowed to use another's property for a certain time, usually in return for payment of a rent or hire charges. Chapter 9 deals with the use of property as security to ensure performance of an obligation, typically the payment of a debt. Chapter 10 is concerned with neighbours' rights over land. Chapter 11 covers the basic principles governing the devolution of property on the death of its owner.

8

Leases and the Like

GENERAL PRINCIPLES

We turn now to the very common situation where one person has the use of property for a period which is fixed or can be fixed by giving notice: for instance, you may rent a flat for a year or a video for a day, hire a car or a skip for a week, or charter an oil tanker for six months. The vast range of objects, periods, and purposes involved in lease transactions means that all that can be attempted in an elementary work is an account of the key features. The task is made more difficult by the fact that, as regards occupation leases of dwellings, business premises, and farms, Parliament intervenes frequently to adjust the balance of power between lessor and lessee.

Why people want to hire things is easily understood. They may not want them permanently but only for a time, and it may be inconvenient for them to buy and resell. Even if they want them for a long time, they may not have the capital to buy them outright, or may prefer to invest that money elsewhere. Sometimes they may be prepared to provide what is called the working capital (livestock, equipment, and the like) while someone else provides the fixed capital (i.e. the land). This is the key to traditional tenant-farming in England. As to residential accommodation, on the other hand, many people do not have and cannot borrow the capital needed to buy, and so must rent their home. Why people let things out is also easily understood. They have something that can be made to yield an income, and to them taking the income is preferable to using the thing themselves.

Lease and hire are normally created by a transaction under which, at the very least, one party lets the other possess and use the property for a time, and the other undertakes to pay.[1] Usually, of course, there are ancillary obligations as to quiet possession, maintenance, insurance, and so on. These may be expressly agreed by the parties or may be implied by law or

[1] For examples of somewhat artificial leases imposed by statute, see LPA 1925, ss.85(2), 149(6).

may be partly one and partly the other. Furthermore, many common categories have become standardized, with their terms contained in precedent books or printed forms. All this means that much of this topic is regulated by the law of contract. Now in principle contracts do not bind third parties, yet things that are leased—especially land—may well be transferred during the period of the lease. So the law of property steps in to ensure that the obligations run with the property transferred. If the lessee transfers the thing, the successor must pay the rent; if the owner transfers his interest, the transferee can collect the rent. In other words, as far as possible, successors in title stand towards each other in the same legal position as did the original parties. For land, the rules and a technical vocabulary were laid down long ago; for goods, both are less developed. Consequently it is best to start with land.[2]

LAND

The property lawyer looks at leases of land in a familiar way.

An estate in land. In the first place, a lease gives the lessee the right to physical possession and use of the property for a time which is fixed (say, seven years) or can be fixed by notice (say, from year to year terminable by half-a-year's notice expiring at the end of a completed year).[3] Furthermore, in principle the lessee can transfer this right to possession for the remainder of the term, or can sub-lease by conferring the right to physical possession for a period shorter than that remaining; he can also transfer the power to effect further transfers. Finally, the lessee or his successor can, during the term of the lease, recover possession of the land from anyone, including those to whom the lessor has sold or otherwise transferred it. Thus the lessee's entitlement is protected, not just by the law of contract which binds only the original lessor, but by the law of property which binds an indefinite number of persons.

The lessor has the right to recover physical possession at the end of the lease period: the land is said to 'revert', and so the lessor's interest is often called a 'reversion'. Until then the right to physical possession has been replaced by the right to the rent.[4] Like any other asset, the lessor can alienate this 'reversion' and can alienate the power to alienate it.

---

[2] The account will assume that there is only one person playing the part of lessor and one person being lessee, though in practice the lessor might be two or more co-owners and there could be two or more co-lessees; see the section on co-ownership, above Chapter 6.

[3] There is no limit to the period for which a lease can be granted: terms of 99 or 999 years were common in the past.

[4] Somewhat artificially, the LPA 1925 treats the 'reversion' as still an interest 'in possession' because it defines possession as including the right to receive the rent.

This splitting in time of the right to possession recalls the discussion earlier of the life interest and the remainder. To express the legal position of those involved, English law developed the concept of the 'estate' by which a right to possession now or in the future is measured by the time for which it may endure. The concept is easily applicable to leases. If land be let (say for twenty-one years) and sub-let (say for seven years) there exist simultaneously three separate estates, each with a market value: the freehold, the head lease, and the sub-lease. Their content can be expressed by means of a formula. We use p to mean physical possession, T and t to indicate the terms of the head and sub-leases (numbers will not do, since each term is diminishing daily). R and r indicate the rent reserved by the head and sub-leases respectively. We use a to indicate the power to alienate. We need a symbol to show that the freehold interest may never end, so use E to mean this indefinite period.

Fee simple: $a^\infty(p(E - T) + RT)$
Head lease: $a^\infty(p(T - t) - RT + rt)$
Sub-lease: $a^\infty(pt-rt)$

The reason why a is raised to infinity is because any estate owner has the power to alienate the power to alienate the power to alienate . . . that estate. And of course any or all of the three estates could be held by co-owners.

CHATTELS

The technique of the estate concept described above and summarized in the formulae just given could readily be applied to chattels, especially those which are relatively durable and which have an obvious use value, such as a crane or a television set. In fact, and as a matter of tradition, English lawyers do not do this; instead they use ownership and possession. To describe the situation where ownership is in one person and (lawful) possession in another, they use the word 'bailment'. The owner of a crane who hires it out for six months to a construction firm is the 'bailor' and the firm is the 'bailee'. The general notion was described in the chapter on common-law concepts.

Bailment is a category which covers many different situations, from the commercial example just given to the brief and gratuitous loan of a pencil to a friend. All they have in common is that the thing itself is supposed to go back to the owner. So between the bailor who hands over the thing and the bailee who receives it there is a personal relation, for the bailee is under a duty to the bailor to take care of the thing and to give it back. But a bailment for a period (as with the crane example) also confers possession on the bailee, to the exclusion of the bailor. Thus the bailee, and not the bailor, can bring an action of trespass against an intruder, and can recover possession (or the full value of the crane) from a dispossessor. And the bailee's right to the chattel for the rest of the period would be protected against the bailor's insolvency. So far there is nothing to differentiate in principle a bailment for a term from a lease of land. Moreover such interest as the bailee has in the chattel is derived from that of the bailor, as is shown by the rule that, just as a lessee cannot be heard to deny his lessor's title, so a bailee cannot be heard to deny that of the bailor. Thus a bailment presents the same sort of mingling of contractual and property relations as does the lease of land.

There may, however, be one quite important difference. The lessee of land is protected, for the whole period of the lease, against the lessor's successor—someone, for instance, who has bought out the lessor.[5] Such a person cannot evict the tenant, and if he or she does take possession the lessee can recover it. But in the case of a chattel, it is said that a buyer from the bailor could oust the bailee during the period of the bailment, leaving him to a contract claim against the bailor.[6] There is, however, little judicial and no statutory authority for this; in the case of ships, there is case law against it; it is a result which does not seem fair; applied to a lease of a furnished flat it would seem odd to hold that one who buys out the landlord cannot evict the tenant from the flat but can remove all the furniture. In any case it is an event that is unlikely to happen, since a buyer from the bailor would almost certainly know that his seller did not have the chattel and would be unlikely to risk a lawsuit with the bailee. And finally, if the bailee is unprotected by the law of bailment against a bailor's successor, the law of pledge will provide a safeguard: the bailee lends a (nominal) sum to the bailor, repayable at the end of the period of bailment, and takes a pledge of the chattel as security. It is quite certain that this confers a right to possession good against the bailor's successors. They cannot repay the loan until it is due, which is not until the end of the bailment period.

In any event, the business world does not seem to worry about the theoretical frailty, nor does it use the elderly vocabulary, of bailment: it

---

[5] We assume that the formal requirements for the grant (and if necessary the registration) of a lease have been met: see Chapter 8.

[6] This proposition is cogently argued by William Swadling, 'The Proprietary Effect of a Hire of Goods', in N. Palmer and E. McKendrick (eds.), *Interests in Goods*, Ch. 20, 491 ff.

uses the words lease and leasing. Furthermore the chattel lease now serves a multitude of different purposes. In one set of purposes the object is expected to outlast the period of any one lease, so that it can be handed successively to a number of persons, each taking and paying for use for the period they need it: car hire is an obvious example. Quite different is the 'finance lease'. Here the minimum period of the lease is the expected life of the chattel; there is only one lessee; and the total rent covers the sale price plus an amount to reflect the fact that it is paid, not in one sum at the outset, but over a period. It is widely used in business for a number of tax and accounting reasons.[7]

REQUIREMENTS FOR A LEASE

Leases, as we have seen, begin in contract by an agreement between the parties. They may then confer on the lessee a property interest, alienable by the lessee and protected, for the period of the lease, against both the lessor's insolvency and the lessor's successors. But to take the step from being a contract claim to being a property right the lease must comply with certain requirements both of substance and of form. The requirements are particularly stringent (and frequently litigated) in the case of land.

Substance. As we have explained, the estate concept involves rights in space (i.e. to physical possession of an object, or entitlement to its income), for a time. The first of these requires that, to count as a lease, the lessee must have exclusive possession. If land is the object involved, then occasional visits by the landlord, say to inspect or to repair, are of course not ruled out; but if an occupant (genuinely, not merely as a sham) actually shares occupation with the landlord or the landlord's nominee, then there is no lease, no matter how formal the document embodying their arrangement. In the case of residential accommodation the occupant is at best a lodger, not a lessee or tenant. Another example is the grant of 'front-of-house-rights' by which a theatre owner permits someone else to have the bar, cloakroom, and programme concessions. They are in essence sharing the use of these parts of the building, and so such a transaction, even though it is called a 'lease', is contained in a sealed document, and is to last for twenty-one years, is merely a contract between the parties: it does not create a property right binding on a new owner of the theatre.

---

[7] For a full and lucid account, see Sir Roy Goode, *Commercial Law*, Ch. 28 (2nd edn., Penguin, 1995).

The second factor, that of time, inherent in the estate concept means that to count as a lease the period must, from the outset, be certain or capable of being ascertained: a term of one year, or a monthly tenancy terminable by a month's notice, are both common types of lease. But a grant of exclusive possession 'until the lessor needs the land for redevelopment' does not amount to a lease. The way round this is make the maximum period certain by, say, granting a lease for 'twenty-one years or until the land is needed for redevelopment, whichever first occurs'.

Form. The law does not impose particular formalities for chattel leases (leaving aside consumer credit safeguards). But the formalities for the creation of a lease of land have long been the subject of legislation and of much intricate historical and legal learning. Nothing would be gained by explaining the details in an elementary introduction to the subject. Here it is enough to say that fairly indiscriminate use is made of two types of arrangement. The first is the lease itself, that is to say a transaction by which the lessor *grants* the interest—the exclusive right to possess and use for the term specified. The second is the agreement for a lease (often called 'tenancy agreement') by which the lessor *promises* to grant the exclusive right to possess and use for the term specified. In both of these the other party, the lessee or tenant, undertakes to pay the rent and observe any other relevant obligations (repair, insure, and so on). From the point of view of the lessor the distinction is between a transfer of the interest and a contract to transfer it.

In principle, leases of land for not more than three years at a market rent, if they are to take effect at once, require no formality at all, nor do contracts to create such a lease ('tenancy agreements'). Since this covers the common monthly and yearly tenancies, it could, in theory, save a good deal in transaction costs. In practice, however, the general principle is merely a default status, and written documents are highly advisable, for two reasons. The first is to save later argument; the second is to comply with statutory requirements imposed on landlords and designed to protect residential tenants.

Leases of land which exceed three years must be by deed if they are to bind everyone. Contracts to create such a lease must be in writing signed by both parties, and, if they are to bind the landlord's successors, their existence should be noted on the appropriate register (either the Land Register or the Land Charges Register), although if the landlord's title is registered and the tenant is in actual occupation, even an informal lease will amount to an overriding interest.

For leases of most chattels, no compulsory formalities are laid down.

Nonetheless, they are often contained in writing, indeed usually in standard forms supplied by the lessor. If the lessee is a consumer, they may therefore be subject to judicial scrutiny under the relevant consumer protection legislation or regulations.

THE RUNNING OF OBLIGATIONS

Leases, apart from conferring on the lessee possession and the right to possess for a period, also contain promises by each party to the other. These may be expressly set out or be implied (by custom, case law, or statute). An obvious example of the former is the lessee's promise to pay the rent (or hire charges) at the periods agreed. The enforcement of such promises is ensured, in the first place, by the basic law of contract. But the law of property also has a role to play, and this is for two reasons. The first is that the law of leases has developed to deal primarily with *land*— chattel leases were left largely to contract and to commerce. The second reason is that lessor and lessee may well, during the term of the lease, wish to transfer their interests, and their successors will not be in any *contractual* relationship: they will have made no promises *to each other*.

The fact that the law in this area dealt first and foremost with land has left its mark on the remedies available to enforce performance of the obligations and on the vocabulary used to describe them. The parties are called 'landlord' and 'tenant', the lease is called a 'demise', and their promises are called 'covenants', meaning an undertaking contained in a deed. We shall concentrate, then, on the enforcement and transmission of covenants in leases of land.

Enforcement. The key obligation of the tenant is, of course, to pay the rent at the times agreed. This is a monetary obligation, and therefore its performance, in the eyes of the law, can never become impossible: the tenant cannot plead that his obligation was somehow 'frustrated' by the fact that, through no fault of his own, he cannot raise the money.

The landlord can enforce this obligation in three main ways. The first is to sue in debt, like any other unsecured money creditor. The second is an ancient common-law remedy, nowadays much limited by statute: to seize and, if necessary, sell the tenant's goods found on the demised land, and to do this in priority to other creditors of the tenant. The name of this remedy is 'distress' and the landlord is said to 'distrain' on the goods. The threat of the power before its exercise does not, of course, prevent the tenant from disposing of the chattels in the ordinary course of daily life and business. In fact the landlord's right of distress somewhat resembles the 'floating charge' of the company creditor, in that it hangs over the things on the premises but does not prevent their alienation until a debt is unpaid and the goods seized (or the charge 'crystallizes').[8]

The third remedy is to cancel the lease while it is still running, a process called 'forfeiture'. This differs from the enforcement methods just discussed in two ways. First, it is not available by default but must be expressly reserved in the lease. Second, when it is included in the lease, it may be—and always is—stated to be available for breach of any obligation, not just rent. Because the sanction—losing your lease—may be out of all proportion to the gravity of the breach, there have long been judicial and statutory safeguards, which in general make the remedy exercisable only by legal proceedings and give the court power to prevent forfeiture. Even the old, strict, common law did make one concession to the tenant. The normal rule of English law is that a debtor must seek out and pay the creditor. But a landlord could not forfeit the lease for non-payment of rent unless he came to the premises to collect it between sunrise and sunset on the very day it was due.

Transmission of obligations. Leases may well be designed to last for some time such as seven, twenty-one, or ninety-nine years. During that period it is very likely that the landlord will transfer the reversion and the tenant will assign the lease. The successors take the place of their transferor as regards the relevant obligations. So the new landlord can enforce payment of the rent and performance of any other tenant's obligations (such as maintenance, decoration, and the like) but is bound to perform any landlord's obligations that might be contained in the lease (such as structural repairs, insurance). Similarly the tenant's assignee must pay the rent and perform any other tenants' obligations, but can enforce against the new landlord those undertaken by the original landlord. The original parties' contractual liability on covenants of the original parties ends when they part with their interest, as does that of each successor.[9] The rules are on the whole clear and sensible: in these longer-term leases, we may think of the role of landlord and tenant as being filled by a succession of persons, each playing the part for a while and then leaving the stage. There are always two characters on stage, landlord and tenant. The older law expressed the fact that each was bound to the other by saying that, although the successors were not the contracting parties and so were not in 'privity of contract', nonetheless, since one

---

[8] The law on distress is in distress, and proposals for its improvement are found in the Report produced for the Lord Chancellor by Professor J. Beatson QC (Independent Review of Bailiff Law, June 2000), available from pvarney@lcdhq.gsi.gov.uk.

[9] For details see Landlord and Tenant (Covenants) Act 1995.

was landlord of a lease and the other tenant of the same lease, they were in 'privity of estate'.

The result is entirely sensible, but one important feature needs to be stressed: if you take over the lease you have to pay the rent to the current landlord, and perhaps perform other obligations *though you never said you would*. And if you take over from a landlord you may have to do things for the current tenant (such as repair the structure), although you made no promise to that person to that effect. Certainly, you ought to know about these obligations because you could read the lease before buying it from the tenant; or, if you bought from the landlord, then you read his copy of the lease and knew that the landlord had undertaken to keep the structure in good repair. When you bought you will promise your seller that you would perform the relevant obligations. But you do not make this promise to the other party to the leasehold relationship; instead you take over the duty of performing an obligation undertaken by your predecessor. This does not square at all with the law of contract, which does not hold you to a promise that you did not make. But it fits this part of the law of property, and produces a workable system. It means that someone else can make you pay, or spend, money, not because you promised them you would, but because you acquired an interest in property—a lease or a reversion—and they have the correlative interest; they are the landlord and you the tenant, or vice versa.

We have dwelt on this, partly for its relevance to the general principles of private law, but also because it explains one of the strangest features of the English law of property in the early twenty-first century: that if you buy a flat you will almost certainly have to buy a lease of it. It will be for a term so long that it almost amounts to full 'freehold' ownership—leases of ninety-nine years are the minimum, and ten times that is not uncommon. By contrast, the rent will be so tiny as to be fictitious ('a yearly peppercorn if demanded'), while the purchase price will be the market price for the premises. The reason for this bizarre arrangement is that it is the only way to ensure that each successive occupant performs the relevant positive obligations (of maintenance, repair, insurance, and the like). Other countries have schemes that enable the outright ownership of apartments to be burdened with such obligations for the benefit of all— they are often called 'condominiums'. England and Wales are promised a similar scheme, to be called 'commonhold', but at the time of writing the courts will not permit positive obligations to run with freehold ownership, and no relevant legislation has been introduced.

SUB-LEASES

Unless the lease forbids it, a lessee is free to grant possession to another, at a rent, and for a period shorter than that of the lease. This transaction is not a transfer of the lease. The lessee remains tenant under the head lease and is now sub-lessor for the shorter period; the new occupant is sub-lessee or sub-tenant. There are three interests in the property: that of the head landlord, that of the lessee, and that of the sub-lessee. The periods of the two leases are not the same, and the rents and other obligations may be quite different. The sub-tenant owes rent only to the sub-lessor, not to the head landlord, and the same is true of any other obligation undertaken in the sub-lease. The head landlord cannot enforce against the sub-tenant the performance of positive obligations in the head lease. The reason for this is twofold: first, they are not parties to, and so in privity of, contract: second, they are not landlord and tenant of the same lease and so are not in privity of estate. So if a tenant's covenant in the head lease is infringed by an act or omission of the sub-lessee, only the head lessee can be sued. He is, so to say, responsible for his sub-lessee to the head lessor. He is also responsible for acts of the head landlord which cause a breach of the sub-lessor's obligations to the sub-lessee.

The only exception is that *restrictive* covenants in a head lease will bind the sub-lessee who has notice of them. A restrictive covenant does not cost anything to perform: it is an obligation not to do something (such as open a business). The sub-tenant ought to know about the restriction because, under the general law of conveyancing, he is entitled to see the head lease before entering into the sub-lease.[10]

CHATTEL LEASES

The system just described in relation to land has not, on the whole, been applied to leases of chattels, although if one took a lease of a furnished house one might expect that much the same legal regime would apply to both the house and the furniture. In practice (and leaving aside ships and aircraft which have rules of their own) chattel leases are hardly ever granted for long periods, and most of the problems are solved by the law of contract, coupled with the fact that the lessee has lawful possession and the right to possess for the period of the lease. Positive obligations entered into by the lessee, say to maintain and service the chattel, are of

---

[10] This rule is now restated in the Landlord and Tenant (Covenants) Act 1995, s.3(5). Restrictive covenants in leases are not registrable; they are so numerous that such a scheme would be impracticable. See Chapter 10.

course enforceable by the law of contract, which will at least award damages for their breach. It is theoretically more difficult to enforce such obligations against someone who takes over the chattel for the remainder of the lease, but in practice—where durable items are involved—the lessor's consent is required for any transfer. The original lessee will seek such consent in order to escape liability for later hire payments, and this will give the lessor the opportunity to make a contract with the new lessee.

INTELLECTUAL PROPERTY

The holder of a patent, copyright, or trademark can stop anyone else using the invention or mark, publishing or performing the work, and so on. But of course the holder can grant permission to someone to exploit the property for a time in return for a payment. In some ways this is similar to the leases just described but, reflecting the differences, the language used is not the same: the permission is called a 'licence' and the rent is called a 'royalty'. A further difference is obvious and important. If you own a house or a car and rent them out, the only person with the right to occupy the house or use the car is the lessee. But you can let dozens of firms exploit your invention or your creative work—there is no need to give just one of them the *exclusive* right to do so. In practice, such licences are often territorial: for instance permission to use the patent for an industrial process (together with know-how) may be given to a company in Russia, and a separate permission to one in China; and both may be forbidden to export the resulting product into the European Union. With copyright and related rights, the picture is even more complex since permission for live performance can be separated from permission to film, record, translate, and so on. A final point to remember in this field is that, while the law relating to land and chattels applies to England and Wales, that relating to intellectual property is the law of the UK and of the EU, and the main constraints on technology licensing arise from the rules on competition.

STATUTORY PROTECTION

We mentioned earlier that the law of leases in England and Wales is complicated by frequent legislation, introduced throughout the twentieth century in order to protect tenants. Only a brief sketch of essentials will be given here. First of all, the statutes deal with leases of land, not chattels. Secondly, they override any inconsistent agreement between the parties. Thirdly, they tend to fall into different categories, one group concerning residential accommodation, another with very long leases of dwellings, a third dealing with business premises, and a fourth covering farms. Fourthly, they do not restate and enact the fundamental principles of the law of leases. Instead they take these for granted, and introduce complex amendments and corrections to the basic pattern. But they are so pervasive that the reader must be warned. The freely negotiated aspects of the lease, so predominant in the general law of landlord and tenant, have now receded so much into the background that landlords and tenants look for their rights less to the terms of their leases than to the statute book and to the case law which encrusts it. In most leases the legislator waits until the parties have negotiated and concluded a lease and then overrides their agreement by imposing provisions, almost all of which are designed to protect the tenant. Thus in these very common situations the move in legal relations has been from contract to status.

Property owners have tried to escape this by casting the arrangement into some different category so that the occupant is merely a lodger and not a tenant. But the courts have been very vigilant to prevent 'sham' transactions. If the factual result of the arrangement, whatever its name and whatever its provisions, is that the occupier has exclusive possession for a fixed or periodic term and is paying rent or a premium ('key-money'), then a tenancy has been created and any relevant statute will apply.

Dwelling houses. At the beginning of the last century almost four-fifths of the population lived in privately rented accommodation and were subject to the ordinary common law: the rent was that agreed upon and, on the expiry of their lease, they had to leave. The decline in speculative building and the 1914–18 War produced a shortage of accommodation which threatened to put tenants at the mercy of landlords. Accordingly in 1914 the first Rent Act was passed which had as its purpose the fixing of rent (and mortgage interest) and also the protection of tenants against eviction at the end of their lease. Designed to be temporary, it proved the forerunner of a large number of statutes which combined to create one of the most obscure and complex areas of English land law. At the same time housing patterns changed. On the one hand, local councils provided housing. On the other hand, more and more people bought their own home with the aid of a mortgage.

The main effect of the Rent Act scheme was to limit the rent and to give the tenant a status of irremovability, a protection which passed on the tenant's death to the spouse or some family member who had lived in the home.

Towards the end of the last century the system was largely dismantled for tenancies taking effect after 1997: the default status of a dwelling tenancy will be one in which the landlord is entitled to possession as of right at the end of the term, and there are limited means of applying to have the rent redetermined by a rent assessment committee. Nonetheless, the statutes impose obligations on landlords above all to provide the tenant with written information on the terms of the tenancy. A tenant who, before moving in, is given notice in writing that the lease is a 'shorthold tenancy' cannot, without the landlord's permission, remain after the expiry of the lease.

As to repairs and maintenance, in principle, any obligation to repair must be agreed by the parties and contained in the lease: the state of, and responsibility for, repair, is supposed to be reflected in the rent payable. Statute has intervened in leases of less than seven years to impose on the landlord obligations to repair the structure and utility installations.

Long low-rent leases. In the nineteenth century a common way of funding housing developments was for the landowner to grant a long lease of the land to a builder—say for 99 years. The rent was very low, or nominal, but the lease contained strict covenants binding the lessee to build and maintain houses. This arrangement meant that the builder could use his capital to build, and could then rent out the houses at a market rent, thus repaying his outlay over time. The landowner was prepared to forgo any return for many years because, under the common law, at the end of the long lease the landowner would take back the land with the buildings which had been constructed and maintained. In theory, everyone benefited. In practice, the short leases of the houses became subject to rent control during the twentieth century and, when any such lease finally lapsed, the building would be 'sold', i.e. the new occupant would pay a capital sum for the remainder of the long lease. But as the end of that lease drew near, many occupants feared that they would lose the home for which they had paid a significant sum. Statute now gives lessees occupying houses as their home under long leases at a low rent, the right to buy out the landlord's interest.[11] The scheme has since been extended so that, under certain conditions, the tenants of flats in an apartment building can have the freehold transferred to a management company.

---

[11] The European Court of Human Rights held that this forced sale to the lessee was not an infringement of the lessor's right to property (now stated in the Human Rights Act 1998; see Chapter 1).

Council housing. None of the statutory protection used to cover tenants whose landlord was a local authority or other public housing authority, but by legislation of the 1980s, public sector tenants have the right to buy their homes; if they do not choose to do so, they have some security of tenure.

Business premises. Business people would often rather lease premises than buy. First of all, the place they want may be only for lease and not for sale. And then, even if they could buy it, they may prefer to spend their own, or borrowed, capital on inventory, rather than on buildings. So business leases are popular and widespread. But a successful business builds up a goodwill in the form of repeat custom which may well attach to the premises and which would be lost to the firm if it could be compelled to leave at the end of the lease. Consequently the legislature has intervened to ensure that, if leased premises are occupied for a business carried on by the tenant, the lease does not end at the term agreed but can be made to end by landlord's notice, whereupon the tenant can, if they wish, claim a new tenancy. This the court is bound to give (though no doubt at a new rent) unless the tenant has gravely broken the terms of the lease or the premises are needed for redevelopment or personal occupation by the landlord.

Agricultural tenancies. These have been the subject of statutory intervention for longer than any other type of lease. For the latter half of the last century, agricultural tenants were in effect given statutory security of tenure and rent control. But changes in the economics of agriculture, together with entry into the European Community, resulted in pressure for reform and farm business tenancies created after 1995 have little statutory security of tenure, although the rent can be referred to arbitration and the tenant is entitled to compensation for improvements.

9

Security

Used in the plural, the word securities tends nowadays to denote shares and other investments. That is *not* the subject matter of this chapter. Here the word security is used to mean an arrangement which is collateral to an obligation, and makes the creditor more sure of performance. Unlike other property rights, a security interest cannot exist without there being an obligation whose performance it is meant to ensure: once the obligation ends (by performance, set-off, release, and so on) the security interest dies.

The ordinary creditor of an obligation, say to pay money, can enforce the obligation by getting judgment in his favour and then using the machinery of justice to levy execution on the defendant's assets in order to satisfy the claim. But this process has two weaknesses: it will work only if the debtor has enough belongings to cover the judgment; and then only if other creditors do not have prior rights to the various items of property. If this is not the case, the debtor's liabilities will exceed his assets and some creditors are going to be, at least partly, unsatisfied. The point of exacting security is to avoid being one of them.

Personal security. In personal security the creditor insists on having performance of the obligation by its debtor guaranteed by another person. The creditor thus has the assets of two persons to which recourse can be had, though not in priority to their other creditors. A common commercial variant of this is used to secure due performance of substantial contracts: the 'performance bond' by which a person who has undertaken a non-monetary obligation, such as to build a factory, is required to procure from a third party—usually a bank—an undertaking to pay a sum of money to compensate for breach of that primary obligation.[1] These and related forms of personal security belong to the law of contract and will not be discussed further.

Real security. Real security is so called because there is an asset (*res*, in

---

[1] Somewhat similar in function, though part of public law, is the bail bond by which a sum of money is pledged to secure the appearance in court of an accused person.

Latin) by means of which the creditor is entitled to have the debt paid, no matter who holds the asset. It has these main characteristics: it follows the asset (and, if properly constituted, follows it in the hands of anyone); it entitles the holder to payment out of that asset or its proceeds in priority to other creditors; by enforcing the security the creditor may recover only the debt, interest, and costs.

GENERAL PRINCIPLES

There are many different types of real security, and it must be said that, at the edges, the law is far from tidy. Some are created by the common law, some by statute, and most by agreement. Furthermore there is no general word in English to cover the persons who grant and take security: instead we have pledgor and pledgee, mortgagor and mortgagee, chargor and chargeholder.[2] In an attempt at clarity, we first set out the general principles of real security, and then turn to the main categories, to the requisite formalities for each, and to some nuances.

The essence of real security is that an asset is encumbered to secure a claim whose creditor can look to the asset for satisfaction of the claim. The claim may be future, as when you leave share certificates with the bank to cover any possible overdraft. To simplify exposition we shall assume that the claim to be secured is for the payment of money.[3] This is by far the most common case, so it means that we can use the words creditor and debtor, or lender and borrower, to describe the parties to the obligation. The creditor will also be party to the transaction creating the security, playing the role of pledgee, mortgagee, or chargee. Usually the other party is the debtor, and it is the debtor's property which is encumbered with the security interest (pledged, mortgaged, charged).

But this is not necessary—it is perfectly possible to pawn your watch, or mortgage your house, to secure a loan made to your friend. If that happens, the result is as follows. Your friend owes the money and the lender can, by judgment and execution, reach all your friend's assets in competition with the other unsecured creditors. You do not owe the money, since you did not borrow it. So you cannot be sued for the money,

---

[2] This last word is the term used in the English version of the *Model Law on Secured Transactions* issued by the European Bank for Reconstruction and Development (London, 1994).

[3] It is customary to secure performance of non-monetary obligations by some monetary means. As noted above, the firm building a factory may be required to procure a 'performance bond' under which, if it builds badly, its bank has to pay a sum of money to the complainant. And in another area of law, money bail secures the obligation to appear in court when required.

and your other property, outside the watch or the house, cannot be taken to satisfy your friend's debt. But if your friend defaults on that debt, your watch or your house is liable to be sold by the creditor to pay it. If the price for which your property is sold exceeds the debt, you have a property claim against the selling creditor for the balance. If the sale price is less than the debt, you do not owe the balance. In either case, if your friend's debt has been paid out of the proceeds of sale of your property, you are an unsecured personal creditor of your friend: for the entire debt, if it has all been paid off; for less, if the sale of your property did not cover all the amount owing. Finally, to prevent the creditor from enforcing the security, you can free your property by paying off your friend's debt, redeeming the watch or the unencumbered house, and acquiring the creditor's claim against the borrower.

The objects of a security interest can be any asset, tangible or intangible: one can pawn a watch, mortgage a house, charge one's share as owner in common; in order to secure financing, a business can assign to the lender the debts due from its customers. Furthermore, a fund can be used as security: a company can create a 'floating charge' on its constantly changing stock; a remainderman can raise money on mortgage of the interest in remainder, although the actual assets themselves will be in the hands of and managed by trustees and may change as the world's stock markets move. Each different type of asset may require different formalities both to create the security and to enable others to find out that it exists.

Whatever the asset involved, any security interest is merely accessory to the claim which it secures. A lender who has taken a pledge of a watch or a mortgage of a house cannot transfer the pledge or the mortgage without a transfer of the claim, nor assign the claim without surrendering or transferring the security interest. If the claim dies, because for instance the debt is paid, or is set-off, or is released, then the security interest comes to an end (though some tidying-up may be necessary, such as a surrender of the mortgage document and/or cancellation of an entry in a register of charges).

Security is not sale. A lender who takes security over an asset is not buying it. The money paid is a loan secured on the asset, not the purchase price of that asset. Consequently, a provision is void which says that the creditor can keep the asset if the loan is late in being repaid. As long as he is repaid with interest and costs, the secured creditor is not allowed to keep the asset as a penalty for late payment. Furthermore, there is a difference between a sale with an option to buy back at the same price plus interest, and the grant, in exchange for a sum of money, of security which will end if the sum is repaid plus interest. Admittedly, it may sometimes be difficult to distinguish, but an example may help. A wants to raise £100,000. He transfers his house and some shares to B for that sum with an option to buy both back on a given day in six months time at a price of £100,000 plus interest. Is he really selling the house and the shares, or is he borrowing on mortgage? If it is a genuine sale and if A does not exercise the buy-back option according to its terms, then (a) he can never claim the house and shares; and (b) he owes B nothing, since the money he received was the purchase price for the things he sold. But if the transaction is really a loan of £100,000 secured by a mortgage of the house and shares, then A can repay the loan with interest and costs at the six-month date *or at any time thereafter* (since by definition a loan can always be repaid) and can thereby end B's mortgage—in the jargon of lawyers he is said to repay the loan and redeem the mortgage.

How are we to decide between these two quite different transactions? Of course, if both parties agree that their deal was a sale and buy-back option, or if both agree it was a secured loan, then the answers are easy. Usually, however, they will disagree. If, since the start of the transaction, house and share prices have risen, B will argue that he has bought them, while A will want to redeem them; if prices have fallen, the parties might well argue the other way round. On the whole the law leans towards finding that such a transaction was security not sale, and there are two facts which, if proved, will strongly support this conclusion. The first concerns possession: if, after the deal, A stayed in possession of the house, it does not look as if he has sold it to B with an option to buy it back. The second concerns the market value of the house and shares at the outset. If that value was just £100,000, then the transaction looks like a sale at that price. If, however, the value was £200,000, then it is very unlikely that A would have sold for half that sum; and the transaction looks much more like a loan secured by mortgage of an asset worth twice as much. What the parties call the transaction is not decisive. In fact, as we shall see, formal land mortgages used to look like sales and are now-adays occasionally disguised, somewhat improbably, as prodigiously long leases. But if the heart of the deal is a secured loan, that is how it will be treated.

If the asset used as security produces a yield of some sort—the crops of a farm, dividends on shares, rent from offices, and the like—then, until there is some default in performance of the obligation, the yield belongs absolutely to the person entitled to the asset. Normally this will be the debtor, of course, who will have mortgaged the farm, shares, or office block and will be expecting to pay the interest on the loan out of the yield of the asset. But on default in any terms of the loan, the secured creditor can appoint a receiver of the income, and thereafter it goes to the creditor who can use it to pay the interest due and, if he or she so chooses, to repay the principal in driblets.

The 'equity of redemption'. A final important general point can best be explained by assuming the simplest of all examples. If an owner creates a security interest in the thing he owns, there exist two property interests over the thing. The interest held by the creditor will bind the thing until the obligation is performed, the debt paid, and so on. But the creditor's interest in the thing is limited in value, a figure can be put on it: it is the value of performance of the obligation (repayment of the debt) plus interest and costs. The other interest is not limited in value, it is residuary: the only way to put a figure on it is to estimate the value of the thing and compare that with the amount owing to the secured creditor: the balance may be positive or negative. Normally it will be positive—there will be something left over: the creditor will take care to ensure that the value of the thing exceeds that of the debt. The central element of this entitlement is the right to repay the debt and redeem the property unencumbered by the security interest. This is called in common-law countries the 'equitable right to redeem'. It came to be called 'equitable' because, while the common law would enforce the strict terms of the deal which allowed repayment only at one specific time, the Chancellor would override the contract and force the creditor both to accept repayment after that date and to return the unencumbered title to the owner. During the life of the security interest, this equitable right to redeem is crucial, but is not the only element in the owner's entitlement. The owner also has the power, *inter vivos* or *mortis causa*, to alienate the interest (including the right to redeem the security). He can in principle sell the thing, although it is still subject to the security interest. The price will be the market value, minus the amount owing to the secured creditor. The buyer acquires the right to redeem the security by discharging the obligation for which it was given, i.e. paying off the amount owing. The owner could also use the interest as security for other advances, thus creating second and third security interests.

The sum total of the owner's interest in the asset given as security acquired the name of 'equity of redemption'. This occurred at a time when security interests were commonly granted by a transfer to the creditor of the formal title ('legal ownership'), subject to a condition for retransfer on performance of the obligation, i.e. repayment of the loan. So since the creditor has the formal title, though it was held only as security, another name was needed to describe the interest of the person who granted the security: 'equity of redemption'. This is best explained by a simple calculation:

Value of asset	£100,000
Amount secured	£60,000
'Equity of redemption'	£40,000

If the value of the asset falls below the amount secured, the creditor can collect the entire value of the asset and claim the balance (as unsecured creditor) from the debtor. In the late twentieth century the unfortunate debtor in this situation was said to have a 'negative equity':

Value of asset	£50,000
Amount secured	£60,000
'Negative equity'	£- 10,000

Although loosely called an 'equity', in fact the debtor is subject only to a personal claim against him for the balance, enforceable against his other assets in competition with general creditors.

As mentioned in the first chapter, this historical jargon has also left its mark on modern corporation law. Companies are financed in two ways: by loans and by shares. The former may be secured, but the bondholder or debenture holder is entitled only to a fixed amount—the loan plus interest. The shareholders' interest is residuary—a share in whatever is left over after the loan capital has been repaid. So the modern word for this type of investment is 'equity participation'. If a company is seriously insolvent but needs to continue trading, its creditors may be persuaded to 'swap debt for equity'; that is to give up their right to a fixed sum plus interest—a right enforceable only against the inadequate assets of the company—and to take in exchange shares, hoping that the company will trade itself into a situation where its assets exceed its liabilities, at which point their shares will acquire some positive value.

Since security is not sale, provisions are invalid which attempt to give the equity of redemption (i.e. the balance) to the creditor if the obligation is not duly performed (i.e. the loan repaid). In the first example above, if this were permitted, the creditor would get an asset worth £100,000 for an investment of £60,000. The only way in which the creditor can acquire this interest, and thus take the asset free of the right to redeem it, is by a successful application to the court to 'foreclose'. Normally, however, the court will give the person entitled to the encumbered property the time to borrow elsewhere the amount needed to pay off the foreclosing creditor. Furthermore, on the application of anyone with an interest in the property, the court can order its sale. This will invariably be done if the sale price is likely to be enough to pay off the foreclosing creditor. So, although the word 'foreclose' is often used loosely to mean any enforcement of the rights of a secured lender, the real thing rarely happens.

Multiple charges. The same asset may be used to secure performance of more than one obligation. In other words, successive security interests can be created over the same thing so that, for instance, land can be mortgaged to X to secure a loan of half its value, and then a second mortgage can be given to Y to secure a loan of a quarter. The borrower's 'equity' is thus worth one-quarter. The possibility that an asset can be subject at one and the same time to a string of security interests may easily give rise to difficult questions of priority. Some means must be found of enabling a secured creditor to warn others of his entitlement, and to make it easy for a person thinking of advancing money on security to find out if there are prior encumbrances.

There are two main ways of doing this: possession and registration. The simplest example of the first is the pledge of chattels. If you take a watch to a pawnbroker, the very fact that you have the watch makes it probable (though not certain) that it belongs to you. By taking possession of the watch, the pawnbroker is effectively warning everyone else of the existence of the security interest. Something similar can be done with certain types of document such as a share certificate, treasury bond, or life insurance policy. These are good evidence of entitlement to the asset involved and can be deposited with a creditor by way of security. It should be added that a separate security instrument is often drawn up at the same time, often by deed, as this gives the secured creditor certain remedies described below.

But in many cases it is not practicable to hand the asset over to the secured creditor. In the normal case of a house mortgage, the borrower wants to live in the house and the Building Society does not. If a factory is to be used as security, then the owner needs access in order to make the money to meet the debt. There may not be any documents of title which could be readily handed over as security—a company may wish to use as security its stock-in-trade, but this may consist of things that are being made or processed and will then be sold. The answer to the priority problem is to set up a register in which the existence of security interests can be noted; the choice between the two methods—possession or registration—is neatly illustrated by the rule for mortgages of unregistered land—they cannot be registered as land charges if the mortgagee takes the title deeds.

On registration in general in English law, three points should be made. First, there are about a dozen registers, each devoted to a particular type of asset or transaction: there are registers for land, land charges, patents, company charges, plant varieties, ships, aircraft mortgages, and bills of sale (that is transfers of chattels without transfer of possession). Second, there is no overall general law of registration; each register has its own rules of formality and priority, and some types of security interest need to be entered in more than one register.

Third, the public registers just mentioned deal with tangible objects or intellectual property. But a third type of asset is intangible: the 'receivables' of a business, i.e. the debts due from its customers; or the life interest and remainder in a fund. The investments of which the fund is composed may (or may not) be tangible, but they may change constantly. So the only way to publicize transfers of the title to such assets as receivables, or the creation of security interests in them, is to do so privately: that is, to make the priority of the interest depend on giving notice to the debtor, in the case of receivables financing, and to the trustees in the case of mortgages of interests in trust funds.

ENFORCEMENT OF SECURITY

The rights of a secured creditor are given for one purpose only—to ensure due performance of the obligation, normally repayment of the loan plus interest. Normally, and in general, the creditor seeks to enforce the security only when the obligor is in breach of the obligation. In the usual case, where security is given for repayment of a loan, this means that the loan must be due. The remedies which then become available may seem rather harsh to the modern reader, but were designed to do justice in a society where two things were true: money was readily available on mortgage so that a borrower pressed by one lender could borrow from a second and pay off the first; and the security commonly offered was frequently a business asset of the borrower. Nowadays the private investor prefers the stock market where there is a chance of the capital growth denied by a loan on mortgage, so that mortgage business has come to be concentrated in banks and building societies. The other great change is that many borrowers mortgage their home, which they would have never been able to buy in any other way.

The secured creditor has three important rights, but a fourth will be added for the sake of historical completeness.

Sale. The most practical remedy is to sell the asset, pay off the debt, interest, and costs and hand any balance to the person entitled: this will be subsequent secured creditors, if any, and then the debtor. The sale need not be by auction but must, of course, be a genuine sale, and reasonable care should be taken to get the best market price. If the instrument creating the security is a deed, the power of sale is implied by the Law of Property Act 1925. If there is no deed, but some less formal security agreement is entered into, the creditor must apply to the court for power to sell.

The power of sale arises as soon as performance of the obligation is due, i.e. on the date for repayment, or on some other date expressly agreed. This is all that the buyer needs to know: by looking at the instrument creating the security the buyer can ascertain that the power of sale has arisen. But in order to be fair to the debtor, as between him and the creditor, the power of sale must not be exercised until he has been given time to pay off the debt, if necessary by borrowing elsewhere: three months is standard. A sale in breach of this duty is perfectly valid as far as the good-faith purchaser is concerned, but may leave the selling creditor liable in damages to the borrower.

The secured creditor's power of sale permits the transfer to the buyer of the interest of the person who created the security, free of that security and any subsequent encumbrances; the seller's security interest is extinguished and the others are shifted to the price paid on the sale. So if the sole formal mortgagee of a freehold house, or a block of shares, or an airplane, or a lease, or a life interest in a fund, sells the asset, the buyer gets the house, shares, aircraft, lease, or life interest. The interests of the houseowner, shareholder, airline, lessee, life tenant *in those very things* are transferred to the buyer. But the interests do not die to their previous owners, nor do they cease to be property interests: only their *object* changes. They are shifted to the money received by the selling secured creditor. Out of this money the seller meets the costs of the sale and then pays off the loan. Any balance belongs to the person whose property has been sold. Furthermore, their right to this balance is a real right, commonly explained by saying that the seller is trustee of the balance. That means that if the selling creditor is insolvent, the balance is theirs; it is not available for distribution to his own other creditors. And they can trace their property, though its form changes: if the seller pays the balance into a credit account at the bank, or buys a yacht with it, they can claim the credit balance or the vessel. Of course if the seller drinks the balance, or pays off a debt with it, their property right dies; but all property rights die with their object. They are then left to a personal claim against the seller, enforceable against all his assets but in competition with his general creditors.

Receiver. The power of sale protects the lender's right to the return of the capital. But the lender may be quite content to leave that on loan, and yet wish to secure prompt payment of the interest. If the property is producing a yield—for example the rents of a block of offices or the royalties on copyright—then that return belongs to the person— normally the borrower—who granted the security interest. But if there is some breach in the terms of the loan—if interest is paid late or not at all—the secured creditor can, after due notice, appoint a receiver whose main duties are to collect the rent, pay the outgoings, and pay the secured lender his interest. Any balance may, if the lender chooses, be applied towards reducing the principal; otherwise it is handed to subsequent encumbrancers or, if none, the debtor.

Possession. Some security interests depend on the creditor's having possession—the pledge or pawn. In most, however, this is not the case. Nor will the secured creditor particularly want to take possession, except as a necessary prelude to a sale. If the property to be sold is a dwelling house, no one will buy from the lender with the borrower and his family still there. As a general default principle, possession is one remedy available to secured creditors. But in the case of dwellings, this principle has been curtailed by statute, permitting the court to delay an order for possession if the borrower looks as if he will be able to repay the loan or meet the instalments due. The protection is extended to the borrower's spouse, domestic partner, and minor children, but if the borrower is made bankrupt and the house has to be sold, the family have only one year's grace before being subject to eviction.

Foreclosure. The principle of this has been dealt with above. Here it will suffice to say that if the secured creditor wishes to acquire the property as his own and hold it free from the borrower's interest, there must be an application to the court for a foreclosure decree. The borrower is then given time to find the money and repay the loan. On his failure to do so the court order takes his interest from him and vests it in the lender free for ever of the borrower's rights and of those of subsequent secured creditors. In practice this remedy is rare. If the debtor has any equity in the property—that is if its value exceeds the amount due—he will either borrow elsewhere and redeem the foreclosing creditor or he will ask the court to order a sale and a division of the proceeds.

Restraints on the secured creditor

When a secured loan is negotiated, the parties may not necessarily be in a position to bargain equally. The lender can lend to anyone, while the borrower may have only one asset to offer as security. Consequently, both the courts and the legislature have tried to ensure that borrowers are informed and that lenders obtain adequate security but no more. Pawnbrokers Acts are an elderly example, and Consumer Credit Acts a modern version of statutory intervention. In addition there are 'voluntary' codes of conduct and a general oversight by the Financial Services Authority.[4]

But leaving aside such particular provisions, we can still identify certain general principles restricting the bargaining powers of the lender. We have already explained that a mortgage is not a sale and so a mortgage cannot be made irredeemable. It exists only to secure performance of an obligation—usually repayment of a loan. Loans, by definition, must be repaid, so they must be repayable; and on repayment the security interest must end. To this there is one statutory exception, where the borrower is not a human being but a company. Debentures, which are documents issued by companies to acknowledge their indebtedness and may relate to both secured and unsecured loans, may be made irredeemable.

There are two other ways in which the courts restrict the transaction to one of security. First, they will strike out a provision contained in the mortgage giving the creditor the option to buy the property; as we have seen, security is not, and cannot transform itself into, sale. Secondly, when a loan is secured on property, that property must, on repayment of the loan, return to the borrower as unencumbered as it was before. Thus if A's neighbour lends him money on condition that he be given (a) a mortgage of A's house and garden to secure repayment of the loan and (b) a right of way over A's garden for ever, then, when A repays the loan and redeems the mortgage, the right of way must end: otherwise he would, before the transaction, have had land free of a neighbour's right of way and then, after repayment of the loan, the property forming security for that repayment would still be burdened. If, however, the incumbrance affects property other than that mortgaged, it may be valid after repayment and redemption. If A, on taking the loan, mortgaged one house but gave a right of way over another, the latter would bind for ever. The right of way was part of the cost of, but *not of the security for*, the loan.

---

[4] For details go to http://www.hm-treasury.gov.uk.

THE MAIN TYPES OF SECURITY INTEREST

Non-consensual security. A few security interests are created by the common law or by statute, which means that the obligor did not deliberately create the security interest. Examples include: the landlord's right to distrain on goods to secure payment of the rent; maritime liens over a ship and her cargo for salvage, seaman's wages, and compensation for damage caused by the ship. A type of security created by statute is that given to the Legal Aid Board over property recovered in proceedings whose costs were financed by the Board.

In some common situations a person who has not advanced money and who has taken possession of chattels for a reason other than security is entitled to retain the chattels until a debt is paid: this type is known as a 'possessory lien'. The lien arises when the thing is already in the possession of the creditor and secures payment of a debt which is in some way connected with the thing. For instance the garage which repairs your car can keep it until you pay the bill; the hotelier (strictly speaking, the 'common innkeeper') who gives you and your luggage accommodation can keep the luggage till you pay your bill. A lien may cover more general indebtedness giving the creditor the right to retain possession until the general balance of the account is paid: for instance the right of a solicitor to retain clients' papers until the bill is settled. Such liens do not permit the person holding the goods to sell them, unless that power is expressly given by contract or statute; nor can the lien be transferred.

In the context of sale, the unpaid seller of goods who has not agreed to give the buyer time to pay is entitled to retain possession until payment. The vendor of land has a lien on the land for the price; and if the buyer pays the price or part of it but for some reason the sale goes off, a lien on the land secures the right to recover the purchase money.

The main point of these security interests is to give the creditor a prior right to be paid out of the proceeds if the thing itself is sold. If the debtor is insolvent, the creditor can insist on having his or her claim settled by the trustee in bankruptcy up to the value of the thing on which it is secured, and is entitled to this in preference to the ordinary creditors of the debtor.

Consensual security. By far the largest and most important types of security interest are those which are deliberately created by some transaction. In the most common situation there are two parties to the transaction: the debtor confers on the creditor security over the debtor's property, and we shall assume this to be the case. The reader should remember, however, that there may be three parties, where the creditor's security is given over property which belongs, not to the debtor, but to another person.

Possessory security. A transaction very easy to understand is the pledge, or pawn, by which the creditor's security consists in taking possession of an item of property. It is the most practical low-cost way of securing a debt on tangible movables. Pledge is a form of bailment, but it is more than a contract between pledgor and pledgee. It confers on the latter two rights in relation to the object, one relating to possession, the other to ownership. These rights are 'real' in the sense of being exercisable against an indefinite number of people; and, of course, the world is warned that the pledgee has these rights because he has the thing itself. The first such right is the right to retain *possession* until repayment of the debt. If the pledgor sells the thing to a third party, the buyer cannot collect it from the pledgee until the debt which it secures is paid off. The second is the power, if the debt is not repaid, to sell the object, thereby transferring *ownership* from the pledgor (or his transferee) to the buyer; and on completion of the sale the buyer will, of course, also take possession. At that point the previous owner's right to the object is gone, but, if the sale price exceeds the amount of the debt (plus interest and costs), it is replaced by a property claim over the balance in the hands of the selling pledgee, a claim that may give priority over the pledgee's ordinary creditors.

Pawnbrokers, that is to say persons who carry on the business of lending money and take, as security, possession of goods and chattels, have long been governed by special statutes which require them to be licensed and to observe certain rules in the conduct of their business.

Proprietary security. Although pledge affords excellent security to the creditor it is awkward for the pledgor since it deprives him or her of the use of the thing. Accordingly it is not a good way of raising security on anything which the debtor needs to use, such as a home or the plant of a business, and it is impossible to give a creditor possession of something which the debtor is still manufacturing.[5] What is wanted in these cases is some arrangement whereby the debtor is left in possession and therefore free to use the object, while the creditor has the right to take possession if the debt is not paid and to sell the object, or perhaps even to keep it as owner, free from any rights which the debtor may have in it.

---

[5] Pledge is also impossible if the asset itself is intangible, such as the debts owed by the customers of a supplier.

It is easy for us now to think of these various powers as constituting in combination a separate institution which needs no justification for its existence except that it furnishes an excellent form of security. But originally lenders did not think this way, and they were in a position to dictate the form which their security would take. So if a lender wants to have, as security, rights over an item of property, and if he is not to be given *possession* until repayment, then he would insist on being made *owner* until then.

From this grew the *mortgage*, a transaction in which the mortgagor transfers to the secured creditor his entire title, on condition, or subject to an undertaking, that when the debt is repaid the title will be retransferred. This is a formal conveyance, or transfer, and complies with the technical rules appropriate to the particular object involved. If it is a chattel, ownership is transferred though the thing itself remains in the debtor's possession. If the property is company shares, the mortgagor executes a share transfer and the mortgagee is registered as shareholder and becomes a member of the company and entitled to the dividends, if any; but the parties also execute an instrument making it clear that this transfer is by way of security only. If the asset is a life interest, or a remainder, the entire asset is transferred with a provision that it will be retransferred on repayment of the debt (and the trustees are given notice of the transaction). If it is an insurance policy, the policy is assigned as security. If it is the debts due to a firm from its customers, the debts are assigned. If a patent, the patent is assigned.

In all these cases the creditor has title to the asset but the debtor has possession of it (or, if it is intangible, appears to be entitled to it). There must, therefore, be some way of making the situation clear to third parties, of providing publicity to the fact that two parties have real rights in the asset: the creditor has a security interest and the debtor has possession and the 'equity of redemption'. Such publicity serves both creditor and debtor: the former needs protection against the debtor's using the fact of possession (or entitlement) to pretend to unencumbered ownership. The debtor needs to warn the world that the creditor, though apparently the owner, is entitled, not to the full value of the thing, but only to the amount needed to cover the debt. The solution is to provide some machinery of registration or notice.

It must be said here and now that the present law is far from simple. The leading English authority has described it as 'profoundly unsatisfactory' and devoid of 'a rational policy'.[6] Only the bare outlines can be

---

[6] Sir Roy Goode, *Commercial Law*, 702–3 (2nd edn., Penguin, 1995).

given here, but it is worth reflecting on the basic problem. Assuming that a register is set up, how is it to be indexed: by the asset itself or by the name of some person? An index by asset enables anyone to search and discover the existence of any adverse interests, whether created by the present holder or someone earlier. But such an index is feasible only if the assets involved are relatively permanent and individually identifiable such as land, ships, aircraft, patents, and the like. A register organized under the names of persons entitled may be a register of holders, such as the shareholders of a company; or it may be a register of debtors, such as that used for chattel mortgages and company charges.

Chattel mortgages are governed by elderly and opaque legislation, whose repeal has long been urged. First of all, the name is strange: the Bills of Sale Acts 1878 and 1882. One might think that a bill of sale is just a document drawn up when something is sold (and indeed, that is what it means in the case of ships). But this legislation deals with the situation where a document transfers ownership of chattels, absolutely by gift or declaration of trust, or as security for a debt, but the things themselves stay with the transferor. It is intended to prevent injustice to the other creditors of the transferor who may well have trusted to his apparent ownership of the things in his possession. The Acts require such documents to be attested and registered in the Supreme Court by the creditor against the name of the transferor. If not registered, security bills are void.[7]

Mortgages of patents are protected by notice in the Patents Register. The mortgagor of shares can obtain protection by serving a 'stop notice' on the company; this will afford some protection against a sale by the mortgagee who has been registered as shareholder. If the asset mortgaged is an interest in a fund, such as a life interest or remainder, notice is given to the trustees. If it is an insurance policy, notice is of course given to the insurer. If it is a receivable, notice can be given to the person who owes the money that the entitlement to the money has been transferred. If the mortgage is by a company on its assets, fixed or circulating, registration must be effected in the Companies Registry.

Land mortgages. The mortgage developed in relation to land, which has

---

[7] The Acts apply only if a document is drawn up, which produces paradoxical results. If a chattel is given as a present by an *oral* declaration of trust, then, although it remains in the possession of the donor, the gift is completely valid and the donee is safe against the donor's creditors. If the declaration is written but not registered, the gift is void against the donor's trustee in bankruptcy or other judgment creditors levying execution on the present. Unregistered *written* declarations by way of security are absolutely void.

long been the most important form of property to be used as security. In the old days the mortgage was effected by a transfer of the entire interest of the mortgagor (fee simple or lease) subject to a proviso that it would be reconveyed when the debt was discharged. The first mortgagee then took the title deeds. This provided a cheap and simple way of warning anyone else thinking of buying, or lending on the security of, the land, for you would ask to see the deeds before entering into any serious transaction. You would not hand over money to someone just because they live in a house; they might be the lodger.

The old form of land mortgage worked quite well but looked very strange. In the first place it stated that the loan was to be repaid in six months' time. Normally neither party wanted this to happen; the debtor because it would have been a waste of the costs, the creditor because the mortgage was a long-term investment. The point of having so short a repayment date was to ensure that at that moment the mortgagee's powers arose, so that if things went wrong and the lender needed repayment, the loan could be called in by a notice to repay and the remedies (especially that of sale) would become available. In the second place, complications arose from the fact that the mortgagor apparently transferred his entire interest to the creditor. Yet in reality he was regarded as owning the property, and the creditor as having a security interest and no more. The drafters of the 1925 property legislation knew this perfectly well and tried to put it right. Unfortunately the method they were forced to adopt is extremely artificial.

They decided to abolish the method of granting a mortgage of land by conveying the fee simple to the lender. They did not, however, dare to reduce the lender's interest to a mere list of remedies. Mortgagees had always, as security, taken an estate in the land—as real to their lawyers as the gold watch to the pawnbroker—and the drafters feared an outcry and a freezing of the money market if lenders found themselves deprived of an estate in land. Consequently they had to give the lenders an estate in land; but here they were trapped by their own logic. Section 1 of the Law of Property Act 1925 was to say that there were only two possible legal estates: the fee simple and the lease. So if lenders were still to have an estate, but were not to have the fee, there was only one choice: they had to take a lease. The artificiality of this is apparent from the fact that it is no ordinary lease: it is for a prodigiously long period (such as 3,000 years) at no rent, and when the loan is repaid the lease ends. Under the Land Registration Bill 2001 this method will cease to be available as a form of security interest.

A second method—that of granting a security interest which is basically a list of powers and remedies—was provided by the Law of Property Act which introduced the 'charge by way of legal mortgage', and that is nowadays the form most commonly used for a formal mortgage. Its statutory definition, however, provides an even more bizarre creation: the chargee is to have the same protection, powers, and remedies as if there had been created in his favour a term of 3,000 years without impeachment of waste but subject to a proviso for cesser on redemption.

A third method is the straightforward charge of the land with repayment of the money plus interest, and is widely used for the ever-increasing amount of land whose title is registered. Such a charge when registered gives its proprietor the powers conferred by law on 'the owner of a legal mortgage'.[8] After it has been created the lender takes the Land Certificate from the borrower and sends it, with the charge, to the Registry. The Registrar enters the transaction against the particular property, so that anyone who consults the Register will see that it is mortgaged. He also keeps the Land Certificate, so that, without it, the landowner will have difficulty in deceiving anyone into thinking that the title is unencumbered. Finally, he sends the lender a Charge Certificate into which is bound a copy of the mortgage.

The charge. The form just mentioned—charge by way of legal mortgage—can be used only in relation to land and only by one who holds a legal estate in the land—a fee simple absolute in possession or term of years absolute. The registered charge is available only to proprietors whose title is registered, which means that they have the fee simple or a lease of over twenty-one (soon to be seven) years. These two forms of charge give a legal security interest, that is to say one which will bind everyone. In the case of land whose title is unregistered, the result is similar if the chargee takes the title deeds or, if not, registers the charge against the name of the landowner in the Land Charges Registry.

But the word 'charge' is also the generic name for a wide range of transactions which create a security interest by any arrangement less formal than the full mortgage. There is a variety of such devices, but in general they transfer to the creditor neither possession nor property, nor do they give the right to take possession or to foreclose the debtor's interest. They can however be enforced by sale of the object over which

---

[8] LRA 1925, s.34(1); LR Bill 2001, cl.52(1). Thus, for reasons of economy, the effect of the new and simple form is defined by reference to the old. With the advent of electronic conveyancing the lender will no longer obtain a paper charge certificate.

they exist. That sale may have to be by order of a court, though the power of sale may be bargained for by the creditor in the agreement by which it is created, and is implied by statute if the charge is by deed. If the charge is created by agreement, it does not attach to any property until there is an obligation whose performance is to be secured. This means in practice (and quite rationally) that there is no charge until the creditor has lent the money. A simple example would be that of a person who has overdraft facilities and deposits with the bank, by way of security, his share certificates, or his Land Certificate. In the latter case, because of the formalities imposed on dispositions of an interest in land, the transaction should be in a document signed by both parties; in practice the bank will use a deed.

The floating charge. In this example the property charged was quite specific—these shares, this land. One great advantage of the charge, however, is that when it is created the property charged need not be specific, although of course at the moment of enforcement it must belong to the chargor and must be identifiable. In other words, charges may be fixed or floating. The former burdens, from the outset, the particular property charged, whereas the latter hovers over a changing class of assets. The floating charge is particularly useful for companies which are in the business of producing and selling goods. If all goes well, such a company will always have assets whose value is constant or growing, but whose form changes: money is disbursed to buy raw materials, these are worked up into the finished product, and that is sold, often on credit, so that the company has debts owing to it.

The floating charge hangs over this mass. When created there must of course be a general description to identify the class of assets, though not each individual member. Although under the normal rule an asset subject to a security interest cannot be transferred free of that interest, the exception afforded by the floating charge enables the company to dispose freely of any particular item in the ordinary course of business: the price replaces the item in the class of things charged. The company must indeed continually buy, make, and sell if it is to earn money to pay the interest on the debt and eventually perhaps to repay the principal advanced. However, if anything goes wrong, the floating charge can crystallize and fasten on the specific articles belonging at that moment to the debtor. From that moment the company can no longer dispose of anything, even in the ordinary course of business, without leave of the creditor. In practice a receiver is appointed to manage the business, or insolvency proceedings are begun. To prevail over other creditors, the charge has to be registered in the Companies Register.

An individual (i.e. not a company) cannot create an effective floating charge because the Bills of Sale Acts require attestation and registration of every specific article in his possession over which security has been given. But the floating charge has distant echoes in other areas. One is the right of a landlord to distrain for the rent on the tenant's goods. The second is the charge over a beneficial interest in a fund. The third is more muted: it is the relationship of the ordinary unsecured creditor to the solvent debtor's entire assets. For such a creditor's claim to attach to a specific item of the debtor's property requires default, judgment, and a charging order by way of execution (or seizure by a bailiff). One can almost see the floating charge as a consensual, unofficial, and speedier version of this: it requires default, crystallization, and a receiver. In neither case can the creditor, before default, point to any specific piece of the debtor's property. Before judgment and execution no particular asset is available to the unsecured creditor, but until then the claim throws a faint shadow over the debtor's wealth. Only in contracts for personal service does a creditor have a claim to an action on the part of the debtor; most claims are claims on the fund of the debtor's property. It is only if a debtor is insolvent that the difference between an unsecured personal claim and a property claim becomes important.

Nomenclature

A final word should be said about the somewhat loose vocabulary of secured transactions. We can broadly distinguish between the 'mortgage' and the 'charge'. In the former case both parties deliberately and scrupulously comply with the formal requirements so that a property right is firmly vested in the creditor; the latter class covers common but informal transactions where the debtor undertakes to give the creditor a security interest. To take a simple example: you may create a formal security interest in your shares by transferring them to the creditor who is then registered as shareholder; or you may create an informal security by simply leaving your share certificates with the bank to secure your overdraft. These examples recall the ways of solving the problem of warning others that you have borrowed money on the strength of your shares. In the formal method your name is no longer on the register of shareholders; in the informal example, you no longer have the share certificates.

Roughly speaking, mortgage is the name given to a transaction by which the mortgagor's entire holding is transferred to the creditor by way of security. If done by formal transfer of a legal interest, it is a legal mortgage, while it is 'equitable' if effected informally—say by a contract by which the creditor advances the loan and the mortgagor undertakes to transfer his interest. A security interest by way of charge is simply one in which property is burdened with the creditor's right of enforcement.

We said 'roughly speaking' because in practice each word is used to mean the whole class of security interest. The Law of Property Act 1925, section 205(1)(xvi) defines 'mortgage' to include 'any charge or lien on property for securing money or money's worth'.

HIRE PURCHASE AND RETENTION OF TITLE

As an addendum to this chapter, mention should be made of two other common devices which provide security in function but not in form. Strictly speaking, a security interest is a right over someone else's property—the pawnbroker holds your watch, the Building Society holds the mortgage on your house, and so on. You cannot pawn your watch or mortgage your house to yourself. But you can give someone the power to acquire your property although you still remain owner until they pay you what they owe, so you are using your title to ensure that you are paid. Hire purchase is a common consumer version of this, while retention of title is a commercial version: both are used only in relation to tangible movables.

Hire purchase

Hire purchase is a somewhat complex legal figure, much affected by consumer protection laws, and in an elementary book we can give only the basic structure. The need for such a type of transaction arises from two perfectly rational desires. The first is that of ordinary citizens to acquire goods now and pay later rather than save up and find that inflation has pushed the price beyond their means. The second is the need of the supplier until the full price is paid to enjoy some security over the goods both in the hands of the customer and of any third party.

If the supplier simply sells on credit, then he parts with ownership at once, and has merely a personal, unsecured, claim against the customer and no claim at all against anyone else who acquires the goods from the buyer. At the other extreme, if he merely hires out the goods, then he retains full ownership and, when the hiring period elapses, may reclaim them wherever they may be. But he would probably not want the return of used goods and his customers would hope that some day they might be theirs.

As its name suggests, the contract of hire purchase is a mixture of two legal figures. The customer hires the goods for a period at the end of which, if all the instalments have been paid, she has an option to buy the goods for a nominal sum.[9] The supplier is bound to sell, eventually, if called upon to do so but, since the buyer does not have to exercise the option, and cannot do so until all instalments are paid, there is no sale until then. This has two consequences: first, if, in breach of contract, the customer purports to sell the goods during the period, the buyer does not get a good title to them and is vulnerable to an action by the supplier.[10] Second, as the option merely empowers but does not bind the customer, she has never agreed to buy so as to be able to pass title under the Sale of Goods Act.[11]

Retention of ownership clauses

When goods are sold, in principle the parties decide the moment at which the buyer becomes owner; in the language of the Sale of Goods Act, section 17 'property passes when it is intended to pass'. This means that a seller who gives credit can stipulate that the buyer does not become owner until all the price has been paid; or, indeed, until all debts have been settled between them. Such a provision has the economic function of giving the seller some protection in the event of the buyer's insolvency, though in formal legal terms it is not a security interest since the goods belong to the seller, not the buyer.

The device gives rise to a number of issues that can only be mentioned here. First, since the buyer has the goods then, in the absence of registration, there is no easy way that purchasers from the buyer can find out that they do not belong to him and that, strictly speaking, he cannot pass title. Second, if the goods are raw materials which become incorporated into something else, there must be a moment when the seller's ownership ends: if a supplier of hay stipulates that she is to remain owner until paid, there will come a point in the digestive tract of the buyer's horse when the seller's ownership ceases. Third, the seller does not retain ownership of the goods for their own sake, but only as security against non-payment. There is no objection to this provided that other potential creditors can be warned. The USA utilizes such a system, and the Uniform

---

[9] In practice the supplier often sells outright to a finance house which then sells on hire purchase: for an example of the documents involved, see Sir Roy Goode, *Commercial Law*, 769 (2nd edn., Penguin, 1995).

[10] There is an exception protecting the innocent private purchaser of a motor vehicle: see above Chapter 4. Hire Purchase Act 1964, Part III.

[11] See Chapter 4.

Commercial Code states that the retention or reservation of title by a seller of goods notwithstanding shipment or delivery to a buyer is limited in effect to a reservation of a security interest, which requires filing to be effective against others.

FINAL REFLECTIONS

A few general comments may be made on the overall law of security at the present time.

Interests in chattels. The first observations apply to both reservation of title clauses and hire-purchase agreements. From the point of view of the law of property, the most interesting feature is the mismatch of the legal concepts and the economic realities. The traditional legal analysis assumes that only two interests may subsist in chattels—ownership and possession—and that the former remains with the supplier until full payment (and, in the case of hire purchase, exercise of the option to buy). So it concludes that the buyer who has paid 99 per cent of the price has only possession, while the seller has total ownership of the goods and of almost all the money. This seems unfair. Perhaps a more realistic approach is to recognize that there are two *proprietary* interests in the goods, that of the supplier diminishing in value while that of the buyer increases. In the case of land and of funds a similar technique has been used for centuries. The estate concept has been applied with perfect ease to the dwindling lease and life estate and to the growing remainder or reversion in both land and in government stock. Acts of Parliament speak of an 'estate' in the funds or in a ship.[12] Yet fine scholars continue to insist that in the case of personalty there is only ownership and possession, although they are quite ready to recognize both co-ownership in undivided shares, and the coexistence of property interests where one is by way of security.

If you hire a television set for three months, you pay only the value of possession, plus something for depreciation. But if you hire *purchase* the same set over three months each instalment would be far greater and by the end of the second month you will have paid some two-thirds of the capital value. Although, on the traditional view, you still merely have possession for the three months with the option to become owner at the end, some part of each instalment is in fact the price of a fraction of ownership.

---

[12] For instance, Government Annuities Act 1695, s.6; Merchant Shipping Act 1894, s.32.

The approach just suggested has been used by English courts to deal with a very practical problem. Suppose in our example of the television set on hire purchase over three months the customer pays punctually ten weekly instalments but then, in breach of the agreement, sells the set to an innocent purchaser and disappears. In an action by the supplier against this purchaser, the traditional view is that there is only possession and ownership, that the supplier has ownership and that therefore the innocent buyer must either return the set or pay its full value. But the consequence is manifestly unjust, since the claimant has already been paid five-sixths of the price of the set. A recognition that he has merely an estate in the chattel with a present value of one-sixth of the set's worth would protect the innocent defendant and prevent over-compensation of the claimant. The traditional approach would award the claimant money for something that does not belong to him, and in modern practice the courts award the lesser sum, which the trade calls the 'buy-out price'.

Land mortgages. Since the days when the law of mortgages was worked out, a number of important changes have taken place: there are far more borrowers and far fewer lenders. As to the borrowers, most ordinary people have to pay for their home by instalments. The old way to do this is to take a lease and pay a weekly or monthly rent, so that the landlord is providing the capital in the form of a dwelling and the occupant is paying the price attributable to possession; but (in the absence of legislation) at the end of the lease the occupant will not own the home. The twentieth century saw the great rise of the domestic mortgage business. The occupants still pay instalments, but each covers interest and some part of the capital advanced by the lender, so that at the end of the mortgage period the occupant will own the home free of the mortgage. This explains the growth in the number of borrowers.

The fall in the number of lenders does not mean that less loan capital is available. It means that private lenders have ceased to play the role of the mortgagee who makes an individual advance to a borrower. Instead they put their money in a building society or a bank, which plays the role of intermediary between many lenders and many borrowers (at a ratio of about seven to one). These institutions lend money to enable us to acquire a home and stipulate for repayment of both capital and income by instalments, so that after twenty or so years the debt and the mortgage are both extinguished. The money that they lend comes to them from deposits made by many savers, so that in one sense they are merely conduit pipes. Ordinary people hand over their savings to them and receive interest on the money; and the funds thus amassed are lent to other ordinary people at interest.

Thus a mortgage looks two ways. The lender benefits the borrower by financing him or her, perhaps in the purchase of a home; the borrower benefits the lender by offering a sound and safe investment. Any problems that might arise over a lender who, because of some emergency, suddenly needs repayment of the loan, are solved by the intermediation of the Building Society or other financial institution so that both lender and borrower are relieved from the risk and anxiety of a one-to-one transaction.

Furthermore, these institutional lenders collect a pool of mortgages large enough to lessen the impact of the default of any particular borrower. The pool protects their entitlement to the interest on the loans and to eventual repayment of the capital and can itself be used as security to back the issue of shorter-term financial instruments by which the lenders borrow on the financial markets both in Britain and overseas. The process is called 'securitization' and is developing rapidly, but its details have no place in this book.

Corporate insolvency. A debtor's insolvency tests the strengths of the various devices described in this chapter so, although the field is extremely technical, a summary may be useful. The assets of the company available for distribution do not include those goods ownership of which has been retained by suppliers. Nor do they include property subject to a fixed charge or mortgage (the advance so secured will very often have provided the capital to acquire the asset in the first place). Here, the mortgagee will usually sell the asset; any balance remaining after his debt and costs have been paid (the 'equity of redemption') does form part of the fund to be distributed among other claimants. These are, in this order: the expenses of the insolvency procedure; then the State for certain tax and social security liabilities, and the employees for some back pay; then come creditors whose security is a floating charge, then the unsecured creditors, and finally the shareholders. If the assets amount to less than the debts and if the shares are not fully paid up, the shareholders must contribute the sum unpaid on their shares. It is rare nowadays for companies to issue shares that are not fully paid up, but their existence reminds us that the 'equity' holding of shareholders is ownership in that it can be reached by creditors and carries the chance of profit or loss. If the company thrives, the holdings will produce income in the form of dividends and the market price of the shares will be robust. If the company collapses, it is the shareholders who take the ultimate risk. This risk does not extend to their other property, but it can swallow up their shares.

10

Real Property: Servitudes

GENERAL OBSERVATIONS

We have now to consider the use of tangible objects. The first thing to understand is that, save for servitudes discussed below, the private law of *property* has little to say on the matter. It may tell the rest of the world not to interfere without permission, though in the common law that seems to be the function of the law of tort. As mentioned before, the law of property imposes no positive duties on an owner: since you can destroy your own belongings, you can certainly neglect them; since you can throw them away, you can give them away.

But in a crowded island the use or neglect of one piece of land may well enhance or diminish the amenity or the value of the land near by. Perhaps in a perfect world such matters would always be resolved by agreement between the neighbours. The basic proposition is that the private law of property does not intervene. If your neighbours have a beautiful garden, clearly visible from your house, this may well enhance the amenity value of your land. But the law gives you no right to this amenity. No matter how long it has been there, you cannot insist that your neighbours keep the garden, still less that they maintain it. If you care enough about it, you will have to make a contract by which you pay for the amenity.

On the other hand the law (though not the law of property) may impose restrictions on occupiers of land in favour of their neighbours, in the absence of any agreements they may have entered into. Thus they must not commit nuisances, that is to say, must not do anything that interferes to an unreasonable extent with the comfort of their neighbours or the proper use of the land. The law of nuisance is properly dealt with in books on the law of torts and criminal law, and all that need be said here is that it imposes liability on an occupier to compensate for any injury caused by excessive noise or the escape of fumes, smells, and so on, or by interfering with the neighbour's natural right to support for the land or the natural flow of water in a stream. The occupier can be restrained directly by an injunction or perhaps indirectly by a prosecution from allowing the injury to continue. Furthermore, by fairly recent legislation, the courts can order a person to give access to the neighbour in order to facilitate the carrying out of reasonably necessary repairs and the like.

On the whole, however, it has more and more fallen to Parliament to regulate by statute such fields as public health, recreation, planning, and the environment. This body of legislation operates mainly by imposing duties and conferring powers on local authorities and other public bodies.

SERVITUDES

The name servitudes is given to certain real rights which burden one piece of land and benefit another owned by someone else. They are real rights in that they bind one property and benefit the other, no matter who has them. They never impose on the person who has the burdened land a positive obligation (i.e. one whose performance will cost money). Their existence is justified by legal and economic arguments, and their source is a long chain of case law punctuated by sporadic statutes.

The legal argument is this: an owner can, in principle, do anything he or she chooses on the land and can keep out everyone else. What the servitude does is withdraw some part of this freedom and say that, for the benefit of the neighbouring property, the burdened owner cannot do certain things (such as build so as to block out the neighbour's light) or must permit the neighbour to enter for certain purposes (such as to make use of a right of way). The economic argument is that land can sometimes be used more efficiently if its owner can control in some way the use of the neighbouring land, and that the value of the benefit may outweigh the cost of the burden. A simple example is property which is landlocked, with no way out at all except along the neighbour's path.

This is the one part of the common law of property which has derived some of its ideas and vocabulary from Roman law. That explains why such rights are called 'servitudes', the benefited property is called the 'dominant' land (or 'dominant tenement'), and the other is called the 'servient' land (or 'servient tenement'). The two main categories of such servitudes are (a) easements, and (b) restrictive covenants.[1] The first have been recognized since time immemorial, in response originally to the

---

[1] The elderly common-law category of 'profits' comprises the right to take something from land—grass by grazing, game by killing, fish by catching, and so on. The rights may be held by someone who is not a landowner. Details will be found in the standard works on real property.

needs of farming. The second were born in 1848 and arose from urban development.

Easements

No one has yet been able to frame a completely satisfactory definition of an easement, but they can be said to comprise two classes of rights. The first are rights for the holder of the dominant land to do something on the servient land, other than taking something from it. The second are a strictly limited number of rights to stop the servient owner from doing certain specific acts on his or her own land. Thus, from the point of view of the owner of the dominant land, easements are said to be either positive—the dominant owner can do something on the neighbour's land—or negative—the owner can stop the neighbour doing something. Neither category entitles the dominant owner to require the servient owner to do anything.

Positive easements are unlimited in variety and number, but are constrained by the requirement that they benefit the dominant land—it is not enough that they please its owner. They include, for instance, rights of way, the right to park a car on neighbouring land, rights to lay gas mains or electric cables together with the ancillary rights to enter the land in order to inspect and maintain them. They do not include freedom from competition: thus a person with land adjoining a canal may be given a valid easement to put boats on it, and this will bind later owners of the canal; but an *exclusive* right to do so is a business monopoly which will not enable the grantee to stop competitors, although there may be a right of action in contract against the party who granted the right in the first place.

Negative easements, which give a right to restrain activity on the servient tenement and thus to stop the neighbours from doing things on their own land, seem to be strictly limited in number and comprise only (i) the right to light, that is to say that the light flowing to a window shall not be unreasonably obstructed; (ii) a similar right to a free flow of air through a defined aperture, such as a ventilator shaft; (iii) the support of buildings, that is to say, a right to restrain any use of the servient land or building upon it which will interfere with the support afforded by them to adjoining buildings on the dominant land; (iv) a right to restrain any interference with the continued flow of water through an artificial water-course. It is worth noting that although they are all in a sense negative, they start with some positive act by an owner of the dominant land, namely the construction of a window or a ventilator, the erection of a building, or the creation of an aqueduct.

Creation of easements. Easements can be created in two ways: consensually, and by prescription. The first method requires a grant of the easement by the servient owner to the dominant owner or, if an owner is selling part of his land, a reservation for the benefit of the land retained of an easement over the land conveyed. The instrument should be a deed, in which case the easement (if for ever or for a term of years) will bind any subsequent holder of the servient land. If not created by deed, a contract for value signed by both parties and registered will have the same effect.

Prescription requires the holder of the dominant land to exercise the prospective easement openly, without force or permission, for a good number of years. The exact number is laid down by somewhat elderly statutes, but here it will suffice to say that, in general, twenty years such user will probably, and forty years will certainly, confer an easement. It is the only example in English property law where the passage of time *creates* (as distinct from kills) a right, of 'acquisitive' as distinct from 'extinctive' prescription. During the period it is always open to the servient owner to interrupt the exercise of the prospective easement, for instance by locking a gate across a path, or by insisting on the payment of some small sum of money as an acknowledgement that the exercise is by permission only.

It may be said that the last sentence can hardly apply to the so-called negative easements, since the only way their use can be interrupted is by doing the very thing which it is going to be claimed should not be done. This means that if the neighbour opens a window overlooking your garden you have twenty years in which to build an obstruction very close to it. The legislator has responded to this by allowing a notional obstruction notice to be filed with the local authority. But in general, since these negative easements are definite and few in number, they escape the difficulty that arises when restrictions are sought to be derived from mere general and indefinite inactivity. And in the days before town planning, when much work was done by hand in houses and shops in the narrow streets of congested towns, it was very important that occupiers should not be deprived of necessary light by the building operations of their neighbours.

It is precisely the availability of prescription as a means of acquiring easements which leads the courts to limit them to so few categories: you cannot, by enjoying television signals over your neighbour's land for twenty years, prevent the building of a skyscraper which will cut them off. If you want, for the benefit of your own land, to keep the neighbouring land undeveloped you must make a deal with your neighbour: *and pay for it*. This is the function of the restrictive covenant.

Restrictive covenants

Like easements, restrictive covenants presuppose the existence of (at least) two pieces of land, one of which benefits from the burden imposed on the other. Like negative easements, they restrict what can be done on the burdened land. Unlike positive easements, they give the dominant owner no right to enter the servient land. Their economic function is much wider than that of easements, since they serve to protect the amenity value of the dominant property, or of the neighbourhood. Their content is always negative (hence the name 'restrictive'); for instance, that, for the benefit of the dominant property, the other land may not be built on, or may not be used for a factory or a shop or any business premises, or for any purpose other than that of a private dwelling house. The obligation imposed is always strict: it does not say merely that the servient owners will do their best, or will take care, not to build a factory; it says they will not do it.

The source of restrictive covenants is always consent, never prescription. This means in economic terms that, one way or the other, the benefit is paid for. If you want to enjoy for ever the view over your neighbours' land you must persuade them to promise, for the benefit of your property, never to build. For this you will have to pay, and pay dearly, since you are effectively attaching to your land the development value of theirs. Furthermore, since you are creating a property right that will always benefit your land and always burden the land next door, there are legal requirements to be met, covering both the formalities for the transaction itself, and notice to any future owner of the burdened land. The undertaking should be by deed (hence the name 'covenant') or at the least by written contract signed by both parties. Notice is given by registration, nowadays at the Land Registry under the title number of the burdened land. This will refer any potential purchaser to the covenant itself which will reveal what must not be done on the servient land and which neighbouring land can enforce that restriction.

The preceding paragraph used a very simple example in order to explain the principles. In practice almost all restrictive covenants arise when an area of land is developed. In a new housing development, for instance, the fields are divided into plots on which dwellings are constructed. In order to preserve the residential amenity value of the whole area each buyer, for the benefit of the others, undertakes not to do certain things on the land purchased: run a business, open a shop, and so on. The existence of such restrictions is noted in the Land Register and the result is a kind of local law preserving the residential environment of the development. As the houses change hands each new occupant is bound by certain restrictions and has the benefit of those affecting the other properties.

Unlike easements, which have been recognized for many centuries, it was not until the mid-nineteenth century that the courts first began to recognize and enforce such amenity-protection covenants against the successors in title of the covenantor. In this way the negative obligation moved from being merely a matter of contract to being a servitude binding an indefinite number of persons. A person on selling part of his land would exact a promise from the purchaser not to do certain things that would reduce the value of the part of the land retained by the vendor. At first such a promise took effect only between the original contracting parties; no other person could be bound by the promise. However, it came to be thought that subsequent purchasers of the burdened land who had notice of the covenant and had therefore perhaps paid less for the land, would be acting unconscionably if they disregarded the restriction. Furthermore, the person who took the benefit of the restriction would not be satisfied with money damages for its breach, but would want an injunction forbidding breach. Until 1873 this entailed an application to the Chancery court and in 1848 an injunction was issued against someone who had bought land within Leicester Square in London with notice that his predecessor had, for the benefit of the houses round the square, covenanted not to build on it. In the years that followed restrictive covenants were subjected to the general requirement applied to other servitudes, that they must exist for the benefit of a dominant tenement. Unlike easements, however, their enforcement depended on the defendant's having notice of their existence. This requirement stems from the fact that they were the creation of equity, but it also accords with common sense. Most easements—rights of way, rights of support, and so on—can be seen by a prospective buyer, or at least by his or her surveyor. But no inspection, however scrupulous, will reveal that a piece of land is not supposed to be built on, or is to be used for only one purpose. Nowadays notice is given by registration.

Restrictive covenants imposed by a lease bind the land for the benefit of the landlord's reversion. For practical reasons—they are so numerous—they are not registrable. But anyone taking an assignment or a sub-lease is entitled to see the last lease and so will usually have notice of the restriction.

Something remains to be said about the interrelation of these servitudes and about one large gap in their operation. Suppose that a developer is building a square of houses around a central garden. Both seller and buyers will want to ensure that the garden is not built on: this can be done by a restrictive covenant which, if registered, will bind all later acquirers of the garden. They will also want to ensure that successive occupants of each house can use the garden for recreation. The law of easements will do this: the houses are the dominant tenements, the garden is the servient. But they will also want to ensure that the garden is looked after—that money is spent on it—no matter who owns it. This cannot be achieved by the law of servitudes. The law of contract will ensure that the *first* buyer of the garden can be required to look after it, but no successor is bound by that contract. The law of servitudes applies only if the burden on the servient land is negative—not to build, not to stop the neighbours strolling in the garden. At the time of writing the highest English courts still refuse to permit a positive obligation to be enforced against a successor in title, even one with full notice of its existence. The Law Commission has recommended reform and has drafted a bill, but Parliament has not acted. So developers and householders are compelled to use more elaborate and expensive legal devices in order to ensure the upkeep of the neighbourhood. One way is to form a company, vest the garden in the company, and issue shares to the householders. The second, even more complex, is to carry out the whole development by leasehold conveyancing. The burden of maintenance and repairing obligations entered into by a tenant for the benefit of the landlord, or vice versa, will run with the lease and the reversion, but their use for an entire residential development is both expensive and prone to error.

11

Succession

GENERAL

A question that can never be avoided in any system of law is: what is to happen to your property when you die? The matter is complicated by a number of factors: along with tangible belongings such as land or goods, the property of a deceased person may include debts due from others and there may well be debts owing by the deceased which need to be paid; furthermore, it may not at once be obvious who among the living is the person to collect debts due, pay debts owing, and generally deal with the balance. In its treatment of these issues, the common law uses the word 'estate' to mean either the totality of property or specific classes of property left by a deceased—the relevant legislation says, for instance, that 'where a person dies intestate, his real and personal estate shall vest in the Public Trustee until the grant of administration'.[1]

This last word—administration—indicates that it is impractical, if not undesirable, that as soon as a person dies their property should be handed out to others: some administration must precede distribution, a requirement made all the more necessary by the fact that, since the end of the nineteenth century, dying is taxed in the shape of death duties or inheritance taxes levied on the estate. It would be possible to choose one or more of the ultimate recipients of the property and impose on them the duty of administration. This is done in many countries where the 'heirs' both administer and then distribute the inheritance. It is not the plan pursued in England. Here administration is carried out by so-called personal representatives, whose duty is to get in and collect the deceased's estate, pay taxes and debts, and then divide what is left according to the last will of the deceased or, in default of a will, in accordance with rules set out by the law. To the extent that an estate is not disposed of by will there is said to be an intestacy. Personal representatives may be outsiders, professionals,

---

[1] Administration of Estates Act 1925, s.9.

but may also be relatives, often those to whom the deceased's property will eventually be given.

Accordingly the law of succession falls naturally into four parts: one deals with the appointment and duties of personal representatives, one with wills, and one with intestate succession; and something needs to be said about the few situations where property may pass on death outside the law of wills or intestacy. However, the law is most easily understood if one deals first with wills.

WILLS

In the law of succession the word will has two shades of meaning, covering what you want to happen after your death and what you have to do to make it happen. To make a valid will you must be in your right mind. Unless you are a sailor at sea or are in actual military service, you must be an adult and your directions must be recorded in documentary form complying with certain statutory formalities. This will has no effect until its maker dies. Until then it can be revoked or altered and, if not revoked, it 'speaks from death'—that is it applies to the property belonging to the testator at the time of death. Virtually every will deals with property, but this is not strictly necessary—it might, for instance, deal only with family matters such as the appointment of a guardian to look after the children.

The 'privileged wills' of mariners and service personnel need no formality at all, merely the expression (which can be by word of mouth) of their testamentary wishes. All others must be in writing (or typing or print) signed by the testator or signed for him in his presence. It must appear that by this signature the testator intended to give effect to the will and the signature must be attested by two witnesses, present at the same time, who then sign in the testator's presence. The fact that the will gives a benefit to a witness does not invalidate the attestation but does invalidate any gift in the will made to the witness or the witness's spouse. Thus in an indirect way the impartiality of the witnesses is as far as possible ensured. There is no need for a solicitor, nor, while the testator is alive, is the will recorded anywhere.

The will is automatically revoked by the testator's subsequent marriage, presumably because the law of intestate distribution is generous to a surviving spouse. But marriage does not revoke a will made when the testator was expecting to marry a particular person and intended that that will should not be revoked by marriage to that person.

A will may be subsequently altered, usually by adding a codicil which must itself be executed in the same way as a will. A will may be revoked entirely either by deliberately destroying the document or by making a new will which expressly revokes, or is entirely incompatible with, the old. The interpretation of wills has given rise to copious litigation and intricate commentary; neither will be discussed here. A testator need not deal with all his or her property by will; the part undisposed of will be distributed according to the intestacy rules, so that a person may die partly testate and partly intestate. However, the normal simple and sensible will does the following things: it appoints an executor or executors; it makes specific gifts; and it includes a clause leaving the 'residue' of the testator's estate to someone.

Freedom of testation

In many jurisdictions, including Scotland, a testator is not free to 'disinherit' the family entirely. The moral claims of close kin are translated into a legal entitlement to some of the testator's property and only what is left over can be dealt with by will. Once upon a time the common law of England had a version of this custom: realty could not be left by will but descended to the eldest son subject to a life estate for the surviving spouse. All this disappeared in the sixteenth and seventeenth centuries, to be replaced among the wealthy by the family settlement.

In principle today the common law treats a testator as entirely free to ignore the family and leave all his or her property to a cats' home. The harshness of this principle was recognized by New Zealand in the early twentieth century and the statutory amendments there adopted have spread throughout the Commonwealth. Their scope is shown by the title of the English legislation: Inheritance (Provision for Family and Dependants) Act 1975. The new technique does not, however, give these people any automatic right to a share; instead it adopts the more costly course of allowing them to go to court, and it authorizes judges to modify the will, or the rules of intestacy, or the combination of both and make the applicant an award out of the deceased's estate. A surviving spouse (or domestic partner) may claim such financial provision as would be reasonable; children or other dependants are limited to a claim for maintenance. Thus only the former need not prove that he or she needs the money.

INTESTACY

The law of intestate succession is very important because it provides the default rules for the distribution of property on the death of its owner. If those rules accord with the wishes of any particular individual, they save the trouble of making a will. The basic structure of distribution in force today was adopted by the Administration of Estates Act 1925. It is based on a study of actual wills and of the standard forms of wills in the books of precedents used by lawyers, so what ensues is a kind of will for the average testator.

The first point to be made is that there is complete equality between the sexes and that no preference is given to anyone on account of age. The rule of primogeniture, which favoured the eldest son, was abolished in 1925. Secondly, the only persons who can conceivably succeed on intestacy are the surviving spouse, the issue (i.e. children and grandchildren and so on), and the four grandparents of the deceased and their issue. Where there is no surviving spouse but there are issue, they take the entire estate to the exclusion of any remoter relative. Failing issue of the deceased, parents can take and also brothers and sisters and their issue, grandparents and uncles and aunts and their issue. Nearer relatives exclude the more remote. That is the whole relevant family group. If the deceased leaves no such relatives, the estate goes to the Crown (i.e. the State) as ownerless property (*bona vacantia*), although out of it the Treasury Solicitor may make compassionate allowances to dependants whether kindred or not.

Thirdly, all other relatives take subject to the rights of the surviving spouse, i.e. the person to whom the deceased was married at the time of death. Ex-spouses and domestic partners have no rights under the intestacy rules.[2] In contrast to earlier times the widow or widower is now greatly favoured. He or she now always takes all the deceased's personal chattels, i.e. personal effects including the car but excluding money. The reason for this last exclusion is that the surviving spouse is also entitled to a fairly generous 'statutory legacy'. If there are no children or grandchildren, this amounts, at the time of writing, to £200,000 plus one-half of whatever is left, the other half going to parents or their issue. If there are issue of the deceased, the spouse takes £125,000 plus a life interest in (i.e. the income on) one-half of the balance; or else the spouse can elect to

---

[2] Though they may apply to a court under the Inheritance (Provision for Family and Dependants) Act 1975 described above.

take its discounted capital value. The issue take the other half. If there is a spouse but not issue, parents, siblings etc., the spouse takes everything. In all these situations, the spouse may insist on taking the matrimonial home instead of the statutory legacy, with any necessary financial adjustment being made.

If there is no surviving spouse but there are issue, they take everything; if there are none, the estate goes to the deceased's parents or, if they are dead, siblings and so on. In all these cases if property devolves on a class—such as siblings—one or more of whom are dead leaving issue, the latter take equally the share their parent would have taken. Furthermore, no member of the family is entitled to a vested interest until majority or marriage, whichever happens first.

ADMINISTRATION OF ESTATES

So far we have discussed the ultimate distribution of the property of a deceased. If we had followed the chronological order, we should have started by discussing the administration of the estate for, as pointed out earlier, distribution must be preceded by administration. However, we have followed the more practical course, because administration varies to some extent depending on whether or not there is a will. The manner of appointing the personal representative will be different because if the deceased made a will it will usually specify an executor to administer the estate as personal representative. If there is no will, or if it fails to name anyone, or if the person named is dead or declines to act, some other means must be found of appointing a personal representative who will, in that case, be called an administrator.

Executors derive their office and powers from the will of the testator. They are free to decline the office but, if they accept, they may at once take various steps which will bind the estate. To regularize their position they must obtain a grant of probate. This involves depositing at the probate registry the original will together with the executor's oath, i.e. an affidavit identifying and verifying the will as the last will of the deceased (whose death certificate is produced), and undertaking to administer the estate. In addition the Inland Revenue must be given particulars of the property contained in the estate. The executor is then given a grant of probate with a copy of the will and is fully authorized to deal with the deceased's property of all sorts. This, the normal procedure, is called probate in common form. It is technically an order of the court and so protects the executor even if, for instance, a later will is then found and the original grant revoked. If there is any dispute about the validity of the will, probate must be sought in solemn form which is equivalent to an action and entails a court hearing.

If there is no executor, some person interested in having the estate administered applies to the probate registry for letters of administration. On intestate succession, preference is given to the surviving spouse, then children, parents, and so on. If any likely beneficiary is a minor, administration will be granted to at least two individuals, or to a trust corporation. Once letters of administration are granted, the grantee becomes the personal representative of the deceased and entitled to act.

Personal representatives—whether executors or administrators—succeed to all those rights and obligations of the deceased that do not die with him (as is the case, for instance, with a claim for damages in defamation). They can claim property belonging to the deceased and collect debts due. They can be sued to recover property belonging to someone else which the deceased possessed and on debts or for torts which the deceased owed or committed. In all these cases they act, not for themselves, but as a representative. Their own creditors cannot reach the deceased's estate, nor can the estate's creditors go against the private assets of the representative.

In all these the office closely resembles that of a trustee—indeed the legislator says that the estate of an intestate is held 'in trust by his personal representatives with power to sell it'. On the sale of land by a personal representative the buyer takes free of any interests of the beneficiaries, which are overreached and shifted to the price.

OTHER TRANSFERS ON DEATH

For the sake of completeness, a few words should be said about two of the events whereby property can pass on death otherwise than by will or on intestacy.

Gifts in contemplation of death

Midway between a gift and a bequest is the rather unusual transaction known by its Latin name of *donatio mortis causa*. It is needed to deal with the case where a person who expects to die soon makes a gift, which is conditional on death, by parting with possession of the item, be it a chattel, a share certificate, or a mortgage or land certificate. Nowadays the courts speak of parting with 'dominion' rather than possession; they do not use the word in other contexts nor define it in this. If the donor then dies, the gift becomes absolute. If the donor revokes the gift, or recovers in health, the gift fails.

Devolution of the office of trustee or personal representative

It is perfectly possible that, during the life of a trust or the administration of an estate, a trustee or personal representative will die. If others survive, the deceased merely drops out: neither the office nor any property connected with it passes on the death. But if the last trustee or personal representative dies the law must find a successor to the office and to the property.

For personal representatives, the position is as follows. If an executor proves the will and dies having made his own will appointing an executor who proves that will, the latter is the executor of both wills with the usual rights and liabilities in respect of both estates. If an administrator dies before completing the task, fresh letters of administration must be applied for by someone with an interest in the estate. In other cases, where, for instance, an executor dies intestate, application must be made to the probate registry for a grant of letters of administration of the estate of the original testator: the grant is made in the normal way to someone interested under the will and is made 'with the will annexed and in respect of property not yet administered'.

On the death of the last trustee of an ongoing trust, the trust property devolves on the trustee's personal representatives (executors or administrators) who must not, of course, distribute it under the trustee's will or to his intestate beneficiaries. They must transfer it to new trustees, if necessary by applying to court for their appointment. In the meantime they are treated as trustees of the trust property for the appropriate beneficiaries.

Part 5

Property as Wealth

This final Part turns to the use of property as an investment, as an asset that will yield an income and keep, or increase, its capital value. As such it forms the means by which wealth can be spread over time and over generations. The mechanics of a basic endowment regime are described in Chapter 12, and the legal limits on its operation are outlined in Chapter 13. The last chapter offers some reflections on the subject as a whole.

Wealth

INTRODUCTION

We can treat things for themselves, or we can treat them as investments. Being mortal we must have access to, and power over, some things in order to stay alive, especially the tangible objects which give us food, clothing, and shelter. We have to use them, and we thereby use them up, quickly or slowly. But to their producers and distributors these objects are part of a business, items in its constantly changing inventory. They have invested resources and talent in the production of certain objects but, so long as it conforms to the norm, no particular item is uniquely important to them: it is simply stock-in-trade and exists only in order to be made into something else or, if it is the finished product, to be exchanged for money. Just as this part of the process ends in money, it begins with the money, or credit, needed to acquire premises, staff, raw materials, equipment, and so on. Those who provide the necessary finance are investing in the production of things or in the provision of services. The existence of the joint stock corporation means that between their money and those things and services are interposed other forms of property in the shape of shares, bonds, debentures, and so on. These then become items to be bought and sold by the billion on the stock and bond markets, whose operation in turn gives rise to other assets like derivatives and traded options.

The point of these observations is to recall that a thing may be treated for itself, and be possessed, used, and disposed of for its own qualities, however banal they be. In this case the law treats that object as specific and unique: it is this house we own and live in, this book we buy and no other. When an object is transferred from one person to another it is treated for itself, so it must be specified and the transaction must comply with any formalities required by the law for that particular type of property.

On the other hand every thing may be treated merely as the clothing (in-*vestment*) worn by a certain amount of wealth. In this case the law accords it the modest role of a member of a class, perfectly replaceable, and subject to an implacable regime whereby it can be exchanged for money or for something else.[1] It is true of course that some things are more suitable for one function than the other: unless we are in the dairy business we would hardly invest our life savings in milk, nor would we buy a National Savings certificate just to admire the printing. But many things fit both roles, and this is obviously and especially true of land.

The key concepts of the English law of property were created for and by the rich at a time when the bulk of their wealth was invested in land. Those concepts are the estate, the trust, and the fund. There was no general family property regime created by the common law or statute, and so the wealthy and their lawyers used these concepts in structures called 'settlements' to ensure that succeeding generations of the family could share control and enjoyment of its assets. The techniques now flourish as a means of handling the wealth held in stocks, shares, bonds, and the like, capital which is not just movable but *mobile*, crossing oceans at the touch of a key-pad in response to movements in the Dow Jones or the Hang Seng index.

As explained in a previous chapter, where land is treated for its own sake (as farm, factory, shop, or home) it will be held as freehold by the 'fee simple absolute in possession' or under a lease, the 'term of years absolute'. Where, however, it is treated as an investment, it may be the object of a much more elaborate structure which divides its value in terms of income and capital and distributes entitlement in fragments over time. The complexities of this structure are reconciled with the needs of the market by statutory rules which ensure that the land itself may be sold but the money takes its place, as does whatever is acquired with that money. Thus land held as investment is nothing special and may always be exchanged for something else. Similar techniques apply to other objects, some by statute, others by consent of those affected, so that if the entitlement to chattels like great paintings or rare books is divided, the objects themselves will be almost as marketable as stocks and shares. The key to understanding this whole process is the notion of the fund 'dressed up (invested) now as land and now as current coin, now as shares and now as debentures'.[2]

A fund, or portfolio, of things treated as investments needs to be held

---

[1] The technical term is 'real subrogation', the process by which one thing (*res*) takes the place of another; it was introduced in our discussion of tracing, above Chapter 5.

[2] F. W. Maitland in H. D. Hazeltine (ed.), *Maitland: Selected Essays* (1936), 134.

and managed by someone. If only one person is involved, managing their own property for themselves alone, there is no need to introduce the concepts of trust or fund so long as the individual is sane, solvent, and alive. The concepts usually make their appearance to handle the situation when two or more persons are entitled to share something successively or concurrently—'pay the income to my daughter, then divide the property among her children.' We shall first describe the general principles of managing the property; then the common types of entitlement to it; then the legal limits on management and entitlement.

MANAGEMENT

A fund of property is not, in the common law systems, a legal person, so the objects which comprise it must be held by someone who is: human beings or a legal entity such as a company. The property is not for that person's sole benefit (though they can be one of the beneficiaries) so, in relation to it, they hold the office of trustee. A trustee holds property and usually has the power to sell it, with the price replacing the item sold in the trust fund. The power of sale is given by statute if the item is land and, for other objects, is usually given by the instrument creating the trust. Trustees are also often empowered to use trust property to secure a loan if the money is to be spent on improving existing or acquiring new investments. It will be remembered that the trustee's private creditors have no recourse against the trust property.

Setting up the trust

There are three ways in which you can set up a trust of your property for the benefit of someone else. In all of them you must make three things clear: what you intend; what property is involved; who is to benefit. The first method is to declare oneself the trustee; the second is to transfer the property to one or more trustees; the third is to provide for this by will and die; it will not be discussed here.

Declaration of trust. This is a striking instance of a unilateral legal act which operates to transfer the beneficial ownership of property and change the status of its current holder from owner for their own benefit to trustee for the benefit of others. The owner of property simply declares that he or she now holds as trustee for the specified beneficiaries. This enriches them, even though they do not know of it, and protects them against the donor's own creditors. If the property is land, the declaration must be evidenced in writing signed by the person able to declare the trust. Otherwise, no formality is needed, no visit to a solicitor, no writing, nothing but the expression of intent. Thus a person can set up a property structure affecting millions of pounds worth of their stocks and shares by singing in the bath. In practice, of course, more formal steps are taken.[3]

Appointment of trustees. The second and more commonly used method is to appoint others to the office of trustee. Unless the owner who sets up the trust includes himself as trustee, he will then drop out of the picture. If humans are appointed, there should be at least two, both to guard against the risk of mortality and to ensure that, on the sale of land, the overreaching mechanism operates and the buyer takes free of the trust.[4] Trustees are commonly professionals and often a trust corporation is appointed, that is a company whose business is to act as trustee. All trustees are entitled to have their expenses reimbursed from the trust property. The separate matter of their remuneration is usually dealt with in the instrument of appointment. In default of such agreement, trust corporations are entitled to reasonable remuneration, as are professional trustees if the other trustees so agree in writing; lay trustees work for nothing.[5]

The trust fund. When the trust is set up each item of trust property is transferred to the trustees by the procedure appropriate to its particular type: at this stage each asset is treated for its own sake, being specified, described, and transferred correctly. For land, a conveyance plus registration of the trustees as proprietors; for shares, a transfer plus registration as shareholders, or the electronic (or intermediated) equivalents; for receivables, a written assignment plus notice to the debtor, and so on. The fact that the new holders are trustees will appear on no register, though in the case of land a restriction will warn the world that no dealing will be registered unless capital money is paid to the requisite trustees.

In addition to the various documents relating to the transfers of the different types of asset, a single trust instrument will make clear that this is not a present, nor a loan, to the new holders but that they are trustees. It will go on to spell out the beneficiaries and their entitlements under the trust. It may also give the trustees powers of investment and management which differ from those conferred by statute, and may exclude their

---

[3] If the trust property includes chattels possession of which is to be retained, then a written declaration of trust must comply with the Bills of Sale Acts to be safe from the declarant's creditors, and may well be liable for stamp duty: so the best course may be to effect an oral declaration followed by a written acknowledgement that this has been done.
[4] See above Chapter 7.
[5] For details see Trustee Act 2000, Part V.

liability for breach of their duty of care.[6] It may name the person entitled to appoint new trustees and, especially for offshore trusts, may provide for the office of 'protector of the trust', that is someone who is not a beneficiary but is given powers to remove a trustee, to appoint new trustees, and generally to enforce the trust.

STRUCTURE

Broadly speaking the beneficial interests in trust property fall into two kinds, depending on whether the holders are concurrently or successively entitled to possession. 'Possession' in this context may mean the occupation and use of tangible trust property, but it also covers the right to the income or capital of the trust assets. Beneficiaries entitled to hold concurrently may take as joint holders, so that the survivor takes all, or each may have a distinct but undivided share. A further, very common, refinement is to give the trustees power to determine at their discretion whether a particular class of beneficiaries are to get anything at all, and if so how much. Concurrent interests may entitle their holders to enjoyment for ever—in which case they amount to absolute, if shared, ownership of the wealth invested in the trust assets—or they may be limited in time. Similar limited interests may be given to one person alone. Whenever a limited interest is conferred (whether on one person or on two or more together), someone must have the right to the assets when the limited interests cease. That person's identity will usually be spelled out in the trust instrument; in default of any such indication, since the trustees cannot take the property for themselves, it must go back to the settlor.

Example. Here is a simple example. Sarah is the settlor, T1 and T2 are the trustees, Ann is Sarah's only daughter. Sarah is rich and wishes to set up a trust to ensure that her daughter receives an income and that Ann's children eventually succeed to their grandmother's fortune. By a trust instrument she appoints the trustees and 'declares the trusts', that is she spells out exactly for whom they are trustees: T1 and T2 will be told that they are going to hold the trust property 'to pay the income to Ann for her life and then to divide the capital equally among Ann's children.' The instrument will be in writing signed by Sarah (though this is strictly necessary only if land is involved) and will, in practice, be signed by the trustees to indicate acceptance of the office, and contain details of their remuneration and so on.

---

[6] See Trustee Act 2000, s.1 and Sched. 1, s.7.

So far, the trustees have accepted an office but are 'trustees' of nothing. Sarah must transfer to them the trust property. Suppose that this consists of land, investment securities, money, and works of art. In order to be transferred correctly each particular asset must be specified, and the transfer must comply with whatever formalities are appropriate to that particular type of property. So the settlor must execute a deed of transfer of the particular parcels of land, and sign share transfers (or set in motion their electronic (or intermediated) equivalents); the trustees then ensure that their names appear on the Land Register as proprietors, on the company registers as shareholders, or on the books of their broker as holders of the appropriate security entitlement. If the settlor wishes to hand money over, the transfer will be effected by delivery, cheque, or credit transfer and must be paid into an account in the trustees' names which is quite separate from their own private bank accounts. Finally, each work of art must be handed to the trustees or, if it is in a bank vault or on loan to a museum, the holders must be told and must acknowledge that they now hold it for T1 and T2. When all this has been done Sarah has neither rights to nor entitlement in the transferred property and has no say in what is done with it. She has given it all away.

But no one has succeeded to the totality of rights, powers, privileges, and immunities that Sarah used to have. That totality has been divided three ways: management and control of each asset is in the trustees; use, possession, and the income of the fund belong to Ann for her life; each child on being born gets a present right to a future enjoyment of capital when her mother dies, the extent of her share being dependent on how many siblings there are; and on Ann's death the trust will end and her children can do what they like with whatever they get. If a child dies before Ann, the child's estate will succeed, since the trust did not make the children's entitlement dependent on outliving their mother.

When the life interest ends, and the capital is distributed to those entitled, the trust comes to an end as does the office of trustee. Only at this very last stage might anyone lawfully exercise the supreme rights of ownership by giving the shares to charity, neglecting the land, and burning the works of art. But until then the assets need to be looked after and Ann is expecting an income, so T1 and T2 have powers and responsibilities, the result of which is that the trust acts as both screen and pivot.

The trust-screen. Essentially the trustees have the power to sell any given asset and the purchaser need know nothing—or may know everything—about Ann and her children. As to the land, statute provides that *'for the purpose of exercising his functions as trustee'*, a trustee of freehold or leasehold land has all the powers of an absolute owner in relation to the land.[7] This cannot mean that trustees have the power to neglect the land or give it to a stranger for nothing. Those are certainly among the powers of an absolute owner, but their exercise would be inimical to the functions of a trustee. The key provision, however, is the power of sale, given by statute for land and by the trust instrument for other things. This means that in the vast majority of cases sale is always authorized, it is not a breach of trust. The purchaser need not ask whether the seller of land or shares or painting really owns the object or is 'just' a trustee of it. The only mandatory safeguard is that, in the case of land, the buyer must pay the price to the trustees, of whom there must be at least two, or a trust corporation. The Land Register which attests the trustees' title as proprietors of the land also contains a restriction warning of this requirement.

The trust-pivot. When a particular asset is sold, its place within the trust fund is taken by the price. However, since this will almost always be paid not in cash but by some form of credit transfer, the actual object which replaces the land in the hands of the trustees is the 'chose in action' of their claim against the debtor bank. That credit balance may then be used to acquire other assets—freehold or leasehold land, shares, bonds, and so on. Trustees now have general powers to invest, prudently, in a wide range of assets and to appoint and pay agents, brokers, and the like. This power of sale means that, from the point of view of those involved, no particular object is unique, nothing need be held for its own sake, everything is an investment. What matters is the wealth, the total trust fund, abstracted from any particular object. Ann's entitlement is to the income derived from this fund, while each of her children receives on birth a vested right to a share in the capital and to the income that that share will produce when their mother dies.

Protection of beneficiaries

If, in breach of trust, T1 and T2 give any trust property away for nothing, the beneficiaries are protected in two ways. First, they can sue the trustees in a personal action to make them restore the trust fund out of their own private wealth, though in this the beneficiaries are merely unsecured creditors. Secondly, if they can locate the donee they can bring a proprietary action to recover the trust property or its proceeds in priority to any other creditor of the donee. If the trust forbids the transfer of some

[7] Trustee Act 2000, s.8 in relation to land acquired under that section; see also Trusts of Land and Appointment of Trustees Act 1996, s.6(1).

particular asset and, in breach of trust, T1 and T2 sell it to someone who knows or ought to know of the breach, the beneficiaries are protected in three ways. They can sue the trustees in a personal action; they can claim the property from the buyer by a proprietary action; and the price which the trustees received for the asset is part of the trust fund and can be recovered wherever it can be traced. The only limit to the enforcement of their interests is that they have no claim against a person who in good faith acquired and paid for trust property without notice that it was being sold (or charged) to him in breach of trust. But *by definition* such a person has handed the trustees something (usually money) in exchange, and that something will be treated as trust property.

It may be worth emphasizing these points. Normally it is the trustees' duty (now codified by statute) to review the particular items of trust property and to decide whether to sell particular things.[8] In the general law of trusts there are two functions of the technique whereby one piece of property replaces another ('real subrogation'). The first is peaceful and by far the more common: on an authorized sale by honest trustees, the price replaces the thing sold. The second function is found in a more hostile context. Where an asset is alienated in breach of trust, the price may still replace the thing sold in the sense that the beneficiaries can, *if they wish*, treat as their own anything acquired in exchange; alternatively they may treat it as an asset over which they hold a charge securing their claims. But they may also bring a personal action against the trustees, and even a proprietary claim against the recipient of the asset unless he or she paid for the asset and acted in good faith without knowing of the breach of trust.

If, in breach of trust, the trustees sell to a good-faith buyer who has no notice of the breach, and if the trustees then squander the money, the beneficiaries become merely unsecured creditors with a personal action against them. There is nothing left to replace the perished property, and all real rights end with the destruction of the object—the fund—in which they subsist. In the final analysis the result here is much the same as if you had wrongly eaten my loaf of bread. While it existed it was mine, the bread or its value being recoverable by me and safe against your creditors. Once it has been eaten I cannot own it and have only a personal claim against you for its value. A judgment for that amount may be executed on your assets, but only in competition with all your other creditors.

---

[8] See generally Trustee Act 2000, Part II.

THE INTERESTS OF THE BENEFICIARIES

We shall now assume that the trust property is being honestly and efficiently managed by the trustees and that they are doing so for the benefit of the persons specified: Ann is to take the income for her life and her children will then take the capital in equal shares. Their interests are well described in the old jargon of the land law. Ann has a vested life estate (nowadays called life interest), and each child obtains on birth a vested fee simple absolute in remainder in the fund in common with the other children, if any. It is a *fee simple* because the children are not entitled merely for their own life; if they die (whether before or after their mother) their entitlement will pass under their will or by the rules of intestate succession. It is a fee simple *absolute* because there is no provision which might deprive a child, once born, of his or her entitlement. The interest is a fee simple absolute *in remainder* because while their mother is alive no child is entitled to the income produced by the property, yet on birth each acquires a vested right to a future slice of it. It is held *in common*, meaning that the children are to have shares.

As a matter of the precise statutory vocabulary applied to land, the beneficial interests in this example are called 'equitable interests', because, although they have been created according to the correct formalities, neither of them amounts to a fee simple absolute in possession or a term of years absolute.[9] What is much more important, however, is to understand that the beneficiaries' rights relate directly to no specific object: as has been explained, they are interests in and entitlements to the fund in general, not to any particular item in which it may be invested. Yet Ann and her children own all the wealth comprised in the fund. It is managed for them by others, but only they and no one else can decide to neglect, abandon, or give away their assets, and the creditors of each can reach their debtor's entitlement. Furthermore, each beneficiary can dispose of her interest by sale or charge. Ann can sell her life interest or charge it as security for an advance. On attaining majority, each child can do the same with his or her 'fee simple absolute in remainder'.

Proving entitlement

But how could they prove their title to a potential buyer or lender? And how would their interests be valued? Title to each specific object in the trust fund is held by the trustees: T1 and T2 are the registered

[9] See Chapter 7 on the 1925 legislation.

proprietors of any land, registered shareholders (or the electronic or intermediated equivalents) of any shares, account-holders with the bank. The beneficiaries have no title deeds or certificates, and their names appear on no register. The answer is as follows. T1 and T2 are trustees and must provide an up-to-date and accurate statement of account of the fund and its holdings. The accounts deal with the assets and do not reveal the identities or interests of the beneficiaries, but this information is in the trust instrument. The trustees must produce it on request and let Ann and her children have copies.

Armed with this information Ann can show (a) the present state, capital value, and income yield of the trust property; (b) that the trust instrument gave her the right to all that income for her life.

Valuing the entitlements

This right to income for the remainder of her life has a present capital value. In Chapter 2 we explained the discounting mechanism used to ascertain the value of present rights to future income which will be paid every year over a number of years. We need to know two things: the amount of income and the period over which it will be received. To keep the arithmetic simple, let us suppose that the trust fund has a capital value of £2,000,000 which is bringing in a net return of 5 per cent, so A can look forward to £100,000 a year for the rest of her life. We do not know, of course, exactly how long she will live. But if we know her age, there are experts—actuaries—who will consult their tables and give us her life expectancy as a matter of statistical probability. Of course she might die tomorrow or live much longer than predicted, but these risks can be covered by insurance.[10]

Valuing the life interest

Let us suppose that A is 55 and, statistically speaking, can expect to live to the age of 75. This means that her interest in the trust fund will yield £100,000 a year for the next twenty years. This adds up to £2m. but A is *not* a double millionaire today. Her interest is dwindling in value—a 'wasting asset'—rather like a goldmine that will produce a profit of £100,000 every year but at the end of twenty years will be worked out and worthless. No one will pay £2m. for A's life interest or for the mine; for if, instead, they keep the money and invest it at 5 per cent, not only will

---

[10] For a similar operation on intestacy, where a surviving spouse elects to capitalize the life interest, see Administration of Estates Act 1925, s.47A, (3A) and 3(B); Intestate Succession (Interest and Capitalization) Order 1977, SI 1977/1491.

they get the same income as if they had bought, but at the end of twenty years will still have capital worth £2m. So to find the present value of the life interest we must discount over time. One way to do this is to ask how much you would need to buy an annuity of that amount for that time. Another way is to work out what sum invested at 5 per cent and left alone for twenty years would add up to £2m. A third way is to assume an annual payment of £100k at the end of each year, work out the present value of the payment due next year, add it to the present value of the payment due the year after, and so on. The total is some £1,256,000. This is the best estimate of the present value of the life interest. It is the figure around which negotiations for its purchase would circle, and it must be remembered that with every day that passes the value of the life interest decreases and that of the subsequent interest grows.

Protection by notice

We now know the present capital value of the life interest and we know that this interest was given to A by the trust instrument. What we do not know is whether she still owns it, free of any burdens. She might already have given it to Oxfam, or sold it, or charged it as security for a loan, or her judgment creditors might have their teeth in it. We can ask her, of course, but she never had any title deeds so we need not go looking for them. Furthermore there is no public register on which she appeared as owner of the life interest or on which any secured lender might register a charge. What is done, then, is to set up a kind of private register held by the trustees (or a nominated trust corporation). In other words any transfer of, or dealings in, the beneficial interests can be protected by giving written notice of the transaction to the trustees and thereby obtaining priority over any competing claimant. So while negotiating to buy A's life interest a prospective purchaser will, as we have seen, study the trust accounts and the trust instrument, but will also enquire whether the trustees have received notice of any prior dealings. If A has already given her life interest to Oxfam, then it is the charity and not her which is entitled to the income for her life. Oxfam should have notified the trustees who will, in turn, reveal that disposition to any person with a legitimate interest. If Oxfam has not written to the trustees, a later good-faith buyer from A will obtain priority and, on notifying the trustees, will get the income for A's life, leaving Oxfam to whatever frail claim it might have against Ann. Any later disposition of the interest during Ann's lifetime will also be notified to the trustees, since it is they who are sending out the income payments. Thus in practice the trustees keep a kind of register of dealings in the interests of the trust fund which, behind the screen of the trust, serves a function similar to the public registers of dealings in land, shares, and so on.

Dealings in the remainder. Ann is not the sole owner of the trust fund. She is entitled to the income only for her life. Her children are then to take so, if she dies childless, the property must revert to Sarah, unless there is some different provision in the trust instrument. Let us assume, however, that Ann has two children. On birth each acquires an unconditional right to a share in the capital of the trust fund. While their mother is alive they are not entitled to the income produced by that capital, as that must be paid to her or her assignee. But she is certain to die and it does not matter if a child dies first, since the child's interest is not a mere life estate: it will form part of the inheritance and go under the child's will or intestacy. The civil-law systems call this interest 'bare ownership' to indicate that it will endure but, during the mother's lifetime, is not clothed (vested) with the income.

The previous section used the example of a fund of £2m. with a 5 per cent net yield, and a life estate with a current expectation of another twenty years, hence a present value of £1,256,000. This leaves £744,000 which is the present value of what common lawyers call 'the interest in remainder' and civil lawyers call 'bare ownership', i.e. an interest which includes the vested right to receive £2m. of income-producing capital in twenty years and the current power to do anything you like with both the present right to the future capital and the power of disposition of that right. Furthermore, it is an interest whose value increases daily as that of the life interest dwindles to death.

On the example given, this interest is divided among the two children but may be reduced in value if others are born since birth gives an equal share. Consequently the exact value of each child's share cannot be known, though precision sharpens as time passes, so that if the mother is 55 there are unlikely to be more children. We could then fairly safely estimate the value today of each child's interest at £372,000. Each of the two shares is a property interest which belongs to the child, and whose object of inherence is the trust fund, not any specific investment thereof. If the child has attained majority, he or she can deal with it as their own, give it away, sell it, charge it as security for a loan, and so on. The dealings are carried out in the same way as that described above. The total fund can be valued, that of the life interest deducted, and the remainder divided to reach the present value of the child's share. The trust instrument attests the child's entitlement at the time it was executed. Enquiry of the trustees will be made to ascertain if notice has been received of any assignment of the child's interest. Finally, a donee or buyer of the child's interest will give notice of the transaction to the trustees and so be sure that, when the life interest ends, they will receive half of the capital.

The market in beneficial interests

One question may well have occurred to the reader. To say that A and her children are each worth a great deal of money today implies that each now owns an asset which can be immediately put on the market. But who, it may be asked, would be prepared to buy? The likeliest purchaser from A would be her children when they grow up. This is because (apart from tax reasons) if they buy her out they are then entitled to both the income and the capital of the trust fund: they and they alone own the wealth invested in the various assets. They can get together and break the trust by telling the trustees to transfer all the investments to them or at their direction and then to relinquish the office of trustee. But if A is not bought out and does not want to buy her children's interests, who might do so? The likeliest buyers would be an insurance company or the trustees of a pension fund. Both are in a business which receives annual income payments—premiums and pension contributions—and in return undertakes to provide capital sums to policy-holders or pensioners in the future. So it may be a good investment for them to balance their risks by buying from the children in a transaction which involves their parting with capital now (capital which, if retained, could be used to produce an income) against the certainty of acquiring a larger amount of free capital when the children's interest falls into possession, on A's death. There is in fact a small but professional market in what the dealers in them call 'reversionary interests'.

Sub-trusts. It should be added that the owners of these interests in the fund, whether the life interest or those in remainder, can, instead of selling or giving away their interest, set up a trust of it by declaring themselves a trustee or by transferring it to selected trustees and, in either case, by spelling out the trusts. This must be done in writing and be signed by or on behalf of the person constituting the trust. The children, if they retain their interest until their death, can also set up a trust of it by will. These are all 'sub-trusts' within the framework of the main trust: the trustees are different, as are the settlor, the property, and the sub-beneficiaries. The asset held by the sub-trustees is not the investments in the main trust portfolio but the right to the income flowing from the life interest or the (ever-growing) capital value of the remainder.

The estate concept. In dealing with interests in property treated as wealth, the above pages make it clear how important is the element of time and the passing of time. Historically speaking, the common-law concept of the 'estate' captures that element precisely. Nowadays, in English law, we need to distinguish: on the one hand, the word is used in relation to land treated as such, as a specific object; on the other, the concept serves to evaluate interests in land treated as investment, and indeed can be applied to interests in a fund, regardless of whether or not the portfolio includes landholding. In the first situation land is the specific object in view and if you have a farm, factory, shop, or home either you have the freehold estate or the leasehold estate. It is described as a 'legal' estate, meaning that, if the correct formalities have been observed, it will prevail against everyone.[11]

In dealing with funds, however, instead of overworking the word 'interest' to describe the various entitlements, we can call on a precise, if elderly, vocabulary of life estate, fee simple absolute in remainder or reversion, and contingent or determinable varieties of these.[12] These concepts have the advantage of indicating the elements of each entitlement without at the same time asserting that their holder is the person with the very best title in the world and without necessarily implying that he or she holds for their own benefit and not as trustee.

The elements which matter are four: the right to the income value of an asset; the time for which that right can be enjoyed; the power to alienate the right to the income value for that time; and the power to alienate the power to alienate. By 'income value' we mean the right to occupy or use the thing, or the right to take the rent, royalties, dividends, interest payments, and so on produced by some thing or some loan. The concepts can then be formulated as follows. We use i to indicate the income value of anything and a to signify the power of alienation. Some symbols must then be found for the element of time, so E stands for eternity, or at least a time without limit, and l for a human life.

> Fee simple absolute in possession $= a^{\infty}(iE)$.
> Life estate $= a^{\infty}(il)$.
> Fee simple absolute in remainder $= a^{\infty}(i(E - l))$.

---

[11] The LPA 1925, s.1(1)(4) extends the phrase 'legal estate' to cover other rights which bind the land itself, such as easements and mortgages. Certain other elderly entitlements may also be so described, such as a protected right to hold a market, or certain fishing and gaming rights: Land Registration Bill 2001, cl.3.

[12] The fee tail, or entail, was abolished in England and Wales in 1996; it never caught on in other parts of the common-law world.

In each case a is raised to infinity because the power to alienate includes the power to alienate the power to alienate the power to alienate and so on.

13

The Control of Endowment

There are few limits to the kinds of interests that can be created in funds. In other words, the enjoyment of the income from a fund may be made to pass from one person to another on the happening of any kind of event, or fulfilment of any kind of condition whatever, so long of course as it is not against public policy, or specifically prohibited. An example of the first would be a gift of the income 'to Jack until he dies or marries'—the last two words would be crossed out, by a court if necessary. An example of a recent specific prohibition is that concerning a very ancient type of property interest, the entail. Dating from the thirteenth century, this was an endowment designed to keep capital and its income within the line of descent of a particular family, so that each generation was to take the income, being succeeded by their children and their children's children and so on. Originally limited to land, its application could be avoided and the entail broken by means first devised by the courts and then spelled out by statute. Since 1996, however, an attempt to grant someone an entailed interest in a fund does not work: instead it operates as a declaration that that someone is absolutely entitled.

Two particular types of legal control must be briefly described: they are designed to cover different problems, one relating to unspent income, the other to unowned capital.[1]

Unspent income: the rule against accumulation

The use of a fund of investments to spread wealth over time may lead to the accumulation of unspent income. A simple example would occur where the beneficiary is a baby. In this and similar situations the trustees are given statutory powers to spend the income on the upbringing and education of the beneficiary and to accumulate and invest any which is not disbursed. But more serious problems arise if they are *forbidden* to spend

---

[1] In 1998 the Law Commission produced a Report and draft Bill (Law Com No. 251) recommending changes in the system of control. They can be found at http://www.lawcom.gov.uk.

the income but are told to reinvest it each year for a long period at compound interest. Suppose, for instance, that by a will trustees are given assets worth £1m. and are told to add the income to the capital until the first of the testator's granddaughters reaches her majority and then to hand the entire sum to her. If, at the date the will takes effect, the testator's children are tiny, it could be several decades before any of them has a daughter, and almost twenty years more until she reaches majority. This has two effects: it seeks to ensure a potentially enormous sum for the fortunate person who has yet to be born; and it does so at the expense of the living, that is the testator's children, who are to see not a penny of the income.

The will of Peter Thellusson who died in 1797 directed that the income of his considerable property be tied up in this way for, as events turned out, fifty-nine years, thereby depriving his widow and children of any benefit from his wealth. Parliament intervened in 1800 and the rules are now contained in modern statutes.[2] Their basic effect is to permit accumulation of income only for certain periods. The first, applying to inter vivos trusts, is the life of the settlor—who could anyway, if she wished, keep all her wealth on deposit all her life. The other periods are either twenty-one years or the life of some child alive at the date of the disposition. If attempts are made to order accumulation beyond these periods, they fail. Thus if a will directs that the income be accumulated during the life of the settlor's children, it is permitted for only twenty-one years. Thereafter the income of the accumulated fund must be paid out to the appropriate beneficiary.

In actual practice directions to accumulate income for long periods are nowadays uncommon. The Law Commission recommends abolition of the statutory controls, except over accumulation by charities.[3]

It is important to remember, however, that, even without any current statutory control, if a settlor gives property absolutely to an adult beneficiary and at the same time orders that its income be accumulated, the donee may, whereupon the trustees must, disregard the direction to accumulate. The point is basic: if property or an interest in property is all yours and you are grown up, your wishes are decisive.

Unowned capital: the rule against perpetuities

A more difficult problem arises when we know there is wealth but we do not yet know whose it is. In the example used above we assumed that T1

---

[2] At the time of writing, LPA 1925, ss.164–6, Perpetuities and Accumulations Act 1964, ss.13–14.
[3] Law Com No. 251 (1998).

and T2 are holding and managing a portfolio of property worth altogether £2m. and yielding an income of £100,000 a year. This income is being paid over to Ann (or her assignee) and is statistically likely to be so paid for twenty years, so the present, though dwindling, capital value of the life interest is £1,256,000. Deducted from the £2m., this leaves an asset worth £744,000 (and growing) which does not belong to the holder of the life interest. To whom does it belong? If Ann has a child, it will belong to the child; if she has children, they will share it. But suppose at the moment she has none: the asset certainly does not belong to the trustees, nor to the holder of the life interest. If Ann dies without having had a child, the trust ends and the entire property will have to go back to Sarah or her estate. But until Ann either has a child or dies childless no one owns the ultimate capital. Someone will acquire ownership. If a child is born, the baby will become 'bare owner' with a vested irremovable right to capital, the income of which is going to its mother. If Ann dies without children, Sarah (or her estate) will become full owner, entitled to the £2m. and its income. But at the moment we just do not know which.

It should be repeated, at this stage, that this uncertainty in no way hinders dealings in the specific objects in which the wealth is invested. If, for instance, one (or all) of those objects is freehold or leasehold land, legal title to the particular property is held by the trustees who have statutory power to sell it. The purchaser need know nothing about the state of Ann's family, though it is of no importance if he does know— the price when paid to the selling trustees simply replaces the land within the trust fund. The uncertainty we are concerned with here is about who owns the wealth, not about who can handle any particular investment of that wealth.

The law's response to this uncertainty is known by the historical title of the Rule against Perpetuities, which applies to interests in any kind of property treated as wealth; in other words it applies to all interests in funds. The Rule says that this uncertainty as to the ultimate ownership of any interest is perfectly tolerable provided that the uncertainty does not last too long. The permitted time-frame *at common law* underlies the operation of the Rule in most common-law jurisdictions, though to it have been added individual variations. The basic common-law rule states that uncertainty as to the ultimate ownership of an interest in property is tolerable provided that it is certain to be resolved, one way or the other, within the lifetime of someone alive at the start of the period plus twenty-one years. Thus in the above example there is no problem. Two interests are conferred. First, the right to the income for life is given at once to

Ann, so it is hers from the start and she can do what she likes with it. Second, the right to the capital is given to Ann's children: when born they get the right to the capital, with 'full ownership' including the right to the income on it coming to them on their mother's death. If, when this trust is set up, Ann already has a child, that child instantly benefits by being given the present (alienable) right to the capital, though not, at the moment, to its income. If when the trust is set up Ann has no child, we do not know if she will have a child or not but we know that we will know one way or the other at the latest when she dies. So our uncertainty cannot last longer than the lifetime of someone alive at the start of the trust. That someone is Ann because only she can have her own children. If she does, they take; if not, the assets go back to Sarah.

If the terms of the trust give the income to Ann for life and the capital to such of her children as reached majority, then two events have to occur: a child has to be born and has to survive to the age of 18. Once again, we do not know whether this will happen. But we do know that if it happens it must do so within the permitted period. Ann is alive; Ann's children must, if born at all, be born during her lifetime; and if they reach 18 must do so within twenty-one years of their mother's death. If they do, they take; if not, the assets go back to Sarah.

But if the terms of the trust give the income to Ann and the capital to such of her children as marry, and if at the start of the period Ann has no married child, we cannot say now that our uncertainty must be resolved, one way or the other, within the permitted period. It is perfectly possible that a child of Ann may marry within Ann's lifetime and twenty-one years. But it is also perfectly possible that the first child of Ann to satisfy the condition is one born after the trust began who marries more than twenty-one years after his or her mother's death.

Before the Rule against Perpetuities was amended in 1964 (for England and Wales) this prolonged possible uncertainty was instantly fatal to the gift to such of Ann's children who marry. The entire gift to them was simply crossed out and the trustees thus found themselves holding on trust for Ann for life, with the remaining interest (presently worth, remember, £744,000 and growing) going back to Sarah: in technical jargon it is said to 'result', i.e. 'jump back'. Since 1964, however, the trustees must wait and see if a child of Ann marries within the lifetime of someone alive at the start of the trust and a period of twenty-one years. This does not mean that they can search the world for the longest life. The relevant lives, spelled out in the statute, are essentially those of the family, so they wait, first, for Ann's life: if she dies childless, that is that. If not, the trustees wait and see if a child marries within the next twenty-one years. If this happens, the child takes the interest on marriage. If, at the end of the twenty-one years no child is married, they lose their chance. The gift to them is crossed out and the property reverts to Sarah or her estate.

The Act also introduces some practical presumptions as to the ability to beget or bear children, especially that which assumes that a woman over 55 is sterile, and it also permits evidence of (male or female) sterility to be given where relevant. So, in our example of a gift to Ann for life and then to her children who marry, if A is unable to have children, then, if there are none, the gift to them fails at once and the interest goes back to Sarah; if there are children but they are not married, then there will be no more, so the only ones who might marry must be alive now and must marry, if at all, within their own lifetime, so the gift is valid.

Finally, to save all this calculation the Act allows the use of a specific number of years up to eighty. Thus a gift to Ann for life then to her children who marry within the next eighty years is perfectly valid and the trustees must wait out that period. If at any point it becomes clear that the event cannot happen—if, without having children, Ann reaches 55 or dies before then, the remainder interest results back to Sarah. If, however, children are born they must, to take under the terms of the trust, marry within the period set.

The reforms proposed by the Law Commission in 1998 would abolish all reference to lives in being and simply substitute a perpetuity period of 125 years from the date of the trust instrument. If the event on which entitlement depends (usually things like birth or marriage) occurs within that period, the gift takes effect. If by the end of the period the relevant event has not happened, the gift fails. So under the proposed regime, if property is transferred to trustees on trust to pay the income to Ann for her life, and then to divide the income among her children for their lives, and then to divide the capital among those of her grandchildren who marry, the trustees (and their successors) can wait to see what happens. If Ann dies childless, they must look to the trust instrument to see what to do and, if it fails to tell them, they hold on trust for Sarah (or her successors). If Ann has a child or children, they get the income of the fund after their mother's death. If her children die childless, there can be no grandchildren and, once again, the trustees must, if all else fails, return the capital to Sarah or her estate. If grandchildren are born, however, the trustees wait to see if they marry. If at the end of 125 years from the creation of the trust none is married, their chance of taking the property dies and the trustees wait no longer. They must deal with the capital as provided by the trust instrument and, in default, return it to Sarah's estate.

Charities. The law permits certain forms of charity, which it regards as beneficial to the community, to be the objects of permanent endowment: that is to say an amount of wealth may be tied up for ever with only the income going to the charity. Any gift to a charity is subject to the Rule against Perpetuities in that it must get to the charity within the permitted period. On the other hand a gift over from one charity to another is valid even if it is to occur at some remote time in the future. It is said that all charity is regarded as one single object and the change in recipient is merely a matter of internal arrangement. But that is merely a way of restating the exception to the Rule (which is preserved by the Law Commission's latest scheme). Probably the true explanation is that the law regards the endowment of charity as taking property permanently out of commerce, but has to admit that a particular charitable object may become obsolete. It is not permitted to set up a perpetual endowment for an impersonal but non-charitable purpose because that would, for private purposes, take capital for ever out of commerce.

Rationale for the Rule

Let us now try to see why, throughout the common-law world, there is, in one form or another, a version of the Rule against Perpetuities. By way of preparation, two points must be recalled.

First, although the Rule does not overtly strike at restrictions on alienation but only at the remote vesting of uncertain interests in property, it has very much the former effect. For as soon as a beneficial interest vests in an ascertained individual—which must occur within the perpetuity period—the interest becomes easy to value and to market. Moreover once all the beneficial interests are in the hands of living persons of full age and capacity, they can make the trustees wind up the trust and distribute the assets.[4]

Secondly, the original purpose of the rule has long since disappeared. It was devised in the seventeenth century when land was the main investment of the wealthy, and had some effect (along with other devices) in preventing land from being kept for too long out of the market. Since legislation of 1882, however, much more rigorous means have been devised to ensure that land is freely alienable. Indeed, there is no longer a danger of freezing any particular asset, since in almost every case any

---

[4] Statute allows the court to give its consent on behalf of those who are not *sui juris*.

specific item of property in which the fund, or part of it, may be invested can be sold at any moment by the trustees. The price, of course, replaces the asset within the fund.

It would seem, therefore, that the Rule against Perpetuities can no longer have any relation to the markets in so far as they deal in specific land, goods, shares, bonds, and so on. It relates only to contingent rights to receive income from a fund and to their capitalized value. Accordingly, some writers regard the Rule as effecting a compromise between the living and the dead. If we had no such rule, a person might, by trust or testament, be able to fix for all time to come the interests that his or her unborn descendants are to take. On the other hand, it would be too great a restriction on our freedom to say that we can give interests in property only to the living. There is no particular virtue in our Rule as it stands. Civil-law countries have different rules which are not obviously worse. But from a comparison of those rules with our own, there does seem to be a consensus of opinion that people should be allowed to give property to a person unborn at the time of the gift but that this power should be limited so as to return to the hands of the living within a reasonable time full control, not merely of the specific investments but of the beneficial interests in the wealth they represent.

Such a rationale sees the Rule more as a restriction on legal personality. During a person's lifetime he or she may do anything or nothing with their property. Further, for some time after death, the will (in both senses) of the dead can control the fortunes of the living. But there comes a time when even the dead must die; and the effect of the Rule is to fix the latest date for this at the time when our grandchildren grow up.

Other writers prefer a different but not incompatible explanation. They say the Rule still has some application even to the specific objects or investments comprised in a settlement because they are held by persons who, being trustees for others, must act prudently. In general, although trustees may make any kind of investment that they could make if they were absolutely entitled to the assets of the trust, it is still only a power of *investment*, exercisable with prudence, if not caution. Wherever the kind of interest exists which calls for the application of the Rule against Perpetuities, then it will be an interest in a trust fund. Trust capital and venture capital are very different. There are many risks that owners can take, but not trustees, who may not in principle make an unsecured loan, even though providing the financial backing for a latter-day Leonardo da Vinci might lead to enormous returns through the development of new technology. And since economic progress demands bold speculation, it is a matter of public concern to preserve a proper balance between trust capital and venture capital.

Where entitlement to the income of a fund is spread over time but the interests of the beneficiaries are vested, each adult beneficiary can realize his or her asset and use the proceeds to take what risks they please. In our example above, if we assume that A's children are adults and that, as she is 55, there will be only two of them then all three have presently marketable interests, Ann's being worth about £1,256,000 and each of the children's being worth about £372,000. They can sell out and spend the money as they please. But if the children's interest were contingent on their marrying it would be much more difficult to assess present market value. The effect of the old rule would be to strike them out and to give back to Sarah the present (instantly marketable) right to the capital on Ann's death. Under the Rule as amended in 1964, the trust cannot last longer than the three lives. If the children marry, they take a vested alienable interest consisting of the present right to the future income when their mother dies. If not, on their death the interest goes back to Sarah (or her estate) and the person entitled will own the marketable asset of the present right to the future income when Ann dies. If she has predeceased her children, that is the immediate right to the £2m. and its income for ever.

All these justifications for the rule have had to be made up. The law in the hands of legislators or judges gives no such reasons; it simply applies the rule, often to the testaments of ordinary people and to dispositions that are in fact quite harmless. It also operates without regard to the advances in medical science, which may make it possible for the dead to become parents. The costs of learning, debating, and litigating it may well outweigh any benefits which are in practice obtained. In 1983 the entire Rule was repealed in Manitoba, and since then in the offshore trust laws of several other jurisdictions.

14

Conclusion

The law of property remains very complicated and not entirely free from confusion. Too many kinds of people have had a hand in producing it to admit of a simple orderly system, consistent in all its parts. Its vocabulary veers between precise technicality ('fee simple', 'term of years absolute') and extreme ambiguity ('owner', 'property', 'interest'). Merchants have built up the law governing goods and services, the financiers have moulded the law of stocks and shares, the managers of popular musicians and the bioscientists have both developed the law of intellectual property, and the desire of ordinary people for security in their home has prompted much legislative intervention. Machinery has replaced horse power in the means of production and our attitude to animals has changed, so that they are no longer the typical chattels of property relations, and the law intervenes more and more to protect them from us.

The traditional heart of English property law was that of realty, which treated land as an investment of the wealthy and an endowment of their family line, with their 'strict settlements' forming a kind of dynastic property regime within a structure built by their lawyers. During the last two centuries, however, much wealth has become invested in other forms of property or in a fund which might be land one day and shares the next. At the same time those of more modest means have aspired, often successfully, to own the freehold of their homes, offices, and shops. The attractions of the 'strict settlement' had so diminished that its abolition from 1996 raised few objections.

Where many people start from different points and pursue different paths they do not always meet. So there is a lack of coordination in property law. Moreover, so vast is the field covered by it that no mind has hitherto been capacious enough to master it all and at the same time familiar enough with the details to make their opinions acceptable outside a part only of what is a most technical branch of the law. The best academic writing is almost forced to operate in separate compartments, so that a recent excellent publication of over 1,500 pages describes itself as a work on the *elements* of *land* law.[1]

If property law had been codified after the Continental fashion, the codifiers would have introduced more order into it and in particular would have asked whether certain techniques accepted for one kind of property might not also be applied to others. A case-law system like ours naturally deals with problems as and not before they occur in practice; and some problems arise for some kinds of property and have not yet occurred for others. Furthermore, some parts of the law of property, especially those protecting entitlements to tangible objects, have grown up around the common-law actions of tort, while in the law of trusts the trail of the Chancery is everywhere evident.

As we have seen in the preceding chapters, the entitlements protected by the law of property are those which relate to some object or some asset, can be asserted against an indefinite number of persons, prevail against their insolvency, and can almost always be alienated by their holder and be reached by their holder's creditors. It would be clear and convenient if we could assert with confidence that there is a closed list of things which can be the object of such entitlements. We know the obvious things—land and goods—because we can touch and, in some cases, move them. We know the main types of intangible assets: some of them, such as cheques, are embodied in documents, some evidenced by certificates or National Savings books, some, such as patents, are registered. But at the edges there are a number of items whose status is uncertain or evanescent. In the financial world this may be the case for some of the derivatives. In the field of intellectual property, problems are posed by developments in medical science, in computer technology, and in show-business.

At the edges, not only are the objects of property law uncertain but so are the interests which it permits and protects. Certainly most of the field is covered by standard interests. Three of them confer the right to possession of the object or to enjoyment of the income or other yield of the asset or fund of assets: they are ownership, life interest, and lease. A separate category is that of the title to, and powers of disposition of, property conferred on a trustee by statute or consent in order to carry out the functions of trustee; it should be recalled that a trustee cannot personally enjoy the property nor may it be reached by his or her creditors.

The other standard types of proprietary interests confer rights over

---

[1] Kevin Gray and Susan Francis Gray, *Elements of Land Law* (3rd edn., Butterworths, 2001).

other persons' property and are not impaired by their insolvency: they are the security interests such as mortgages, and charges whether fixed or floating; and the servitudes such as rights of way and restrictive covenants.[2] Two or more persons may hold all of these interests concurrently.

Most other rights over things do not count as property rights and may be enforced, if at all, only under the law of obligations, typically those arising from contract or kinship; they are thus at the mercy of the defendant's insolvency. Thus the right to enter a cinema is enforceable only against the other party to the contract evidenced by the ticket. If that party does not have possession of the building (because it never had it or because it has sold the cinema), the right to enter cannot be enforced against the occupier. The ticket does not give its holder ownership, a life interest, or a lease of the building, nor a mortgage, nor a right of way. Similarly a lodger, who shares the accommodation, has rights only against the other party to the contract, not against an indefinite number of persons and certainly not against one who has newly bought or taken a security interest in the premises. A spouse or domestic partner may well be in a somewhat similar position.

The real rights summarized above cover most of the field, and it is tempting to conclude that they cover it all, and that there exists only a closed list of interests in property that will bind an indefinite number of persons. We would then have a clear system in which property interests would be *exclusive*, because a right could not at one and the same time be of more than one type, and *exhaustive* in that a claim which did not fall within one of the recognized categories would be merely personal. Certainly the law will not be bound by the name the parties choose to call their relationship. If you give someone else exclusive possession of your house for six months at a rent, you have granted a lease, even though both of you called the transaction a licence and the occupant a lodger. Conversely, if you grant a concession in your store to a firm selling perfumes, this is not a lease, whatever name be given it. Outside the land law, if you sell your watch or your shares to someone with an option to buy the thing back at the same price plus interest, the deal looks like pledge or charge, whatever you both call it.

In practice it is not so simple. Interests arise which ought to confer real rights but are difficult to fit into the standard patterns—one example is the time-share in holiday accommodation. There we can readily

---

[2] There are a few other customary and ecclesiastical real rights, not mentioned here.

identify the object—the apartment, seaside cottage, or whatever—and the holiday-maker's rights can be defined in the contract. But the traditional patterns of property law do not help us decide whether the arrangement confers a real right which will prevail against the grantor's successors or on his or her insolvency, so specific legislation, or recourse to company law, is desirable. Another awkward example is the tenacious rule that, to bind freehold successors in title, obligations must be negative, they must not cost money. This permits the enforcement of *restrictive* covenants, but means that the performance of positive obligations by successors can be ensured only by the use of some largely fictitious figure such as the lease or the rent-charge.

In relation to housing, and in the absence of a system of family property, the courts are sometimes faced with situations where it would be unconscionable not to provide a remedy for someone who deserves protection but who cannot lay claim to one of the standard property interests. At one extreme a court may order the defendant to convey the freehold to the claimant; at the other they have ordered a monetary payment to be made secured on the defendant's land. In between there is a variety of remedies tempered to the individuals and the conduct involved. Since these remedies do not fit the standard patterns, and for lack of a better name, the claims they enforce are called 'an inchoate equity' or 'a mere equity'. To varying extents these 'equities' are recognized as proprietary rights, a status confirmed by the Land Registration Bill 2001.[3] In an introductory book it is impossible to be more precise, since such interests arise more by discovery than by definition.

We have referred earlier to the inveterate habit of the common law in dividing land law from the law of property in other things. This is still found in many areas. For instance, the Law Commission's draft bill on Limitation of Actions, published in 2001, treats the two types quite differently. A civil claim to recover land *may not be made* after ten years from the accrual of the right of action, whereas in other claims the expiry of the limitation period is merely a defence. This seems to suggest that, where land is at stake, the court must take judicial notice of the limitation period, whereas for other claims, if the defence chooses not to plead limitation, the court will not raise the issue.[4]

The intellectual gulf in our treatment of the two types of property goes deeper—at least in England and Wales—by insisting that we do not own

---

[3] Land Registration Bill 2001, cl.114.
[4] Draft Limitation Bill, cl.1, 16 (Law Com No. 270).

our land, we own the freehold or leasehold estate in it; but that we cannot use these two concepts to describe our entitlement to any other sort of tangible property—for that we must speak of ownership and/or possession. Complete harmony in the law is probably undesirable and certainly unattainable at any reasonable cost. Nonetheless, writers on the principles of property law might profitably enquire whether some uniform doctrine could not cover all limited interests in physical objects and whether, for instance, the solutions found for leases could not be applied to bailments. They might find that the doctrines common to all kinds of property are more numerous than is at present apparent; and where there is doubt, the courts might be persuaded to apply to one kind of property by analogy doctrines developed for other kinds. In that way, for instance, it might become possible to devise straightforward and consistent principles for the law governing the lease of a furnished flat.

The universalizing tendency of the trust has produced much more uniformity in the treatment of beneficial interests, whatever the physical object or other investment on which their value depends. Trustees almost always have the power to sell any particular asset and the beneficiaries may well not know the current composition of the portfolio in which the trust fund is invested. Their interests, whether concurrent, successive, or both, can be defined, alienated, protected, and reached by their creditors, without much regard to the specific rules relating to particular types of property.

Looking at the system as a whole, however, it seems that one broad distinction now outweighs all others, namely that between objects regarded as things to be used, enjoyed, or treated for themselves, and objects which may in the broadest sense be called investments, of which the money value alone is relevant. It may be expressed summarily as the distinction between things and wealth. It is not a distinction between different kinds of things: the same object may be treated for its own sake or as an investment. We may live in a house or rent it out, read a book or keep it in unopened mint condition. To the hungry customer food and drink are things to be consumed; to their producer they are things to be sold. Of course some things are likely to be thought of primarily in terms of their value—savings bonds for instance—while others are more likely to be used and used up. If funds, such as trust or pension funds, can be regarded as composite things, they of course are wealth and nothing else.

The matter is complicated by the fact that, since all human beings need food, clothing, and shelter, we cannot treat all our belongings as investments. Furthermore, there is a potential for conflict when the same object is a necessity to one person but an investment to another. In the latter half of the last century, housing was the focus of such conflicts. For its occupants the house is their home; but their mortgagee can truthfully say that they would never have been able to buy it without the loan. Furthermore, the lender is almost always a building society or bank using the savings of their depositors. Problems are multiplied by the absence of any legislative regime of family property, so that the respective property rights of spouses or domestic partners or children are worked out as if they were all strangers: for instance a co-owner of the family home can sell his or her share to whomever he chooses without asking permission of the other owners, or even informing them. It should be added that some sort of solution to the housing problem has to be provided by public law, which imposes on local authorities the obligation to house the homeless.

The law is bound to be influenced, and the balance of its parts in large measure determined, by the ways in which the various groups constituting a nation think of property and by the balance existing between them from time to time. If the dominant groups think of things mainly as investments, the law will tend to disregard the desire of a person to keep and enjoy a thing in specie and will see no great harm in forcing sale and switching the owner's interest to the money obtained. Still less regard will it pay to one person's expectation of succeeding to specific objects. It will in principle give no effect to attempts to tie up land itself. For all property it will ensure that, on the death of its owner, the personal representatives have power to sell any and every thing. If, on the other hand, the groups predominate which attach particular value to the possession of physical objects themselves, the law will be much less inclined to force an acceptance of money compensation or to allow limited interests to be overreached.

In the last quarter of the nineteenth and the first years of the twentieth centuries it was pretty clear that the law generally took a commercial view of property, in that it favoured the circulation of land as well as of other assets, and declined to create, for instance, any serious general system of family property. It was bound to secure tenants in their holdings and mortgagees in their security, but only to the extent that they had bargained for their rights. Such interests had from the beginning been looked on as essentially commercial in character, so their protection formed no exception to the policy of the law.

However, the Rent Acts marked a decided swing away from the treatment of all objects as merely the investment of wealth. Dwellings were different, and it was accepted that the relation between a person and their

home was worthy of protection irrespective of the contract with the
landlord. The legislature was forced to pay special attention to the holding of specific physical objects and to refuse to allow landlords to buy
tenants off with money as the price of eviction. The essential thing was to
secure to a person a roof over their head, and rent restriction was introduced less for its own sake than in order to prevent eviction by forcing
tenants to pay a higher rent than they could afford. The family dimension
was reflected in the fact that, on the death of the tenant, the co-resident
family members remained protected. Here was a direct denial of the
general commercial thesis that every physical thing can be adequately
replaced by its price in money. Introduced as a temporary measure in
1914, the Rent Act system lasted for most of the twentieth century,
though it affected ever fewer dwellings. One reason for its dwindling
scope was the great rise in owner-occupation of dwelling houses whose
acquisition was almost always financed with the aid of a mortgage
advance repayable by instalments over a number of years. Once again the
law was forced to step in, here to protect home-owners in arrears whose
mortgagee wished to evict them and sell the house with vacant possession. First the courts took, and then the legislator confirmed, powers to
postpone the date for delivery of possession to give the owners time to
catch up with the payments and thereby keep their home.

Two other reforms of the twentieth century show the law's recognition of the strength of the desire to own one's home. Where a house is
held of a private landlord on a long lease at a low rent, the house is a
home for the occupier but an investment for the landlord. And in the
case of public housing owned by local authorities the house is clearly a
home to the 'tenant' but for the council it is a means of discharging
statutory duties. In both situations—the long lease and the council
house—legislation allows the occupier to buy out the owner by paying a
sum which is well below the vacant possession market price. It should be
recalled, however, that these methods of protecting claims to one's home
are the exception, and are almost entirely the work of the legislator, not
of the judiciary.

It is worth emphasizing that the student must be prepared at every
turn to ask what it is that the law of property is really talking about. Is it
dealing with physical objects such as things to be acquired, used, and
enjoyed for their own sakes, or is it merely talking about wealth? Sometimes it is only by putting this question that any sense can be made of the
law. For instance, the continued operation of the Rule against Perpetuities
can be reconciled with the policy enshrined in the first two sections of the

Law of Property Act 1925 only if it is realized that the Rule deals with wealth and the statute with land.

Generally speaking the distinction between wealth and the things that it will buy introduces order and system into the law. It explains, for instance, why a floating charge hovers over the mass of assets of the corporate debtor but that when the charge has to be enforced by seizure and sale it is the particular and specific things which are dealt with. It explains why trustees of a portfolio pay close attention to each investment and sell or buy in strict compliance with the formalities appropriate to the particular object involved, whether it be a shop, a share, or a racehorse. Meanwhile, however, their beneficiaries are concerned with the overall fund and the value of their interests therein.

For over a century attacks have been made here and in other countries on what is called conceptualism. It may be described roughly as a tendency not to give a direct answer on the merits of a practical question but to interpose between the question and the answer one or more abstract concepts, to work out a number of legal rules and principles entailed in those concepts and then to see whether the concepts may be made to apply to the situation in respect of which the question arises. Take for instance the simple question: if you find, on someone else's land, something which has been lost, can you keep it? There is a tendency to answer this question by asking whether the person on whose land you found it had 'possession' of the thing, thereby introducing an abstract and far from easy concept into the discussion. 'Property', in the sense, not of things but of rights, is another abstract and difficult concept, yet it features in the solution of practical questions in the sale of goods.

The whole conceptual structure of mortgages has become little more than a nuisance. All that the mortgagee needs, and all that he really gets, is a bundle of powers over the mortgaged property, namely, to apply to the court for a foreclosure decree, to appoint a receiver, and above all to sell and pay off the loan. All of these are governed by practical rules suggested by experience. The borrower in effect remains owner of the property subject to these powers and has a right to repay the loan and thereby free it from the burden. Yet other practical rules decide to what extent the right to repay and redeem can be restricted and how far the lender can bargain for other, collateral, advantages by making the loan. Nothing would be lost if the notion that the mortgagee has an interest in the mortgaged property were entirely given up and the existence of the equity of redemption entirely disregarded. The essence of the mortgage,

Property as Wealth

like other forms of charge, is that it ensures the secured creditor repayment out of certain property in preference to other creditors. A final example, now fortunately abolished, was the mandatory imposition of a trust *for sale* on all cases of co-ownership so that when a young couple bought their home together they held it *on trust* to sell it.

What these examples have in common is that they illustrate the use of artificial concepts in situations where property is being treated for its own sake as a specific object. It is this particular object you found or bought, this land you mortgaged. Where, however, we are dealing with things as wealth, abstract concepts can be more helpful. The doctrine of estates creates an abstract entity comprising a right to income over time and the power to alienate that right and that power. This is certainly artificial but it serves practical purposes and has been extremely useful. In dealing with land as such, we need only freehold and leasehold. But in dealing with a fund we can, and do, make use of a much wider variety of interests in which the entitlement to income is spread over time: the life interest, the life interest determinable on bankruptcy, the remainder conditional on birth or marriage or attaining a particular age, the interest subject to the discretion of the trustees.

In the world of commerce, the various commercial documents such as negotiable instruments, documents of title, letters of credit, trust receipts, and so on have reached a high degree of standardization and are as artificial as could well be. Were they not so, they could not be used as units in a form of commercial mathematics, by bankers and the like. Moreover, the trust fund made up of ever-changing investments is an artificial concept if ever there was one. But it is not merely the plaything of the lawyers—modern finance could not dispense with it. Similarly the components of a private trust fund may comprise all manner of financial and legal abstractions, culminating in the 'uncertificated unit' in a 'Fund of Funds'.

It would seem, therefore, that speaking generally and somewhat crudely, artificiality and conceptualism are on the whole out of place in that dimension of property law which deals with things as objects treated for their own sake. Such techniques are, however, useful and perhaps essential to that dimension of the law which deals with wealth. In any case, what is more abstract—and mysterious—than money itself?

Index

Abstract,
  concepts 21, 200
  person 5
Abstraction 21
Accession 50, 52
Accumulations, Rule against
      184–5
Acquisition 50–62
  compulsory 63
  derivative 53–62
  in good faith 66–7
  original 50–3
Action,
  at common law 10
  right of 72
Administration, Letters of 164
  of estates 163
Administration of Estates Act 1925 8, 97,
      159, 178
Administrator 159, 165
Agent, mercantile 67
Agricultural tenancies 126
Aircraft 28, 122
Alienation 115, 183, 189
Alteration 52–3
Animal 26, 51, 192
Artificial concepts 21
  persons 21
Assignment 61

Bail bond 127
Bailment 50, 115–16
Bank 127
  of England 43
Banknote 43
Bankruptcy 46
Beneficial interests 61, 177–83, 196
Beneficiary 196
Benefit of promise 28
Bill of Exchange 32
  of lading 30
  of sale 141
Bills of Sale Acts 1878–91 141
Bona fide purchaser 83–4
Bona vacantia 162

Breach of contract 60, 66
  of trust 88, 176
Building
  lease 125
  Society 149–50
Bulk goods 94
Business premises 126

California Civil Code 1872 82
Capital,
  and income 46–9
  corporate 45
  trust 190–1
  venture 190–1
Chancellor 10, 82
Chancery 15, 193
Charge 133, 194
  floating 129, 144–5
  legal 143–4
Charity 86, 189
Chattels 22, 115–17, 122
Cheque 32, 174
Cheques Act 1992 31, 67
Chose in action 29–30, 54, 175
  in possession 30
Church 78, 101, 104
Classification of things 20–2
Clogs on equity of redemption 137
Commerce 29, 66
Commercial paper 54, 61, 66
Common law,
  courts 10, 12
  remedies 82
Common ownership 92–3
Commonhold 93, 121
Company law 11
Compulsory acquisition 63
  registration 104
Conceptualism 199–200
Concurrent interests 92–7, 103
Conscience 84
Consideration 85, 86
Constitutions 6
Contract,
  asset, as 37

breach of 60, 66
privity of 120
Conveyancing, electronic 104
Co-ownership 92–7
Copyright 38–41, 54
Copyright Act 1707 11
Copyright, Designs and Patents Act 1988
    14
Coroner 52
Corporation, trust 172, 175
Council houses 126
Court,
    of common law 10, 82
    of equity 10, 82
Covenant 43
    for title 83,
    restrictive 24, 103, 156–8, 195
Creditors,
    of trustee 45, 87
    unsecured 71, 88, 127, 176
Criminal law 3, 89
Crops 20, 46
Crown property 7–8, 78

Damages 69
De Soto, Hernando 5
Death 4, 159–65
Debentures 137
Debt 30, 91
Declaration of trust 171
Deed 54, 55
    mortgage 133, 134, 135
    title 104
        deposit of 134
Dematerialization 34
Demesne land 78, 101, 105
Design rights 38
Discounting 47–9
Distress 89, 120
Dividend 34, 47
Divorce 3
Doctrine of estates 79–81, 115, 182–3
Document 31
Domesday Book 16
Dominant tenement 153
Dominion 164
Droit de suite 40

Easement 153–6
    negative 154
    positive 154
Ejectment, action of 69
Electronic Communications Act 2000 54

Enforcement of security 133, 134–7
Enjoyment,
    successive 99–100
Entailed interest 80, 182
Equitable,
    interest 13, 102, 177
    jurisdiction 15, 82
    remedies 84–6
Equity 10, 15, 82–6
    court of 10, 15
    negative 132
    of redemption 15, 131–2
Estate 15, 79–80, 114, 182–3
    freehold 101–2
    leasehold 15, 101–2, 114–15
    legal 80, 142, 182
    life 15, 79, 182
    of deceased person 15, 159
    privity of 121
    tail 79
Estates, doctrine of 79–81, 115, 182–3
Euro 7, 44
European Union 7, 38, 41, 123
Executor 163
Expectation of life 178
Externalities 24

Factors 30
Fame 42
Family 4
Fee simple 80, 106
    tail 79, 182
Feudalism 77–8
Finding 52
Fixtures 23, 53
Flats 23, 121
Floating charge 144–5
Foreclosure 132–3, 136
Forfeiture 120
Formalities 54, 57, 83, 118
Fragmentation of ownership 90–100
Freehold 101–3
Fund 34, 44–6, 141, 171
    trust 66, 172–3
Fungible goods 27, 61, 68
Future goods 28
    income 47–9
    interest 49

Germany 20
Gift 55–6
    in contemplation of death 164–5
Gilt-edged securities 29

Good faith 66–7
Goode, Sir Roy 140
Goods 26–8
    ascertained 28
    fungible 27
    future 28
    sale of 28, 57–9
Goodwill 42–3
Government Annuities Act 1695 148
Government bonds 30

Hire 113, 115–17
Hire-purchase 67, 146–7
Hire-Purchase Act 1964 67, 147
Holder in due course 16, 32, 66
House 22
Human rights 6
Human Rights Act 1998 6, 125

Immovables 20
Income 24, 46–9, 178–9
    tax 47
Inflation 44
Inheritance 159
Inheritance (Provision for Family and
        Dependants) Act 1975 161, 162
Injunction 14, 38, 68
Insolvency 91, 150
Instalments 3, 149
Instrument, negotiable 31–2
    trust 173, 175
Insurance company 181
Intangible assets 29–49
Intellectual property 38–43, 123
Interest,
    beneficial 173–83
    concurrent 173
    entailed 80, 182
    in chattel 148–9
    in trust fund 177–81
    life 177–9
    limited 173
    overriding 106–9
Interest on investment 178
    on loan 46–7
Intermediation 34–5
International law 6
Intestacy 178
Invention 38, 39
Investment securities 33–6, 60–1

Joint ownership 93–5
    tenancy 93

Jurisdiction, equitable 82

King 77
Know-how 123

Land 22–6
    certificate 105, 143
    Registrar 104–6
    Registry 11, 59, 98
    sale of 59–60
    unregistered 143
Land Charges Registry 59, 143
Land Registration Act 1925 44, 72, 102,
        104, 107
Land Registration Bill 2001 12, 51 72, 80,
        85, 102, 107, 108, 142, 143, 195
Landlord 119
    and tenant 120–1
Landlord and Tenant (Covenants) Act
        1995 120, 122
Law of Property Act 1922 12
Law of Property Act 1925 10, 11, 15, 80,
        102–3, 108, 113, 114, 142, 143, 185
Law of Property (Miscellaneous Provisions)
        Act 1994 83
Lease 97, 113–26
    agreement for 118
    finance 117
Leasehold 101, 102
Legal charge 143
    estate 80, 142, 182
Legislation 11–12, 101–9
Lessee 114
Lessor 115
Letters of administration 164
Licence 123
Lien 138
Life,
    estate 97
    in being 186
    interest 49, 97–100
    tenant 103
Light 154, 155
Limitation,
    of actions and rights 71–3
    Statutes of 71
Loan 46–7, 61–2, 130
Lost property 52

Maitland, F. W. 82, 170
Mattei, Ugo 9
Merchant Shipping Act 1894 148
Milk quota 7, 24

Mint 43
Money 21, 43–4, 46–7, 62, 66, 70, 72, 174, 200
Monopolies 38
Mortgage 91, 140–3, 149–50, 199
  charge by way of legal 143
  deed 133, 134, 135
Motor vehicle 147
Movables 20

Negotiable instruments 31–2, 66–7
Neighbour 153
New Zealand 161
Non-charitable purpose 189
Notice 59
  to debtor 61
  to trustees 61, 179–80
Nuisance 152

Oath, executor's 163
Overreaching 102
Overriding interests 106–9
Ownership 57, 90–2, 147
  bare 180
  concurrent 92–7
  content of 90–2
  fragmentation of 92–100
  in common 92–3, 95
  joint 93–6
  legal 131
  retention of 147–8
  risks 91

Parliament 9, 30, 44, 148
Partner,
  business 95
  domestic 4, 91, 161, 162
Partnership Act 1890 9
Passing off 41
Patents 30, 38–41, 54, 141
Patrimony 46
Pawn 129
Pawnbroker 139
Pension fund 35
Perpetuities, rule against 185–91, 199
Perpetuities and Accumulations Act 1964 185
Perpetuity period 186
Personal belongings 162
  property 22
  representative 46, 164
  security 127

Personal Rights Protection Act 1984 (Tennessee) 42
Planning law 24
Pledge 129, 139, 194
Policy of law 197–8
Possession 52, 65, 114, 133, 136
  estates in 114
Possessory lien 138
  security 139
Power,
  of alienation 115, 183
  of sale 170, 176
Prescription 155–6
Primogeniture 162
Priority 133
Private law 121
Privity of contract 120
  of estate 121
Probate 163
Profits 153
Promise 55
Promissory note 30
Property,
  law of 3–5, 9–12, 63
  legislation of 1925 101–9
  movable 20
  passing of 57, 58
  personal 13
  real 13
  rights 14, 108
Proprietary security 127–8
Protection of property interests 63–73
Protector of the trust 173
Public law 7–9
  Trustee 159
Purchaser's lien 138
Purpose, charitable 86
  non-charitable 189

Quia Emptores 1290 11, 36

Radical title 78
Raw materials 147, 169
Real property 13, 21
  rights 14, 65, 135, 194–5
  security 127–8
  subrogation 77, 89, 170, 176
Realty 13, 21
Receiver 136
Redemption, equity of 131–2
Reform Act 1832 108
Register 28, 133, 140
  Land 104–5

Registered land 104–9
Registration 73, 134, 140–1
  and possession 133
  compulsory 104
  of mortgages 195
  of title 104
  voluntary 104
Relative title 50–2, 80
Remainder 100
Remainderman 100
Remedy,
  common law 83
  equitable 84–6
Rent 119, 124, 198
Rent Act 1914 124
Rent Acts 124–5, 197–8
Repairs 125
Representative, personal 46, 164
Restrictive covenants 122, 156–8,
    195
Retention-of-ownership 147–8
Reversion 100
Right,
  contractual 14
  of possession 51, 52
  personal 36–7
  real 14–15
Roman law 92
Root of title 104
Rule against accumulations 184–5
  perpetuities 185–91

Sale 56–62, 135–6
  bill of 141
  of goods 57–8
  of land 59–61
  power of 135
  proceeds of 135
Sale of Goods Act 1979 9, 58
Sanity 46
Scotland 56, 161
Securities 60–1
Securitization 150
Security 127–51
  enforcement of 134–6
  personal 127
  possessory 139
  proprietary 139–45
Seeds 22
Self-help 63, 69
Services, feudal 77–8
Servient tenement 153
Servitude 152–8

Settlement 100, 103, 161, 170, 192
Severance 93
Share 33–6, 141
  undivided 92
Shareholder 33, 93
Sheriff 69
Ship 28, 122, 148
Show-business 42, 193
Son, eldest 161, 162
Specific performance 84–5
Spouse 125, 161, 162–3
Statute,
  of Frauds 1677 11
  of Monopolies 1623 11
  of Uses 1535 11
  of Wills 1540 11
Stock, government 29
Stock Transfer Act 1982 54
Stocks and shares 33–6
Sublease 22
Subrogation, real 77, 89, 170, 176
Succession 159–65
  intestate 162–3
Survivorship 93

Tangible things 20–8
Tenancy,
  agreement 118
  in common 93
  joint 93
Tenant,
  agricultural 126
  business 126
  in chief 77
Tenement, dominant 153
  servient 153
Tenure 77–9
  security of 126
Term of years absolute 102
Testation, freedom of 161
Theft Act 1968 10, 64
Things,
  abstract 5
  classification of 19–49
  intangible 20, 21
  tangible 20
Time 97
Title 65
  deeds 178, 194
  registration of 104–6
  relative 50–2, 80
  root of 104
Tort 3, 68, 158

Torts (Interference with Goods) Act 1977
70
Tracing 88–9
Trademarks 41–2
Transfer,
consensual 53–62
gratuitous 106
on death 159–67
operating between parties 57
Treasure Act 1996 8, 52
Trees 22
Trespass 68
Trust 35, 45–6, 86–8, 171–5
breach of 175
charitable 87
corporation 172, 175
declaration of 171
fund 35, 172–3
instrument 172, 173
protector 173
Trustee 80, 86–7, 94
in bankruptcy 46
office of 174
Public 159

Trustee Act 1925 10
Trustee Act 2000 172, 173, 175
Trusts of Land and Appointment of
Trustees Act 1996 11, 175

Undivided shares 92
Uniform Commercial Code (USA) 36,
148
United States 33, 42, 86, 147
Unsecured creditors 127, 150

Value 178–9, 180–1
Vendor's lien 138
Vested interest 177, 180
Voluntary registration 104

'Wait and see' 187–8
Wealth 169–200
Will 160–1
Witness 160
World Intellectual Property Organization
40
World Trade Organization 41
Writing 59, 60

CPSIA information can be obtained at www.ICGtesting.com
Printed in the USA
BVOW04s0953110816

458590BV00001B/10/P